Voices From the Past

Hong Kong 1842-1918

For Alison, Beverley, Elizabeth,
Judith and Rosemary,
with affection

Voices From the Past
Hong Kong 1842-1918

Selected and Annotated by

Solomon Bard

香港大學出版社
HONG KONG UNIVERSITY PRESS

Hong Kong University Press
14/F Hing Wai Centre
7 Tin Wan Praya Road
Aberdeen
Hong Kong

© Hong Kong University Press 2002

ISBN 962 209 574 7

A CIP catalogue record for this book is available from the British
Library.

Secure On-line Ordering
http://www.hkupress.org

Printed and bound by Kings Time Printing Press Ltd., Hong Kong, China

Contents

Acknowledgements

I am very grateful to:

Lo Tak-shing, of Lo & Lo Solicitors, for generously allowing me to use material previously published in the column 'Past Perspectives' in his magazine *Window*;

Joseph Ting, Chief Curator of the Hong Kong Museum of History, for giving me full access to and the use of the Museum's rich library of historical photographs;

James Hayes, Robin Hutcheon and David Moore who offered useful suggestions for the text and whose support and friendship were a great comfort;

The Hong Kong University Press, who helped and encouraged and have finally brought to fruition the publication of this book.

I owe special thanks to my team of tireless snippet seekers, Rosemary Lee, Beverley Hirschel, Elizabeth Heinz, Judith Lingard, and Alison Hunter, to whom this book is humbly dedicated.

Lastly, to my daughter Monica and son Paul who strengthened my resolve whenever it wavered.

Solomon Bard

Message

There are various approaches to the study of history. In *Voices From the Past: Hong Kong 1842–1918*, Dr Solomon Bard has chosen to view Hong Kong's history through the columns of newspapers of the time – an approach which has perhaps not been sufficiently explored before. Through these newspaper excerpts, people from the past speak directly to us expressing contemporary views, ideas, daily concerns, both important and trivial. Although compiled from the English-language newspapers only, I believe it is still a valuable contribution to our knowledge and appreciation of this period of Hong Kong's history. It gives me much pleasure to announce that the Hong Kong Museum of History is the sponsor of some 200 photographs from its collection to be included in the book; they will, I hope, add to its merit and appeal.

Dr Joseph S. P. Ting
Chief Curator
Hong Kong Museum of History

Introduction

'News is the first rough draft of history'
Ben Bradlee

Much of this material was first published as a weekly column called *Past Perspectives* in the Hong Kong magazine *Window* between 1992 and 1996. The present publication assembles these columns together in a revised form with many added photographs. In this assemblage of historical snippets, or excerpts, taken from contemporary English-language newspapers, we look into Hong Kong's past from the beginning of its acquisition by Britain.

In the early 19th century, trade between China and the West was confined to Canton alone, where it flourished despite rigid restrictions imposed by the Chinese authorities. Among a large variety of merchandise traded, importation of opium into China, prohibited by the Imperial Edict of 1800, played a prominent role. Britain, determined to keep the trade channels open, and China, equally determined to stop the opium trade, came into armed conflict in 1839, in what is generally known as the First Opium War. In 1841, the two sides signed a convention at Chuenpi, near Canton, by which the island of Hong Kong was ceded to Britain. But before the treaty ending the war was signed (in 1842) and ratified (in 1843), a small British naval contingent landed on Hong Kong Island on the 26 January 1841, at a small promontory on the western shore of the Island, later to be named Possession Point, and claimed Hong Kong Island for the British Crown. Since this de facto possession of the island was probably the most important milestone in the history of Hong Kong as a British enclave, it is worth quoting the description of the landing by Captain Edward Belcher of HMS *Sulphur**

---

* From Captain Belcher's *Voyage Round the World*, Vol. II, 1843. Captain (later Sir Edward) Belcher commanded the survey ship HMS *Sulphur*. Belcher's Street and Belcher's Gardens on Hong Kong Island are called after him. The sea passage between Hong Kong's West Point and the Green Island is called Sulphur Channel after HMS *Sulphur*.

who landed at Possession Point the day before the formal ceremony: '... On the return of the Commodore [to Macao*] on the 24th [January 1841] we were directed to proceed to Hongkong and commence survey. We landed on Monday the 25th 1841 at Fifteen minutes past 8 a.m. and being the bona fide first possessors, Her Majesty's health was drunk with three cheers from Possession Mount. On the 26th the squadron arrived; the marines were landed, the union hoisted on out post, the formal possession taken of the island by Commodore Sir J.J.G.Bremer, accompanied by the other officers of the squadron, under a *feu-de-joie*** from the marines and a royal salute from the ships of war ... .'

There is little doubt that the spirit of commercial enterprise was the leading motive in the early British colonial policy, and it was the British pursuit of trade in the East which brought China and Britain into confrontation and heralded the birth of Hong Kong. It has been stated, with some truth, that when an expeditionary force was being organized early in 1840, Lord Palmerston, the British Foreign Secretary, was still far from committed to the acquisition of any base on the China coast. The vital thing was trade security and he was not yet convinced that another addition to the British Empire was necessary. Whatever the motivation, Hong Kong became a Crown Colony and was administered as one.

The early years of Hong Kong had not been encouraging. Lack of level land, unhealthy climate, murders and piracy — all pointed to an unhappy outlook. Several people who were in the best position to judge could not visualise any future for Hong Kong. Yet Hong Kong confounded the gloomy forecasts and grew to become a major trading, financial, and cultural centre. It was the combination of the tenacity and resourcefulness of the Colonial Civil Service, the entrepreneurial ability of local traders, and the determination of its people that secured a prosperous future for Hong Kong.

Today, the world has largely discarded imperialism, colonialism and the right of strong nations to rule over weak ones, and has recognised the right of all peoples to self-determination. But in the 19th century imperialism was still the way of the strong. Nevertheless there were

---

* Macao: English spelling for the Cantonese transliteration 'Ou Mun'. 'Macau' is the Portuguese spelling.
** *Feu-de-joie* (French): a firing of guns in token of joy.

colonial administrators with progressive visions who passionately believed in improving the welfare of the people they ruled. Were such visions to be dismissed as a mere facade for economic exploitation? Was all colonialism bad? And can it account for Hong Kong's success and a rapidly growing population? Anton Chekhov, the famous Russian playwright and humanist, who visited Hong Kong in 1890, was clearly impressed. 'Wherever you turn,' he wrote, 'you will note evidences of the most tender solicitude on the part of the English for men in their service; there is even a sailors' club.'* The answer, of course, is that colonial rule and economic success are fully compatible. Inevitably, the system creates two distinct classes — the more privileged expatriates, who rule the colony and occupy all the senior positions in the government and private sector, and the less privileged locals, in the lower ranks. A large social and economic gap which is formed between the expatriates and the locals is further aggravated by discriminatory regulations and restrictions. In Hong Kong, the vast majority of 'locals' would be the Chinese, but anyone domiciled in Hong Kong, for instance long-time Indian residents, Portuguese of Macao descent, Eurasians with roots in Hong Kong, and a sprinkling of other, often stateless, persons such as White Russians, would be regarded as locals. British economic policy in Hong Kong, characteristically *laissez faire*, gave much scope, however, for individual ambition and enterprise so that not a few 'locals' did achieve wealth, power, and distinction.**

Hong Kong had been fortunate in having a succession of capable governors in its early formative years. They worked hard to ensure law and order and to provide safe and stable living conditions for the people of Hong Kong. However, reared in the strict colonial mould and with a firm belief in the superiority of the system they represented, they were averse to any reforms or changes which would remove some of the existing inequalities; with one exception: Sir John Pope Hennessy, a governor with liberal, progressive views — a man ahead of his time.***

---

* Hellman, L. (Ed.) *The Selected Letters of Anton Chekhov*. London: Pan Books, 1984, p.132.

** Example is usually given of Sir Robert Ho Tung, Eurasian long-time compradore of Jardine, Matheson & Co. who became a wealthy merchant, a philanthropist, and a baronet, and who established a wealthy and powerful dynasty.

*** Sir John Pope Hennessy, who governed Hong Kong from 1877 to 1882, appointed the first Chinese, Ng Choy, to the Legislative Council.

He may well have initiated a sequence of changes, slow at first, which signalled the decline of the colonial system, and which in the end proved unstoppable.

The book covers the period under British administration from 1842 to 1918. In compiling the items I attempted to select them from a wide range of subjects, in a contrasting way: instructive and entertaining, serious and amusing, important and trivial, agreeable and disagreeable. The text deals mainly with Hong Kong and to a lesser extent with Macao and China, but a few world items of outstanding interest are also included. Accompanying the text are many historical photographs from the excellent photographic library of the Hong Kong Museum of History. They are of considerable interest not only because they relate to the text but they also depict many items of Hong Kong heritage no longer extant — victims of the massive redevelopment.

The selected snippets reflect the gradual changes over the years in language, style of writing, even humour. It will be interesting to read about the public response to the many inventions which today we take for granted, such as electric lighting, the motor car, and the first attempts at flying. Most importantly, the items reflect the gradual changes in Hong Kong's colonial attitudes, as the people become aware of the new contemporary values and social and political changes. They show, contrary to the still commonly held view that the Hong Kong public remained complacent about elected government, that there were repeated calls for representation on both the governing councils.

Many snippets are followed by my comments or explanations which are in italics. I have chosen the Wade-Giles romanization of Chinese names in keeping with the period depicted. It is my ardent hope that the reader will find *Voices From the Past* informative and enjoyable.

1842

⌒ᵔᵔ⌒

As far as can be gathered, Hong Kong was without an English-language newspaper during 1841, the first year under the British administration. Its small foreign community was probably served by news printed in Canton. In 1842, the Friend of China *became Hong Kong's first newspaper. Since the Government had no printer of its own, its official notices were published in the* Friend, *which became known by its full name —* The Friend of China and Hongkong* Gazette. *The* Friend *was published weekly, on Thursdays, and the first number appeared on the* **17 March 1842** *(the date worthy of celebration by the Hong Kong press). This issue was almost entirely taken up by an impassioned editorial, which today appears somewhat pretentious and self-righteous. It seems appropriate, however, to begin our* Voices From the Past *with some passages from this editorial:-*

After much toil anxiety and expense we are enabled, with grateful feelings to lay before our friends and the Public the First Number of Friend of China.

    On introducing ourselves to the Public it is fitting that we should fully state something of our views objects and plan, and the pretentions upon which we confidently ground our expectations of Patronage and Support.

    A year has scarcely elapsed since the British flag was unfurled on this Island evidence de facto of its being henceforth a part and parsel of the wide spread British Empire that Empire on which the sun never sets, and with whose aggrandizement is linked the regeneration social and political of the vast Empire of China if as we believe she is designed to be the demolisher of the middle walls of partition which for so many ages have separated one third of the human race from communion with the rest. …

    Our columns shall always be open to those who cooperate with us in endeavouring to open up the vast resources of the Chinese Empire — we accept all as auxiliaries (whatever clime or country may claim

Friend of China
17 March 1842

---

* Prior to 1926, 'Hong Kong' was spelt 'Hongkong' — in one word with a small 'k'; the Hongkong and Shanghai Banking Corporation still uses the old spelling.

their origin) who will join us in demanding an unrestricted trade with the Chinese — we inscribe Free Trade on our banner and that it may wave triumphant we shall insist on the permanent occupation of Hongkong, the authoritative declaration by the British Government of its being a Free Port, and the exercise of a generous policy by the Home and Local Governments to foster and encourage this insular settlement on the coast of China, which we earnestly believe requires little aid to become one of the most important commercial emporiums in the East.
...

It might be supposed that we shrunk from the high responsibilities of our position were we not to touch on the Opium Trade. In common with every Philanthropist we must deeply deplore the addiction of the Chinese to this fascinating vice, and whilst we share such sentiments we are still not so over zealous and blinded by our regrets as not to acknowledge the utter inadequacy of all attempts to suppress the cultivation sale and use of this Potent Exhilerant hitherto attempted by the Chinese Government. It must be put down by moral power and sound public opinion, those two mighty promoters of the temperance movement in Great Britain and America.

❖   *In the same issue of the* Friend, *the following two paragraphs appeared:*

On the 10th inst. James Matheson Esq. the accomplished partner of the well-known firm of Messrs. Jardine Matheson & Co. sailed for England in the *Tartar* after a residence of many years in China. ... one of the last acts which he performed on leaving the shores of China was to place at the disposal of His Excellency the Governor of Macao five thousand dollars to be appropriated to some benevolent establishment under the control of the Portuguese Government.

❖   *With the Treaty ending the war not yet signed, and Hong Kong's future far from assured, Mr Matheson might have felt, justifiably, that it was still too early to invest in charity in Hong Kong.*

A day or two ago a portion of the walls surrounding the large Chinese temple at Makok, Macao gave way and we are sorry to learn that two Chinese have been killed by the accident, and a third very seriously injured.

Benjamin Simonds was brought up [before the magistrate] on a charge of having been drunk and riotous the previous evening.

It appeared that the accused who was a seaman belonging to the *Ariadne* Steamer, having a few dollars in his pocket determined according to his own eccentric phraseology to have 'blow-out' at the Britain's Boast. … Vainly did he invoke Ariadne to assist him as she did Theseus and get him out of the scrape; the ruthless constable insisted upon his company to the Gaol.

❖ *Ariadne, the daughter of Minos, king of Crete, fell in love with Theseus of Athens, and gave him a ball of thread which enabled him to find his way out of the labyrinth. The* Friend's *showy reference to Greek mythology is out of place.*

Friend of China
24 March 1842

Attack and Capture of Chuenpi, Near Canton
After negotiations between the British and the Chinese had failed, British warships landed troops on 7 January 1841 near the forts of Chuenpi. The forts were captured, leading to the signing of the Convention of Chuenpi and the cession of Hong Kong to Britain.

(Drawing by T. Allom from the sketch on the spot by Lieutenant White, Royal Marines)

**Friend of China
24 March 1842**

The recent Census gave the total native population of Hongkong as 12,361 souls. Among more than 30 occupations listed, the following are of interest:

	Shops	Souls
Chandlers	67	402
Bakers	6	39
Rice dealers	1	9
Apothecaries	6	22
Masons	1	380
Tailors	14	89
Barbers	11	66
School-masters	2	10
Opium sellers	24	131
Prostitutes	23	439
Labourers		1366
Hawkers		600
Having no ostensible employment		500
Boat population		2100

View of Hong Kong Island and Harbour, c.1845
(Drawing by B. Clayton from a painting by Piqua for Miss Corner, *History of China and India,* 1845)

Name of our town. We have been asked by many subscribers, whether it is intended to call the Capital of the First British Settlement in China 'Queens Town'? ... We believe and recommend 'Victoria' as more suitable.

Friend of China
31 March 1842

Name of our Town. We are very glad to find the suggestion in our last that it should be called Victoria, is universally accepted.

Friend of China
7 April 1842

For a brief spell of time the Friend of China *had indulged in a chatty column called* On Dits, *which my school French tells me means 'it is said'. Here are a couple of items from* On Dits:

The Chinese are making preparations to attack Hongkong. The force is variously estimated at ten to fifteen thousand men. ...

Friend of China
21 April 1842

❖   *A gossip or truth? At the time this was far from amusing, and some panic resulted in Hong Kong.*

Commissioner Lin and his favourite wife have been added to the collection of the portraits in wax of madame Tussaud.* The figures are as large as life, and were modelled by a Chinese artist at Canton.

❖   *In recent years Commissioner Lin has been hailed in China as a hero, and so he was. A zealous and capable official, he used strong measures to stop the opium trade.*

Letter to the Editor
Sir, the disgraceful scenes of which our streets are the arena, call loudly for magisterial interference; each day they become worse and worse. You must be quite sure, I can only allude to the drunken delinquencies of our soldiers and sailors: for the conduct of our native population, by contrast, is truly admirable.

Friend of China
25 April 1842

---

* Madame Tussaud's renowned museum of wax models of famous and infamous people, established in 1802 in London.

Pending His Majesty's further pleasure, I do hereby constitute and appoint you, William Caine Esquire, brevet major, and Captain in Her Majesty's 26th Regiment of Infantry, to be Chief Magistrate of the Island of Hongkong and its dependencies: and I do hereby empower and require you to exercise authority according to the laws, customs and usages of China as near as may be (every description of torture excepted).

[Signed] His Excellency Sir Henry Pottinger

❖ *This amazing announcement showed that more than a year after a de facto acquisition of Hong Kong Island, it was still without a judiciary officer. Captain Caine, after whom Caine Road in the Mid-Levels was named, was to dispense justice according to the Chinese laws and customs but without torture! Hong Kong was not yet officially a British possession and Pottinger not a governor.*

Friend of China
16 June 1842

From the Editorial:
We affect not to be depositaries of official secrets. ... we ask our readers to accept the opinions we may express, as our own. ... we may say it is understood that Nanking and Shanghai will be captured, whilst a simultaneous movement will be made on the Peiho River to the strongly fortified city of Tientsin. Unless the Emperor then gives way, we shall fight a battle, gain a victory, and occupy the Capital of the Celestial Empire. But what then? Is our presence in the Imperial Precincts to be the signal of the demise of the tartar Dynasty and of a total revolution in China?

❖ *A prophetic editorial. The war between China and Britain was resumed in May 1842. Shanghai was captured in June 1842, and Nanking was about to fall when a peace treaty was signed there in August 1842. Tientsin and Peking were also taken but not until 1860, in the Second Opium War, and the Qing Dynasty was overthrown, but that took another 70 years!*

Friend of China
30 June 1842

An American Toast
The Ladies, the only endurable aristocracy, who rule without laws, judge without jury, decide without appeal and are never in the wrong.

From the Peking Gazette, *the Emperor's epitome of past events translated:* I, the Emperor, in consequence of opium flowing in poisonous torrents throughout the Central Kingdom, have already transmitted my commands definitely ordering that in every Province the most rigorous prohibitions should be set on foot.

The barbarian merchants of every nation readily yielded to restraint, but it was only the rebel barbarian Elliot of the English nation, who made false pretence in order to excite disturbance, which occasioned Lin's unhappy management and his banishment to the cold country.

❖ *The unfortunate Captain Elliot, the most misunderstood and misjudged man in Hong Kong's history, shared Commissioner Lin's abhorrence of the opium trade, but had to fight a war for it as the loyal naval officer. Both Elliot and Lin fell foul of their governments, the former for not taking enough, the latter for giving away too much.*

Friend of China
28 July 1842

Possession Point, Hong Kong Island, c.1930
The place where the British naval contingent landed and claimed possession of Hong Kong Island for Britain, on 26 January 1841. Subsequent shore-line reclamations have moved the locality well inland. A small recreation ground has been constructed on the site, and the name 'Possession Point' dropped, but a street nearby is still called Possession Street.

Friend of China
11 August 1842

Captain Elliot took his departure from England on the 1ˢᵗ of June. He proceeded to his official appointment [as British Consul for Texas] via Jamaica, on board the West India Packet Steamer *Clyde*.

❖ *This is what happens to disgraced British officials; by contrast, Commissioner Lin narrowly escaped execution.*

Friend of China
17 November 1842

Advance Hongkong!!!
Theatre Royal
Messrs. Dutronquoy & Co. have at length the satisfaction of announcing to the nobility, gentry and clergy of this flourishing and opulent Colony, that their Theatre is advancing most rapidly towards completion.

It is on a most splendid scale, and what with the pieces that will be performed, the Scenery that will be introduced and the splendid assemblage of rank, beauty and fashion which they hope to be honoured with, there is no doubt but that the blaze of Splendour will dazzle the eyes of all beholders. Vivat Regina.

N.B. The actresses have arrived during the last week, their beauties and talents are only to be surpassed by their spotless virtues.

❖ *This attempt to introduce a professional theatre company into Hong Kong, not yet two years old and beset by war, sickness, and crime, is truly amazing.*

1843

Friend of China
12 January 1843

Hongkong Dispensary
The undersigned, beg to intimate that they have removed the Canton Dispensary And Soda Water Establishment to Hongkong.
Capt. Morgan's Bazaar   A. Anderson
1ˢᵗ January 1843   P. Young

❖ *Hongkong Dispensary was the predecessor of A.S.Watson & Co., the well-known and popular firm in Hong Kong. Alexander Skirving Watson took control of the firm in 1858 though his name was not bestowed on the firm until 1870.*

The same issue contains a list of prices of provisions at the Hongkong Market, some of which are quoted below:

Pork per catty	11 cents	Fish, fresh per catty	11 cents
Beef " "	11 "	Salt Fish " "	8 "
Ducks " "	11 "	Oysters " "	6 "
Frogs " "	7 "	Shrimps " "	7 "
Hen's eggs per dozen	7 "		

Madrigal Society — the absence of the president (Lord Saltoun) was the subject of regret with all and wonder with some, — especially when it was announced that he was gone on a martial expedition to China. ...

**Friend of China
16 February 1843**

❖   *In 1843 there were no major hostilities between Britain and China, only minor incidents. However, there was a good deal of piracy in China waters. General (Lord) Saltoun may have gone on an anti-piratical expedition.*

Tsim Sha Tsui Bay, Kowloon, c.1870
An early photograph of the bay looking north towards the hill soon to be named Blackhead Point after the firm of F. Blackhead & Co., which had built its godowns near the Point. A few matshed buildings, on the left, mark the sparse occupation; Kowloon had only been ceded to Britain ten years previously. In the coming years, the reclamation would straighten the beach line and Salisbury Road would be constructed upon it.

❖   *Flushed with the excitement of a new British possession, the early Hong Kong administration was fond of Proclamations; two follow:*

Friend of China
20 April 1843

His Excellency Sir Henry Pottinger, Bart., G.C.B., Her Britannic Majesty's Plenipotentiary, and Chief Superintendent of the Trade of British Subjects in China, issues this PROCLAMATION. ... To His Excellency, Viceroy of the two Kwang Provinces, on the 13th of this month.

As at present informed, it is impossible for Her Majesty's Plenipotentiary, &c., to particularize, either the firms or individuals, or even the countries to which they belong, who have with the connivance of the Chinese Custom-House officers, entered into this shameless and disreputable system of wholesale smuggling. ...

His Excellency further intimates, that such Smugglers and their boats and Vessels will not receive protection in the Harbour or Waters of Hong-Kong.

God Save the Queen

Dated at the Government House, at Hongkong, this 15th day of April, 1843.

Henry Pottinger

Friend of China
30 June 1843

The Treaty of Peace, ratified under the Signs Manual, and Seals of the respective Sovereigns, between Her Majesty, the Queen of the United Kingdom ... and His Imperial Majesty, the Emperor of China, having been this day formally exchanged, the annexed Royal Charter and Commission ... are hereby Proclaimed and published for general information, obedience, and guidance.

His Excellency, Sir Henry Pottinger ... has this day taken the Oaths of Office, and assumed charge of the Government of the Colony of Hong-Kong, and its dependancies.

In obedience to the Gracious Commands of Her majesty ... the Island and its Dependancies will be designated and known as 'The Colony of Hong-Kong' and ... the present City, on the Northern Side of the Island, shall be distinguished by Her Majesty's Name. ...

(Dated 26th of June 1843)

❖   *Although occupied and administered for over two years, this is surely a milestone in Hong Kongs history, when it officially became a British Colony and Pottinger its first Governor.*

Sir Henry Pottinger (1798–1856)

Sir Henry Pottinger, the first governor of Hong Kong, arrived in the colony in August 1941 to replace Captain Charles Elliot as chief superintendent of British trade in China. In January of that year, Hong Kong became a de facto British possession, and already a great deal of constructive work had been done. Pottinger continued setting up the essential functions of a new colony, and in June 1843, after the status of Hong Kong was formally ratified by the Treaty, was appointed its governor. Although his service as governor was short, barely a year, his achievements were considerable.

A capable administrator with enormous responsibilities, he did not become a popular figure, since, it was said, 'he had never courted friendly relations with the leading British merchants' (E. J. Eitel, 1895).

After leaving Hongkong in May 1844, he served in Cape Colony and in India. He died in 1856 at the age of 67.

Chief Magistrate's Office
Victoria, Hongkong

Friend of China
17 August 1843

It has been lately Notified by Proclamation of the Chief Magistrate, to the Chinese Inhabitants of Hongkong, that between the hours of eight and ten P.M., they are prohibited from being out of their houses without lanthorns, and that after ten o'clock P.M., and until daylight on the following morning, no Chinese will, in future be permitted to go out … unless he can produce a pass in English specifying his object in being out at so late an hour.

❖ *Robberies were frequent, but putting the Chinese population under curfew was hardly the answer. This outrageous order was resented by the local population, but was explained by the authorities as the need to guard against 'crimes of violence committed by the desperadoes of the island and neighbouring coasts'. Note the old use of the word 'lanthorn' for 'lantern'.*

Friend of China
21 September 1843

Mr. Christopher begs to inform the inhabitants of Victoria, Hongkong: that he has opened a Billiard Room, in the Queen's Road opposite the Hongkong Market, and trusts by attention to his customers that he will obtain a liberal share of public patronage.

Mr. Christopher begs to inform the inhabitants of Victoria, that he undertakes funerals in all their arrangement.
N.B. he has got a respectable hearse.

Friend of China
19 October 1843

Canton Markets:	IMPORTS
Cotton Yarn -	$24 & $26 Nothing doing. Stock large
Iron -	Demand is limited and nothing doing
Opium -	*Patna* $820, *Malva* $760, *Benares* $800

❖ *A typically dull market except for opium! In the same issue, the Editorial sneeringly touched on the opium trade saying, 'We were amused at the outbreak of the Imperial wrath, at the recent discovery that the Poisonous Drug was introduced into the sacred precincts of the Palace by some Tartar Horse Dealers ...'.*

Friend of China
23 December 1843

From the Editorial
Robberies, and attempts at robbery, have been very frequent. ... We have more than once called the attention of our fellow townsmen to the subject of *lighting the town*; surely no one can be blind to the benefit which would be derived during the present dark nights from a proper system of lighting. ... We are aware of two instances in which gentlemen had their silk umbrellas snatched out of their hands, and the rogues disappeared in the gloom of night and eluded pursuit. ...

❖ *Street lighting by gas replaced oil in 1864, and electric street lamps were introduced in 1890.*

1844

From the Editorial
We offer our congratulations to our friends on the commencement of another year — may it be more prosperous in every respect than its predecessor. ...

    We have only to add, that we trust it may be our good fortune to have to record from time to time during the present year, the increasing prosperity of the Colony, and the growth of friendly feelings between our countrymen and the Chinese. Under liberal management, Hongkong must and will prosper, and take its place as a commercial mart, among the *first*, if not *the* first. ...

❖   *One can only marvel at the optimistic, even fervent, hope for the prosperity of Hong Kong expressed here. In fact, in 1844 conditions in Hong Kong were still very grim, and few of the people in the position to know thought Hong Kong had any future as a commercial centre. Nor did the foreign and Chinese merchants rush from Canton into the relative safety of Hong Kong as the next editorial laments ...*

From the Editorial
It is a matter of regret, that more of the English merchants have not removed the head quarters of their establishments, to Hongkong. Macao offers no inducements for continuing there, its trade is limited and not likely to increase. As a place for Storing Goods, and giving instructions to the various Agencies at Canton and on the Coast, Hongkong is much to be preferred. The princely establishment built by Messrs. Jardine Matheson & Co. and those by Messrs. Dent & Co. and other firms, are nearly completed. We anticipate at an early date, the removal from Macao to this Colony of every British House in China.

East Point, c.1870
The first land sales on Hong Kong Island were held by auction in June 1841. While most of the original land purchasers bought their lots along the sea shore, in the Central area, Jardine, Matheson & Co bought land in East Point. There, the company established its headquarters in 1841 and built its offices, godowns and dwelling houses.

The photo, right centre, shows the East Point promontory, with the Jardine Matheson & Co buildings around 1870. The company still has extensive property there.

The small island, seen opposite East Point, is Kellett Island. A small fort can be seen on it — one of the earliest harbour defences in Hongkong. The island is now connected to Hong Kong by a causeway and houses the Royal Hongkong Yacht Club.

In the foreground of the photograph is the Bowrington Canal, named after Governor Bowring. It is commemorated today by Canal Roads East and West.

Friend of China
31 July 1844

The recent deaths have caused a good deal of uneasiness among the inhabitants and gloomy forebodings of another disastrous summer. ... During the warmest day this month, we noticed four Europeans passing along with their umbrellas closed, and under their arms, the thermometer at the time 91 in the shade. ... It is to be wondered that such folly (it claims no milder epithet) in many instances is not rewarded with sickness.

1845

From a letter to the Editor by a Dr McGowan, an American Baptist:
The [opium] traffic is the bane of China, it is carried on at Hongkong as briskly as it ever was at Lintin. At the former place it was protected only by the arms of the smuggler. Here it is carried on against the laws, but with the connivance of the British authorities.

The Editor comments:
Every word of this paragraph is untrue, and displays gross ignorance — we will not say deception — on the part of the person who penned it. The opium trade is not against the laws of Hongkong. ... Unfortunately for the prosperity of the colony it is not carried on as briskly as it ever was at Lintin.

❖ *Both the good doctor's virtuous indignation and the Editor's callous response are understandable. Unfortunately, the Treaty of Nanking (1842) which ended the First Opium War, omitted the question of opium altogether. Therefore, from the Chinese point of view its import was still illegal (as before the Treaty), and from the British point of view its smuggling was still fair game (as before the Treaty); only now the centre of the opium trade was transferred to Hong Kong. It also shows how much Hong Kong's very existence as a trading post depended at that early stage on opium trade.*

Friend of China
9 August 1845

Government Offices, Lower Albert Road, Hong Kong Island, c.1870
The buildings, erected around 1843, housed the first government offices on the 'Government Hill', between Lower Albert Road, seen on the right, and Battery Path below. The site is roughly where the Central Wing (the Main Wing) of the future Central Government Offices would stand. The hill also accommodates St. John's Cathedral, the tower of which is seen on the extreme left. A cannon in the foreground marks the location of Murray Battery.

1846

**Friend of China
18 April 1846**

We often hear the question asked, what is the cause of the delay in building the Colonial Chapel? ... We are none of those who believe that the Deity may be worshipped with greater sincerity within the walls of a Cathedral than on a hill side; but in a Christian community, where no religious intolerance compels the members of any particular sect to secrecy, we certainly think that any unnecessary delay in erecting a suitable edifice betrays an indifference to obligations. ...

In Hongkong our Roman Catholic brethren have for years had a decent and suitable place of worship.

❖ *Whether as a result of this criticism or not, the building of the Hongkong Colonial Chapel began in March the following year, and it was opened for services in March 1849; it was consecrated as the St. John's Cathedral in 1852. Although Roman Catholics were able to worship in a church since 1842, their cathedral was not built until 1880s.*

St. John's Cathedral, Garden Road, Hong Kong Island, 1862
This is probably one of the earliest photographs of Hong Kong. The cathedral is seen on the left viewed from the north. Gothic in design, with a bell-tower above the entrance, the cathedral was completed in 1849 as the founding church of the newly-established Diocese of Victoria. A new choir and a chancel extension were added in 1872, lengthening the building. The building in the centre served as the Government House until the proper Government House, seen on the right, was completed in 1859. The Mid-Levels are still largely undeveloped. A portion of the Murray Parade Ground is seen in the foreground.

At a General Court Martial, assembled at Victoria, Hongkong, on Friday, the Twenty-Third day of October One Thousand Eight Hundred and forty-six, Lieutenant Augustus Frederick Hippolito Dacosta, of the Royal Engineers, was arraigned on the following charge:- '… with having, at Victoria, Island of Hongkong, whilst seated at the Mess-table of the Officers of the Royal Engineers, between the hours of four and five o'clock … thrown a tumbler at Captain Edward William Durnford of the same Corps, thereby striking him, the said Captain Durnford, in the Arm; such conduct being unbecoming the character of an officer and a gentleman, subversive of all discipline and propriety, and in breach of the Articles of War'.

[Signed] Edward Aldrich, Major

❖ *Lieutenant Da Costa, of mixed Brazilian and English descent, had distinguished himself in the First Opium War, but was being court-martialled for a minor offence here. He was later murdered, in February 1849, along with a fellow officer, Lieutenant Dwyer, by the villagers at Stanley in very suspicious circumstances which suggested provocative behaviour on their part. Da Costa is buried at the Happy Valley Cemetery.*

Friend of China
7 November 1846

1847

The Opium Farm
The Governor of Hongkong by his fiscal measures has deprived the Chinese of every remaining inducement to settle on the island. The most grievous and impolitic of these measures is what is called the 'Opium Farm'; a monopoly which secures to one man the right of selling opium on this island in less quantities than one chest. … If it is an 'iniquitous' trade let not the British be directly implicated in it, by putting up to auction and letting the exclusive right to sell it … In this country, all classes of statesmen acknowledge the injustice and impolicy of raising money by means of … monopolies. The system is identified in the British mind with the misfortunes of the days of King Charles I.

❖ *The monopoly and franchise still reign in Hong Kong today and have been cited as the reasons, at least in part, for Hong Kong's economic success.*

Friend of China
30 January 1847

Friend of China
17 April 1847

The Emperor denounces Keying
The English have rebelled against us, disobeying our laws and bringing disorder and injury on the 'Flowery Nation'. Keying's heart is inwardly inclined towards them; he disregards our families, and, trampling on the people, he thereby degrades the nation. His crime deserves to be punished with death; it is therefore desirable that every one of us should exert himself, that all uniting together, we may set fire to his palace, and then cast his dead body into the street. To do this is not exceeding the law.

Taoukwang, 27ᵗʰ year, 2ⁿᵈ Moon, 20ᵗʰ day (5 April 1847).

❖ *Although the First Opium War was over, hostile acts by both sides continued. In one such incident, a party of Europeans was attacked by the Chinese near Canton. In a precipitate and out-of-proportion action, Governor John Davis ordered General D'Aguilar to seize the Bogue Forts (guarding the approaches to Canton) and prepare for an assault on Canton. The forts were captured, but Canton was spared after Commissioner Keying agreed to punish the culprits and allow entry to Canton, hitherto denied. Keying had no choice, but his action was regarded as an act of treachery; the Emperor, although angry, spared his life.*

Friend of China
12 May 1847

Mr. Gutzlaff has furnished the Asiatic Society with some curious information regarding China. It is really to be regretted that the Society permit such haphazard, brazen-faced quackery to be read at their meetings, without testing the data upon which he bases his assumptions. … we will not take the trouble of impressing upon our readers the utter absurdity of the document. A man who will gravely assert, that in a city of 30,000 souls, there was only one unmarried woman, must be charlatan of the first water … .

❖ *Dr. Gutzlaff, a Pomeranian missionary, was a colourful and controversial character in the early Hong Kong. His fluent knowledge of the Chinese language made him indispensable to the Hong Kong Government, but many regarded him as a buffoon and a charlatan; he was even suspected of dabbling in opium trade.*

Friend of China
1 December 1847

THE CHIEF JUSTICE IS SUSPENDED; ATTORNEY-GENERAL CAMPBELL APPOINTED TO ACT FOR HIM.
The above notice was put into our hand at a late hour; and we can only say, we trust it is not true.

❖ *But it was, as officially confirmed the following day.*

Further on this subject

Friend of China
4 December 1847

We have received various communicates of this subject; but decline them all. The character of a Judge is too sacred a thing for newspaper disquisition; it now rests with the public ... to declare with one voice that Judge Hulme carries with him their unshaken esteem and respect.

❖ *Chief Justice Hulme was suspended for alleged drunkenness. There was no substance in these allegations, but the real reason was a bitter and long-standing feud between him and the Governor Sir John Davis. When Davis resigned shortly afterwards, Hulme was reinstated. He was a popular Chief Justice and he continued to perform his duties until 1854.*

Sir John Francis Davis (1795–1890)

Sir John Davis, the second governor of Hong Kong first came to the Far East in 1816 as a member of Lord Amherst's mission to China — the second unsuccessful attempt by the British to establish diplomatic and trade relations with China. A scholar and sinologist of considerable merit, Davis had written an authoritative work on China and was much sought after for his knowledge of the Chinese language and the ways of its people. His career proceeded successfully, and in 1844 he succeeded Sir Henry Pottinger as the governor of Hong Kong.

There was still a great deal to be done in Hong Kong, and Davis applied himself to his task with zeal. Like his predecessor Pottinger, however, Davis despised the traders, and this soon made him unpopular with this dominant power in Hong Kong. E. J. Eitel summed it up well when he wrote of him: 'He has spent the best part of his life ... bowing to Chinese officials and frowning upon European free traders.'

Compelled further to introduce a number of unpopular measures, he became unpopular in all circles of the Hong Kong community.

His reputation, already tarnished, suffered a further setback from two unrelated incidents. The first was his long dispute with the Chief Justice Hulme, whom he suspended for alleged drunkenness, but who was finally vindicated to the acute embarrassment of Davis. The second was his precipitate action, in 1847, of seizing Bogue Forts (guarding the approach to China) as a reprisal for the Chinese attack on a party of Europeans. Clearly, governing colonies was not his metier.

When he left Hong Kong in 1848, after four years as governor, his departure was virtually ignored by the Hong Kong community. In retirement, his scholarship had earned him many honours and distinctions.

He died in 1890 at the age of 95.

1848

**Friend of China
27 May 1848**

Ferriery corner of Wellington and Wyndham Street, Victoria. Mr. Duddell begs to inform the community of Hongkong, that he has engaged an English Horse Shoer, and will open a Ferriery in all its branches on the above premises on … ; and is confident that the moderate charge of $1.5 per Horse together with attention and despatch, will procure him a share of Public Patronage.

**Friend of China
9 September 1848**

On Tuesday the Honourable Chief Justice Hulme was providentially saved from a violent death. In crossing a bridge on horseback between Victoria and Stanley it broke down and the Judge had a fall of about thirty feet. Fortunately the fall was broken by a scaffolding put up for repairs; and though the respected gentleman was severely bruised, it is gratifying to know that his injuries are not such as to endanger a life so valued by his countrymen in China.

❖ *It would seem that bad fortune followed the Honourable Chief Justice. If one reads the report correctly, the bridge was under repairs, in which case the good judge had only himself to blame for the accident.*

**Friend of China
23 September 1848**

Hongkong is a butt at which every writer on China launches a shaft, nor has the contributor to the Dublin Magazine spared the unfortunate colony; in his estimation it is but little better than the very place where wicked people go. … he has evidently been in China, however, but even a bad memory and a traveller's licence will not excuse very gross ignorance or very deliberate deception. We are assured that when Hongkong was taken possession of by the British troops it was in such bad repute that there was not a single Chinese inhabitant. This is error number one, there having been several villages and farms on the island with a population estimated at 5,000 souls. Again, we are told that the weather has known the thermometer at 116 in the shade in summer, while during winter 'the nights are so cold that ice is formed in the water Jugs'. If he ever saw the thermometer at 116 in the shade it must have been in an engine room. …

❖ *Misconceptions about Hong Kong abounded. Even the British Foreign Secretary, Palmerston, who should have been better informed, described Hong Kong as 'a barren island with hardly a house upon it'.*

1849

The distressing intelligence of the murder of the Governor of Macao arrived on Thursday morning. … Mr. Amaral, accompanied by his *Aide-de-camp*, went out on horseback at his usual hour on Wednesday afternoon. On returning … a Chinese boy presented him with a flower on the end of a bamboo. His Excellency accepted the flower, when the boy struck him with the bamboo. … he was attacked by *five* Chinese armed with swords. … they bore him to the earth and despatched him with many wounds.

Friend of China
25 August 1849

Macao in 1870
Historians are divided as to whether the possession of Macao by the Portuguese was originally due to Imperial bounty or to right of conquest. The Portuguese first took up their residence in Macao in 1557, and for many years prior to 1848 a rental of 500 taels a year was paid to the Chinese authorities. In 1848, Governor Ferreira do Amaral stopped paying the rental and drove out the Chinese Customs House. This bold stoke cost the governor his life at the hands of an assassin the following year and it was not until 1887 that the sovereignty of Portugal over the peninsula was formally recognized by China in a treaty.

The establishment of Hong Kong as a free trading port, in 1841, posed a strong challenge to the future of Macao, but it survived the competition and continued to flourish.

The photograph above shows the familiar view of Macao with the magnificent Praia Grande stretching in a graceful curve. Beyond, on the highest point at the far end, stands Guia Fort with its lighthouse faintly visible. In the foreground is what appears to be the bishop's residence after it was rebuilt in 1837.

Friend of China
12 September 1849

More about the assassination
It is apparently reported in Canton, and is very generally believed, that the officer upon whom it devolved to organize the assassination of Governor Amaral, has been rewarded with a button of considerable rank for his services! And has the promise of a situation of emolument on the first vacancy (from *Hongkong Register*, 11th September).

❖ *This was denied most forcibly by the Chinese Government.*

1850

Friend of China
2 March 1850

The Opium Revenue. In order to give the reader a view of the gradual increase of this branch of the public Revenue, we have drawn up … a return of the … nett profits of the opium during the last twenty years:

❖ *A list follows in which the last year, 1848/49 shows a profit in rupees, equivalent to 2.5 million pounds sterling.*

The opium revenue has now become so important an element in our financial system that it is difficult to imagine how the machine of government could be carried on without it.

Friend of China
24 April 1850

The past month has been very barren of incident. Business rather dull. A regatta and two balls have been the means of driving away the *taedium vitae* of our Canton neighbours; one of the Balls was given By H.B.M.* Consul J. Bowring Esquire, to H.E.** Mr. Bonham, who with Mrs. Bonham and a large party of Hongkong fashionables honoured the Regatta with their presence.

❖ *Bonham was the Governor of Hong Kong from March 1848 to April 1854. John Bowring succeeded him as Governor in April 1854.*

---

* H.B.M.: Her Brittanic Majesty.
** H.E.: His Excellency.

Sir George Bonham (1803–1863)

Samuel George Bonham, the third governor of Hongkong (1848–1854), was a man of considerable experience in the affairs of the Orient and in the colonial civil administration. At the time of his appointment to Hong Kong, the colony was still in its infancy with many 'teething' problems. Prominent among these were problems of finance, defence and public works. The latter had to be suspended altogether, except for the most urgent needs. With all these, Bonham dealt promptly and efficiently.

He was noted for his concern for the welfare of Hong Kong Chinese residents, and the event which distressed him probably more than any other, was the disastrous fire in the Chinese section of the island (Sheung Wan), in December 1851. The fire, aided by strong winds, swept through the area rapidly, and in spite of heroic efforts by members of the garrison, 472 houses were destroyed and 80 lives lost. Bonham's other major regret was the continuing bad relations between China and Britain which fettered the Nanking Treaty.

He left Hong Kong in 1854, admired and respected, and his departure, unlike that of his predecessors (Pottinger and Davis), was genuinely regretted.

The whole of the 59th Regiment are panic stricken and if there is any wish to save them the experiment should be tried of billeting those who are well … at the Seamen's boarding houses in the Colony. … the contract with the Commissariat baker should be broken immediately, and English made biscuits served out in place of stuff unfit for a dog to eat.

Friend of China
3 August 1850

❖ *The 59th Regiment of Foot was badly stricken with epidemics of malaria and dysentery with high mortality rate.*

1851

The First Criminal Sessions of the year commence on Monday next the 16th. The Calendar contains twelve cases. Two of piracy (Chinese) and one of murder, on the high seas … one of Forgery (Chinese) — George Thomson for a rape — Five Seamen of HMS Hastings for stabbing — Matthew Hopkins for abetting desertion from the garrison — One case of Burglary with wounding — and Five Larcenies.

Friend of China
14 February 1851

**Friend of China
1 March 1851**

The great event of the month has been the capture of Chui-apoo, who, on his own admission, was concerned in the brutal murder of Capt. Da Costa and Lieutenant Dwyer in February 1849.

❖   *The murder of Captain Da Costa and Lieutenant Dwyer was mentioned on p. 21 (Friend of China, 7 November 1846). Chui-apoo, a notorious pirate, was convicted of manslaughter (not murder!) and sentenced to transportation for life (at that time to Van Diemen's Land, later to be renamed Tasmania), but he hanged himself in his cell.*

1852

**Friend of China
14 February 1852**

'We have always been very much at a loss to know how any Governor could possibly have it in his power to benefit this Colony, — especially the *last* one' writes our correspondent referring to Sir G. Bonham.

❖   *Friend of China then concludes with the following description of Governor Bonham:*

… Inefficient as Commander in Chief — neglectful as Vice-Admiral — perverter of justice in his interference or his inattention — tacit sanctioner of extortion mongering — socially deficient in any other sphere than the Race Course, the ball or the Dining Room — careless about the promotion of knowledge — callous to the appeals of sick and destitute — totally wanting in the qualifications that go to make an efficient governor, such has been Sir Samuel George Bonham; and easy though it may be to pass a compliment, — his admirers will find it a task of no slight difficulty to show that aught of what we have now said of him is other than the truth.

❖   *What an indictment! Friend of China certainly did not spare the poor Governor, and yet, going over the historical accounts, it is difficult to see how Bonham could have acquired such a reputation. Historian George Endacott (1958, p. 87) describes him as 'popular and friendly; … his departure was genuinely regretted'. Eitel ([1895]1983, p. 287) describes him as, '… this model Governor, the first really popular and successful one of the Colony's rulers'.*

1854

But the newspaper has not yet finished with Governor Bonham; it goes on: A circular went the round of the town ... intimating to parties desirous of signing a farewell address to Sir S.G. Bonham. ... Among other subjects of laudation the speedy rebuilding of the Chinese town is spoken of; but surely this must be meant in joke. Why, along the whole sea front where the fire occurred more than $2^1/_2$ years ago, there is not one house that may be called finished. ... Personally we have much pleasure in wishing His Excellency farewell.

**Friend of China
8 April 1854**

A meeting of the CHINA BRANCH OF THE ROYAL ASIATIC SOCIETY, will be held on ... 9th May ... at the Society's Room in the Court House, when H.E. Sir John Bowring will preside. Papers have been received ... on the following subjects — Porcelain bottles, — Pagodas of China, — Ancient Chinese Pronunciation.

**Friend of China
29 April 1854**

Sir John Bowring (1792–1872)

Dr John Bowring (later to be knighted), a scholarly-looking man who was a linguist, an economist with an honorary degree from a German university and a writer of hymns in his spare time, chose to pursue government service instead of a more befitting academic career. After a number of civil service posts, which included a consulship in Canton, John Bowring was appointed Governor of Hong Kong in 1854, when he was already 62 years of age. His was not a successful governorship.

It may have been his age or some weakness of character, or both, which were responsible for the lack of determination needed for the job. His intentions were good and he had many splendid ideas, but seemed to lack the strength and courage to carry them out. Although considered liberal and peace-loving, Sir John Bowring made no effort to defuse the strained relations between China and Britain at the time, and, in fact, pursued the second Anglo-Chinese conflict, the so-called 'Arrow War', with vigour.

However, on the home front in Hong Kong, he cared about his Chinese subjects and was popular with them. When he left Hong Kong in 1859, after five years as governor, he was honoured with gifts by the Chinese community, but ignored by the European residents of the colony.

1856

**Friend of China
2 April 1856**

On dit: The Hon'ble Lieutenant Governor Caine, goes to England next mail. — The Colony will gain something by his absence.

1857

**Friend of China
7 January 1857**

Our news from Canton was just a week old when HMS *Coromandel*, Lieutenant Douglas R.N.* Commanding, arrived … bringing the following exciting information … on Sunday last, a boat arrived from Macao Passage Fort advising the Admiral of the approach … of a large number of Chinese War Junks. Steam was got up immediately, and, with all the available boats in company, the *Coromandel* proceeded to a reconnaissance. …

❖ *In October 1856 hostilities broke out again between Britain and China, which became known as the Second Opium War or the 'Arrow War', and which ended in 1860.*

**Friend of China
7 March 1857**

With regret we have to inform the public of a fire which was caused by an incendiary at one of Mr. Duddell's godowns last night. … The Police must have kept a very bad lookout as nearly an hour and a half elapsed after the fire was discovered before an engine made its appearance. …

Mr. Duddell we understand had applied to the Government for a guard for his bakery some time ago, but without effect.

❖ *A merchant and versatile entrepreneur, George Duddell was a well-known personality in the early business community of Hong Kong. He had no success in his protracted claims against the British Government for compensation (for the loss in the above fire), but is remembered in Duddell Street at the centre of Hong Kong.*

---

* R.N.: (British) Royal Navy

Steps and Street Lamps Duddell Street, 1977

A small area of old Hong Kong in the Central District of the island has been preserved as a monument. Fine, broad granite steps lead from Ice House Street above to the blind end of Duddell Street below. Four street lamps, two above and two below adorn the steps. They are the sole surviving street lamps still employing gas, originally lit manually but now operated automatically.

It has not been possible to fix the date when the steps were built, but the old maps of Hong Kong indicate it was between 1870 and 1880. The street was named after a versatile but luckless entrepreneur, George Duddell, a well-known personality in the early business community of Hong Kong.

It is nearly impossible today, when well-lit streets are taken for granted, to imagine what it was like to walk at night on the streets of Hong Kong in the 1840s and 1850s. Original street lighting depended almost entirely on oil lamps suspended before the doors of occupied houses.

In any case, frequent robberies made the streets after dark so unsafe that the police magistrate, in 1846, was obliged to issue a notice warning residents 'not to go beyond the limits of the town singly or even in parties unless armed' (Eitel, [1895] 1983).

By 1856, general street lighting by the existing 250 oil lamps was augmented by a further 100 lamps, extending lighting to Wan Chai. In 1864, the city was at last lit by gas — a milestone and a great improvement over the weak and uncertain oil lamps.

Electric lamps were introduced to the streets in 1890, gradually replacing the gas lamps.

The four gas lamps on the steps of Duddell Street were deliberately left in their original condition as relics of an age long gone, when the lighting of all the streets was done by gas.

1858

**Friend of China
6 March 1858**

The following is a translation of the Imperial Edict by which the Emperor ordered Commissioner Yeh to be degraded:

Holding the office of Imperial Commissioner, for the direction of the affairs of the Barbarians, *Yeh Ming-ching* ought to have devised means to keep in check the said Barbarians. ... also he ought to have conferred with the commandant, the governor, and other officers of the city, so that measures for soothing and controlling them might have been reasonably adopted. ... Thus, day after day, for a long time, he dallied with and put off the Barbarians, till, excited to wrath, they suddenly entered the provincial City (Canton).

So very insufficient and obstinate was he, perverse and reckless, utterly disregarding the duties of his high commission!

Let Yeh Ming-ching, therefore, be immediately degraded from office. ...

This is from the Emperor, dated (28 January 1858).

❖   *The unfortunate Commissioner Yeh was powerless to prevent the fall of Canton against the strong combined British and French force. He refused to negotiate to the end, and was arrested in Canton by the British and sent to Calcutta.*

**Friend of China
24 July 1858**

The Fox is run to Earth — Dr. Bridges, Honourable no longer, has resigned.

❖   *Dr. W. T. Bridges, barrister and Acting Colonial Secretary, a strong and unscrupulous man, was implicated in accepting a bribe from an opium monopolist and was forced to resign. In spite of the disgrace, Bridges Street, in the Mid-Levels, remained named after him.*

1860

Letter in San Francisco, 30 July 1860: The Bishop of Victoria on Chinese Worth:

Friend of China
20 October 1860

My dear Sir, — Until my arrival in this city, I had never become cognizant of the fact that by the legislative action of this State every individual among the 45,000 Chinese immigrants in California, is incapacitated from giving evidence in your courts of law; and under no circumstances of crime, oppression, injustice, or violence, is the possibility of redress open to a Chinese in this State. ... Chinese merchants in this City, of the highest respectability, who received their education under my roof at Hongkong, have called my attention to this exceptional legislation. ... They are pillaged, plundered, assaulted, and even murdered, by European and American miscreants in your gold-fields, and, in the absence of European witnesses, there remains to these poor Chinese no alternative but that of helplessly and hopelessly submitting to the oppression caused by this unequal law.

In the name of all that is just, equable, and humane ... in the name of your American Plenipotentiaries, who, in China and Japan, are demanding for American citizens equal privileges ... in the name of our common Christianity ... I exhort and entreat the Christian citizens of your great and powerful country ... to apply themselves vigorously to a repeal of this obnoxious Act.

1871

No further issues of the Friend of China *were available at this point, but a new daily, the* Hongkong Daily Press *had appeared.*

Hans Ordlhit, a seaman of the *Esmeralda*, was charged with having first got drunk, secondly visited a brothel, and thirdly walked off with an umbrella belonging to one of the inmates. Fined $2 for the umbrella, and 50 cents for the disorderly conduct.

Hongkong Daily Press
10 January 1871

Hongkong Daily Press
13 February 1871

Hongkong & Shanghai Banking Corporation:
Eleventh report of the Court of Directors to the Ordinary Yearly General Meeting of Shareholders. ... The net profits for the period (half-year ending on 31.12.70), including $99,398.33 brought forward from last account, ... amount to $465,968.82 of which, after taking out Rebate on Bills not yet due and Remuneration to Directors, there remains for appropriation $451,141.46.

From this sum the Directors recommend the distribution of a Dividend of $5 per share.

Hongkong Daily Press
23 February 1871

Chinese New Year: We foreigners are apt to treat with disregard or even ridicule the fact that the Chinese have a new year's day different from our own. ... At the lowest estimate, we should say that the day is rigidly observed by some four hundred and fifty millions of people.

Hongkong Daily Press
1 May 1871

Unlicensed Hawking:
Chu Ahong, an unlicensed hawker of salt fish, offered I.P.C. [Indian Police Constable] No. 191 ten cents as a bribe to let him go when apprehended. The market people complained that they could not sell their fish because undersold by the people outside. Defendant said that the constable had struck him, and he had given him the ten cents piece to forbear. Ten cents confiscated, and defendant fined $2, in default seven days' imprisonment.

❖ *After 130 years, unlicensed hawking is still a problem.*

Hongkong Daily Press
22 May 1871

From the Editorial:
The extraordinary fear which the Government of Hongkong entertains against all publicity is one of the most discouraging features in connection with the local administration of the Colony. Not only is no assistance is given to the papers to obtain intelligence regarding passing events, in which the public is deeply interested but every effort is made by the officers to prevent information coming from the numerous channels, from which in every other place it is largely derived.

Wellington Street, Central District, Hong Kong Island, pre-1911
A view of a very busy street lined on both sides with tenement houses and shops. Large number of people are looking at the displayed wares in shops and stalls. The men are shaven and wearing queues according to the Manchu custom.

**Hongkong Daily Press
29 June 1871**

The Opium Trade:

The Trade throughout the past year has been seriously affected by the competition it has met from the native drug. … it may be reasonably deduced that, in order to meet … the native competition effectually, Indian opium must … be placed in the consumer's hands at a cheaper cost.

❖   *The commentator states the obvious — how to deal with competition. But the important point here is that by the early 1870s China had found a partial solution to the opium question — the production of its own opium which was grown in Yunnan and Szechuan Provinces.*

Hong Kong Police, c.1885
Lawlessness and crime were rife in the early days of Hong Kong and concern for law and order was pre-eminent in the minds of the early administration. The initial Hong Kong Police Force, established in 1844, relied on discharged British and Indian soldiers, untrained in police duties. It was not until 1855, under Governor Bowring, that efforts were made to improve the force; at the same time Chinese constables were now recruited for the police. Still, the improvement was slow and painful, and public safety was often put at risk. In subsequent years, the Police Force was often closely scrutinized and described on several occasions as being 'corrupt and inefficient'. The photograph shows a group of police inspectors. In the back row, third from the left, is the first Chinese inspector, though with a European name of William Quinsey.

Extract from Mr. Smale's (Chief Justice) local song on Hongkong Police:-
  They've given you here as 'Guardians of the peace'
  An inefficient staff of mix's police,
  A pretty motley group of roughs I'swear,
  A riff raff, pick's here'n alone knows where,
  Drunken Europeans, and the lanky Sikh,
  Who cannot understand a word we speak,
  Lazy Indians, too, from various tribes,
  Chinese detectives who are fond of bribes —
  In league — if all I hear be true —
  With gamblers, thieves, and even murderers too,
  Shame on the Government, a Shame I say,
  To keep such 'barefac'd' robbers in their pay.

Hongkong Daily Press
12 July 1871

A godown belonging to Messrs. Burd & Co., collapsed on Saturday afternoon at about 5.30, this time not on account of the rain, but of the white ants. A few remaining casks of pale ale indicate the spot.

Of the eight non-English jurors called yesterday, only one declared himself unable to speak English. He was ordered to sit in court and learn.

Hongkong Daily Press
28 August 1871

<u>A flying machine a failure.</u> Mr. Falger of Detroit, made himself two spacious wings of rattan, cork, and oilskin, summoned his friends and the newspaper reporters, repaired to the roof of a one-storey home, and promised just before he commenced to flap that he would telegraph back from Grand Rapids. He flapped, but instead of being wafted upward ... he landed among some weeds on his stomach.

Hongkong Daily Press
16 October 1871

From the Editorial:
HOW, WHEN and WHERE? These interrogatives ... at the present moment they shall suggest only three definite enquiries touching Hongkong. *How* is Hongkong to be governed by Great Britain? *When* shall we have a Government that shall govern Hongkong? *Where* are we to find a Government that shall govern Hongkong? ... We may now reply to our opening question as follows: Hongkong is to be governed by Great Britain through the Foreign Office. We shall have a Government that shall govern Hongkong as soon as a well-matured

Hongkong Daily Press
7 November 1871

scheme of popular representation be combined with a selection of Crown Officers. ... We are to find a Government that shall govern Hongkong in China and not elsewhere.

❖   *By all standards this must be considered an extraordinary statement showing foresight and mature judgement, considering that this was a colonial era at its height.*

1872

**Hongkong Daily Press
23 January 1872**

The public flogging of eighteen prisoners will take place at the whipping post, this day, at 3.30 p.m.

❖   *As far as can be ascertained, the whipping post was near the Harbourmaster's Office, located half-way up Wyndham Street, near the present On Lan Street. Members of the English Club (predecessor of the Hongkong Club), which was located at the bottom of Wyndham Street, would have had an excellent view of the flogging from the upper balcony of the Club!*

Hongkong Club, Queen's Road Central, Hong Kong Island, c.1870–75
The first Hongkong Club, originally called the English Club, shown on this photograph, was opened in May 1846 at the corner of Queen's Road and Wyndham Street. Colonial in style with arched verandahs, and modest in size, it served the British community well for 50 years until replaced, in 1897, by the much bigger and more prestigious building in Statue Square. The Hongkong Club was often referred to in the past as the 'citadel of Hong Kong's expatriate mercantile community', its exclusive membership being in tune with the prevailing colonial tradition of the time.

1873

A Scotch missionary, in speaking of cannibalism, solemnly declares that for his own part, he would rather go hungry for two days, than eat an old personal friend.

Hongkong Daily Press
2 July 1873

Feng-Shui: The Chinese are a materialistic people, almost destitute of imagination, and most of their superstitions are of a material character, and, therefore can best be counteracted by instruction in natural facts. Who would believe in the dragon devouring the sun, if he understood just a little. ... of the Copernican System; or who would believe in Feng-Shui, if the principles of geologic change were clearly taught to him? Superstition rests on ignorance, and ignorance alone.

Hongkong Daily Press
16 August 1873

Foreigners ... are also to blame. They allowed themselves to attach undue importance to the opinions of the Chinese ... the lamentable ignorance under which we have been labouring is quite sufficient to explain our want of success in many affairs, diplomatic and others. ... That we were misled and misunderstood ... is not strange. But now our facts are accumulating, and we can more justly estimate the genius of this wonderful race.

We have much pleasure in noticing a new edition of the Rev. Dr. Eitel's lectures on Buddhism, and also the publication of his excellent work on Feng-Shui. ... This system [Feng-Shui] he views as nothing more than a dim perception of the mysteries of nature ... a sense of its varied power and regulated action ... . Each nation has its own cosmogony, and its explanation of the origin of things, and it seems to us that this peculiar system is somewhat more philosophical than many others, and affords another illustration of Lord Elgin's remarks 'that at all points of the circle described by man's intelligence, the Chinese mind seems occasionally to have caught glimpses of a heaven far beyond the range of its ordinary ken and vision'.

❖   *Dr Eitel's work and publications are well known to students of Hong Kong's early history. His best known book is* Europe in China *(1895), republished in 1983. There is no doubt that his wonderful insight into the Chinese mind and character helped enormously to bridge the gap which existed (and still exists) between the Chinese and foreign communities.*

Tsui Shing Lau, Ping Shang Pagoda, c.1930

The pagoda is thought of as a characteristically Chinese building, but in fact it had developed originally as a repository of sacred Buddhist relics or as a place of Buddhist devotion.

There are few pagodas in Hong Kong compared with the mainland, where splendid tall pagodas are a common enough feature. Among the few, Tsui Shing Lau is the sole authentically ancient pagoda. It stands in Ping Shan in the heart of the Tang clan district.

Though small and modest by any standard, it enjoys a special and honoured place in local tradition, which sets the date of its building in the 14th century, early in the Ming dynasty. Local people relate that it was built as a protection against 'unfavourable influences from the North'.

Its location in alignment with Castle Peak, historically regarded as the Sacred Mountain, was interpreted by the Tangs as being propitious for scholarship and distinction. Indeed, the Tang clan of Ping Shan claims, with historical truth, among its members have flourished a number of distinguished scholars and high officials.

The pagoda is a six-sided structure, about 10m wide and 20m high, built of Chinese grey brick. The intricately arranged brick corbels separating the three storeys form a pleasing architectural feature. It is said to have been originally seven storeys high and subsequently to have lost the four upper storeys in two separate incidents, presumably by the force of typhoons; a geomancer had then advised the villagers to let the pagoda remain at three storeys. By counting the layers of corbelled bricks, however, the author believes that the original height of the pagoda may have been five storeys, not seven.

Its name of Tsui Shing Lau, carved on one of the tablets decorating the pagoda, may be translated as the 'building of many stars'. Two other stone tablets claim for it a heavenly connection, and within is an altar with wooden deities; nonetheless, the pagoda is neither a temple nor a Buddhist shrine, but principally a *fung shui* structure.

An Atlanta doctor advises persons afraid of cholera to stand on their head for one minute three times a day. He argues that arrests abdominal depression, and would be a healthful gymnastic exercise at any time.

Hongkong Daily Press
10 September 1873

A boa-constrictor, in Singapore, has swallowed a young lady who had on a diamond necklace valued at 15,000 dols., and is now in demand.

Hongkong Daily Press
3 December 1873

1874

The Emperor of China and the Railway: The project of a wedding gift to the Emperor of China, to take the form of a short railway complete with carriages and locomotives, has been finally set at rest … the answer … was in substance this[:] 'China not having yet introduced a railway system, the Emperor could not receive such presents as the committee propose to offer, and therefore the presents are to be declined in advance, to obviate the unpleasantness that might arise upon them being rejected on arrival.'

Hongkong Daily Press
10 January 1874

❖   *In fact, we learn later that the present of the railway was accepted.*

William Phillips, a seaman … was charged with being drunk, and refusing to pay chair hire. … He was fined 50 cents, and ordered to pay chair-coolies 30 cents.

Hongkong Daily Press
19 January 1874

From the Editorial:
A Municipal Council in Hongkong … would, we think, be infinitely more satisfactory to the public than the existing form of government. … It might be considered desirable to retain the present Executive Council as a sort of a Upper House … but we think it only fair that the general public should be more directly represented in our local administration than they are at present.

Hongkong Daily Press
9 February 1874

❖   *There is no mistaking this call for an elected representation, and what is suggested here is a replacement of the Legislative Council by a Municipal*

Council. Instead, in 1935, the Sanitary Board was replaced by the Urban Council with two elected members, but very limited powers. It should be clear to the readers, however, that the clamour for a truly representative government in Hong Kong was evident early and was not merely a late 20th century phenomenon.

Hongkong Daily Press 24 September 1874

Terrific Typhoon: On Tuesday night and yesterday morning, Hongkong was visited by the most awful typhoon which has ever been recorded in the history of the Colony ... the damage done to the buildings on the heights has been very extensive. The Governor's bungalow has been completely unroofed ...

Typhoon in Hong Kong, September 1874
This photograph shows the badly damaged pier of Douglas Lapraik & Co., a shipping company, and other signs of devastation at Hong Kong's waterfront. One of the worst typhoons in Hong Kong's history, it struck Hong Kong suddenly and with little warning, on 22 September 1874. In six terrible hours 2,000 lives, mostly fishermen at sea, were lost. Many ships were sunk and extensive damage done to property.

And further on …

… it was ascertained that not a single ship in port escaped undamaged and the loss of life was estimated at 2000 souls.

Hongkong Daily Press
26 September 1874

❖ *This was certainly the most devastating typhoon in Hong Kong's recorded history up to that date. Only two later typhoons would equal or surpass it — in 1906 and 1937. In the latter, 10,000 people lost their lives, mostly fisher-folk caught unprepared at sea.*

1876

Snippets from the China Mail *are now included. Although established in 1845, earlier issues were not available.*

From the Editorial:

We can hardly agree with the London and China Express that the Praya* is the 'White Elephant' of Hongkong. That rarely seen animal is, as we understand, something which, while of no earthly use to his unfortunate keeper, has nevertheless to be maintained at an enormous cost. … Now the Praya is neither useless to those who pay for it, nor likely to lead to the financial ruin of the Colony, and we therefore submit that it is in no way a 'white elephant'.

China Mail
4 January 1876

❖ *The Praya Reclamation, first proposed in 1855, was strongly opposed by the merchants who had their private piers on the waterfront. The reclamation was eventually carried out in 1873. It is amazing that anyone should have doubted the necessity of this and subsequent reclamations, which have expanded much needed flat land for the development of the city. See Hong Kong Waterfront, p.44.*

---

* Praya: a road built along the shore, the waterfront (from Portuguese *praia*, beach, bank).

Hong Kong Waterfront, c.1875–80
Picture after the completion, in 1873, of the first major praya reclamation.
Merchant houses with arched verandahs, uniformly 3-storeys high, of simple
unpretentious style, line the waterfront. Slightly to the right of the centre is
Pedder Wharf, with Jardine, Matheson & Co. offices on the right and Hongkong
Hotel on the left. Behind, the twin domes of the Roman Catholic Church, on
Wellington Street, can be seen.

China Mail
15 January 1876

Town Postage (Victoria) Letter, Newspaper, Book, or Pattern.. 2 cents
Rates by Private Steamer, — to United Kingdom .... 8 cents

China Mail
7 February 1876

From the Editorial:
The Report of the Captain Superintendent of Police for the year 1875
is an interesting document. Commendably concise it gives a good deal
of information. He notes a decrease of reported crime to the extent of
4.89 per cent, on the previous year, an increase of 19.74 per cent on
serious crime, and a decrease of 11.11 percent, on minor offences.

When Darwin informed us that man was descended from the monkey, we thought that man was lowered quite sufficiently. ... However, it appears, we must go a peg lower. The London correspondent ... writes: 'I have just heard Professor Huxley lecture. He calmly proved that we were all vegetables, that there is no real difference between vegetables and men. ... Where are we now? Our ... contemporary wants to know if this is a new discovery, or simply a scientific proof of the old Scripture saying:- 'All flesh is grass'.

China Mail
28 March 1876

❖ *This, of course, is written 'with one's tongue in one's cheek'; Darwin never said that humans were descended from monkeys, but only that we shared a common ancestor with apes.*

Owing to the inclemency of the weather, the intended parade of the Fire Brigade this afternoon was not held.

China Mail
6 April 1876

❖ *What?! Our firemen afraid to get their feet wet?*

The return of the revenue and expenditure of the Colony for the year 1875 is published in the *Gazette*. ... The total revenue for the year was $896,624.31 and the expenditure $869,822.51. Compared with 1874 the revenue shows a net increase of $41,824.40 and the expenditure a net decrease of $51,657.07.

China Mail
25 April 1876

❖ *These amazing figures show that the net revenue for the year was a mere $26,801.80. Barely enough to pay one month's salary of today's junior staff. Even granted the 130 years intervening, and the vastly changed value of a dollar, has any place in the world grown so fast?*

The Postmaster General has issued the following notification ... 'The Italian Post Office has complained that, in the mail for the Continent ... which left Hongkong on the 20th January, was a sample of Indigo, which became loose and damaged the whole mail ... The public are therefore again earnestly begged not to attempt to send dye-stuffs in powder through the Post ... .'

China Mail
1 May 1876

1877

China Mail
27 January 1877

The attention of a great many residents has no doubt been attracted during the last week or two by the picture of a man's head, paraded about the streets on a board by a Chinese. This is the manner in which an exhibition called the 'Speaking Head', held in Wellington Street, is advertised. Our reporter … says that the room in which the loquacious *caput* is on view, has no furniture whatever. … The 'Speaking Head' appears in a basin on a table. The spectators may ask it any questions and it answers accordingly. The 'Head' speaks several languages, and simply astonishes, at all events, the Chinese visitors.

China Mail
5 March 1877

We are glad to learn that Mr. Ng Choy, who has been studying for some years in London, was called to the bar at Lincoln's Inn on the 26th January last. He is now on his way back … but will not probably arrive here till the end of April. … He is the first Chinese who has been called to the English Bar, and will no doubt, prove himself useful to his country.

Ng Choy (伍才), 1842–1922
Portrait taken in Hong Kong, c.1880, wearing barrister's robe and wig. Also known as Wu Ting-fang, he was educated at St. Paul's School in Hong Kong, and qualified as barrister in England. Ng Choy was the first Chinese to be appointed, in 1880, to the Legislative Council. This was due, in no small measure, to the Governor Pope Hennessy breaking with the established tradition of Europeans only on the Council, though Ng Choy's ability and fine qualities were no doubt the deciding factors. Ng Choy served later as the Chinese ambassador to Washington.

Reuter's telegram, London 2 August 1877:
After desperate fighting at Plevna, the Russian troops have been completely defeated, with a loss of 8,000 killed and 24,000 wounded.

China Mail
4 August 1877

❖ *This was the Turkish-Russian War. The author could hardly resist including this bit since his grandfather fought in this battle, on the Russian side (!), who told a different story. The report shows a bias, since Britain, although non-participant in the war, was strongly pro-Turkish; worried about the Russians gaining control of the Bosporus strait and, thus, the entry into the Mediterranean.*

Our Harbour presents quite a lively and business-like appearance, there being this p.m. no fewer than 107 sailing vessels and 19 steamers in the Bay — not to mention the eight or nine men-of-war ships at their usual anchorage. Seldom have there been so many ships at one time lying at this port, and if a typhoon should now visit us — which Heaven forbid — the damage would certainly be greater in proportion to the large number of vessels.

China Mail
15 August 1877

Hong Kong Harbour, c.1875
The Kowloon Peninsula, seen in the far distance, although ceded to Britain 15 years previously, appears still largely undeveloped. In the forefront are the buildings of the Naval Dockyard, showing the main entrance between the two large buildings which fronted Queen's Road.

Several ships are seen anchored in the harbour. This was the age when steam was replacing sail, though many ships combined the two. The ship near the centre of the photograph, with many portholes, is almost certainly HMS *Victor Emanuel* (sometimes spelt Emmanuel). Originally named *Repulse*, she was renamed *Victor Emanuel* in

honour of the first king of united Italy. In 1875 she relieved HMS *Princess Charlotte* as the Receiving Ship, and was in her turn relieved in 1897 by HMS *Tamar*. Receiving Ships generally remained in the harbour for a number of years serving as Naval Office accommodation and providing additional storage to the store depots on shore.

Ships of the Royal Navy were regularly stationed in Hong Kong. Many had given names to familiar places, such as HMSS *Hebe* (Hebe Haven), *Starling* (Starling Inlet), *Plover* (Plover Cove), and *Sulphur* (Sulphur Channel).

China Mail
6 October 1877

<u>Chinese Eunuchs:</u> It would take up too much time and space to specify particularly all the duties eunuchs have to perform in the palace. They may be summed up in a few words; as regards out-door employment, they are water-carriers, watchmen, chair-bearers, gardeners, etc., while their in-door work is such as would be performed by cooks, chamber, parlour, scullery maids, and persons of that class in our countries.

❖ *Ignorance or reticence, probably the latter, explains this misconception. It is generally known that the principal role of eunuchs was to supervise the female household of the Palace, and in particular the numerous concubines. Not a few eunuchs reached positions of influence and even power in the Court.*

1878

China Mail
5 January 1878

The extent to which the several foreign nations having trade relations with China have participated in this trade … is shown in the following table:*

	<u>1875</u> %	<u>1876</u> %
Britain	36.21	36.64
Hongkong	28.99	27.31
Other British Possessions	3.22	2.66
The rest of the World	21.–	23.–

The trade with Hongkong is of course merely a transit trade in goods from all parts of the world. It is also interesting to note the share taken by each flag in the carriage of the commodities comprising the foreign trade in China. The following table exhibits the percentage of this share during … :-**

British	73.93	71.25
American	4.54	2.42
German	4.32	4.28
French	10.36	13.28
Japanese	1.60	2.82
Chinese	0.64	0.86

These tables show that Great Britain and her possessions at present monopolize $77^{1}/_{2}$ per cent of the direct foreign trade, and that $71^{1}/_{2}$ per cent of this trade is conveyed in British keels …

---

* Only 1875 and 1876 are shown.   ** the same two years as previous

An Imperial Edict appears in the *Peking Gazette* on the 9th inst., reiterating the law against the cultivation of the poppy in the various provinces of the Empire. It states that the severity of the present famine in Shansi is due, in some measure, to the cultivation of the drug in the place of cereals; and it threatens all those officials who connive at its planting with severe punishment.

China Mail
23 March 1878

❖   *In this whole messy business of opium trade, it is often forgotten that from about 1870s the Chinese grew their own opium against the explicit edicts of the authorities. It did not stop the import of foreign opium, but it did significantly diminish it.*

From the Editorial:
The Report of the Acting Captain Superintendent of Police for the last year is of special interest … that it contains the first statistics of crime in the Colony since the practical abolition of flogging by Mr. Hennessy. … Being strong advocates of … flogging … we experience a sort of grim satisfaction in observing that the report is … the most unsatisfactory one of the kind that has ever been presented to the Hongkong community. The figures … show that … both serious crimes and minor offences have increased to … an alarming extent. So far as statistics are concerned, there was more crime in the Colony last year than … in any similar period for at least a decade.

China Mail
8 April 1878

❖   *The* China Mail *at the time was notably reactionary. Strongly colonial and anti-progressive, it watched with horror (reflected in its editorials) as the Governor Hennessy tried to remove, one after another, the discriminatory measures practised against the local Chinese community.*

The weather to-day has been anything but encouraging for the Volunteer movement. Recruits could hardly be expected to muster in full force under showers of rain like those we have experienced to-day, whatever they may do under a shower of grape and canister.* We trust that to-morrow, the day chosen for the next parade, will prove to be more auspicious.

China Mail
21 May 1878

---

* 'Grape and canister' here refers to the form of old cannon ammunition consisting of cast-iron balls packed between iron plates and held together by a central iron pin.

❖   *The author, himself a Volunteer with many years of service, suspects that the Volunteers of that period were of a very different breed from those who defended Hong Kong in 1941 with stubbornness and courage. Formed in 1854, and consisting almost entirely of expatriates, the Volunteer Corps was more a social club than a serious fighting force. There was a story of a Volunteer, in those bygone days, going to his training with his servant carrying his rifle!*

Hong Kong Volunteers, Headquarters, Lower Albert Road, Hong Kong Island, c.1890–95
The Volunteers are seen parading in front of their Headquarters, located at the corner of Lower Albert Road and Garden Road. Formed in 1854, when the call of the Crimean War had depleted the Hong Kong garrison, the Corps of Volunteers had been closely connected with the Hong Kong community for 140 years, until its disbandment in September 1995. They were called upon to defend Hong Kong in battle, in 1941, against the invading Japanese forces, and although Hong Kong fell to the superior forces, the Hong Kong Volunteers had fought for every inch of the ground with courage and stubbornness, winning lasting honour.

***China Mail*
1 November 1878**

The drain in Bonham Strand is open again for the fourth time this year, and the neighbourhood is rendered anything but savoury in consequence. It is a pity that once a year is not sufficient to attend to such matters. The natural unpleasant-messes of the neighbourhood are quite sufficient without any additional pests.

1879

There appears to be good reason for believing that the report of a tiger, or of some other ferocious animal of a large size, being at large in this Colony is well founded. The Inspector of Police at Stanley states that one of the … guard there saw … what appeared to be a tiger walking off with a pig … in his mouth.

❖ *Tigers were seen and successfully hunted from time to time, mostly in the New Territories, right into the 1930s. The last report of a tiger was in 1940, also at Stanley.*

China Mail
13 January 1879

Hong Kong Waterfront (The Praya), Central District, Hong Kong Island, c.1870–75
An interesting early photograph of the waterfront. On the extreme right, a portion of Hongkong Hotel (before three more storeys were added) is visible. Buildings which follow to the left contain merchant firms of Melchers & Co. (established in 1866), Holliday, Wise & Co. (established in 1841), Russell & Co. (established in 1850) and others. On the extreme left, the long building is the City Hall. Behind and above is a 4-storey government building on top of Battery Path (still extant though much changed), and still higher and to the right, the bell tower of St. John's Cathedral stands out amidst the surrounding vegetation.

China Mail
24 March 1879

A proposal to light up with gas houses on the Peak and Gap [Magazine Gap], as well as the road leading up the Hill, has been entertained lately; and there is some reason to believe that it will be carried out before the more ambitious project of a railway ... if the Government will only give a helping hand, the idea might soon become a reality.

China Mail
5 April 1879

We would call the attention of those of our readers, who are capable of being amused with the vagaries of the intelligent school boy ... Few of the stories of class-room answers beat the Indian one, which tell of a bright ... youth, who defined matrimony as 'the money you get from your wife's parents for marrying her'.

China Mail
19 December 1879

The annual general meeting of the Shareholders of the Club Lusitano was held last night at the Club for the purpose of electing the committee for the following year with the following result. For the General Management Committee:- Messrs. J. A. dos Remedios (Chairman), F. J. V. Jorge, C. Danenberg, J. L. S. Alves, J. P. da Costa.

Club Lusitano, Shelley Street, Mid-Levels, Hong Kong Island, c.1870–80
The fine, 3-storey building — the centre of Hong Kong's Portuguese community's cultural life — was opened in December 1866 with a grand ball attended by many prominent people of Hong Kong and Macao. The building served the Portuguese community well until 1919–20, when the club was moved to a new clubhouse on Ice House Street. The Portuguese community of Hong Kong came mostly from Macao during Hong Kong's early days as a trading centre; it had made a significant contribution to Hong Kong in many fields.

1880

From the Editorial:
There is a strong feeling among the English or 'foreign' community here that a change is fast becoming necessary in the mode of selecting the unofficial members of the Legislative Council. ... Mr. Hennessy's recent step in nominating a Chinese member of Council who does not in the opinion of many, fairly represents the interests in whose behalf he is put forward, does not fail to strengthen this growing desire to obtain voice in the selection of suitable representatives. ... It is nevertheless patent to the large majority of the mercantile community of the Colony that Mr. Hennessy's policy and sentiments are at variance with the majority of the residents.

China Mail
3 March 1880

❖   *The* China Mail, *staunchly colonial in outlook, consistently attacked Governor Hennessy's efforts to remove inequalities among Hong Kong's people. But one may wonder if this plea for 'a voice in the selection of suitable representatives', however wrongly motivated, is a suggestion for an elected Legislative Council?*

Sir John Pope Hennessy (1834–1891)
Controversy and conflicts between the Governor and the Hong Kong community were nothing new. But with Sir John Pope Hennessy, appointed Governor of Hong Kong in 1877, they reached their peak. What other governors had only cautiously attempted, Pope Hennessy put into practice — an equal treatment for all his subjects. He was a man before his time. His courteous consideration for the Chinese community, and his insistence on a more humane and lenient judicial system (he abolished public flogging), had soon aroused the sharp indignation of the foreign community. He threatened to stop the museum grant unless the rules dictating separate visiting hours for Europeans and Chinese were abolished.

But when he appointed the first Chinese to the Legislative Council, a well-known and respected barrister Ng Choy, this was the last straw. At best, Pope Hennessy was considered a hopeless idealist, at worst a dangerous radical.

In spite of these commendable qualities, the governor proved, in the end, to be a poor administrator. Except for the colony's sound financial position, his record of achievement in other areas was small. Obviously England considered him a good governor, for when he left Hongkong in 1882, he was to become governor of Mauritius, where a statue of him still stands.

China Mail
24 March 1880

A poor crazed Portuguese seaman, known as Phillip, had a narrow escape of losing his life in the harbour to-day. Impressed with the idea that he was a Saint … and imagining that he shared with other saints the power of walking on the water, he jumped from Peddar's wharf into the water with the intention of walking to Macao. A police constable, Gool Mahomed, No. 560, accoutred as he was, plunged in after the madman, and with the assistance of a boat, got him to the shore.

China Mail
28 April 1880

His Excellency the Governor's [Hennessy] appointment to be a K.C.M.G.* is officially notified in the *Gazette*, in all the glory of widely leaded type, with Chinese translation to match.

China Mail
12 July 1880

From the Editorial:
The full report which is just to hand of the recent meeting of the Society for the Suppression of the Opium Trade … [is] deserving of some attention. … It is easy to understand how much more a course of moderate zeal is likely to result in something being done than is an agitation conducted with too much ardour, and striving after impracticable achievements. To come to the facts. The yearly revenue of India from opium is £9,000,000. … To fight for the abolition at one blow of this enormous trade, with the consequent huge loss of revenue to the country, is simply useless. Whatever is to be done must be done gradually. More than a million of acres of land in India are occupied with the cultivation of opium.

❖   *The* China Mail *sees only one side of the problem — millions of acres of land occupied with the cultivation of opium — and ignores the millions of people who are destroyed by the drug.*

On His Lordship the Chief Justice taking his seat on the bench this morning he announced it as the intention of the Court to sit unrobed till the vacation, on account of the excessive heat of the weather.

---

* K.C.M.G.: Knight Commander of (the Most Distinguished Order of) St Michael and St George.

Military Strength of China and its Development. Extracts from an important memorandum by Colonel C. G. Gordon, R.E.* The following ... document ... which we had received from Col. Gordon ... will be found, we think ... of great interest:-

China Mail
25 August 1880

'China possesses a long-used Military Organization, a regular military discipline. <u>Leave it alone. It is suited to the people.</u>'

It goes on to give many lines of advice, e.g.:-

'China should never engage in pitched battles. Her strength is in quick movements. ... Rockets should be used instead of cannon. China should never attack forts ... but wait and starve them out ... Mortars should be preferred to big guns.'

Finally he says:- 'If I stayed in China it would be bad for China, because it would vex American, French, and German Governments who would want to send their officers. Besides I am not wanted. China can do what I recommend herself. If she cannot, I could do no good ...'

And a P.S.:- 'As long as Peking is the centre of the Government of China, China can never afford to go to war with any first-class Power. It is too near the sea. The Emperor (Queen Bee) must be in the centre of the hive ...

China cannot have an army when generals keep 2000 men and draw pay for 5000. Those generals ought to have their heads cut.'

❖ *Colonel Gordon, later general, a brilliant British officer, led the Chinese army in a successful campaign, in 1854, against the Tai Ping rebels. He subsequently became famous as Gordon of Khartoum (Sudan), where he perished in the siege of the city.*

Statue of General Gordon, Khartoum, Sudan, c.1920s
General Charles George Gordon (1833–1885) died a heroic death in the siege of Khartoum, in Sudan. The statue of the general, appropriately seated astride a camel, is on Gordon Avenue in Khartoum. Gordon also distinguished himself in the Crimean War (1853–1856) and in the actions against the Tai Pings in China, where he was known as the 'Chinese Gordon'.

---

* R.E.: Royal Engineers.

Old City Hall, c.1900

Probably most Hong Kong residents know that our present City Hall, opposite the Star Ferry pier in Central, is not the first City Hall in Hong Kong. Its predecessor, shown in this photograph, stood in Queen's Road, Central, opposite the present Cheung Kong Center.

It was opened on 2 November 1869, by His Royal Highness Prince Alfred, Duke of Edinburgh. Built by public subscription on a piece of land granted by the government, it was a splendid building in the old classical style. It housed a theatre — called somewhat pretentiously the Theatre Royal — a library, a museum, and was the centre for many public functions.

In front of the City Hall stood a lavishly ornate drinking fountain (extreme right), donated by the old and well-respected merchant house of Dent & Co. Sadly, by the time the fountain was installed in 1869, the company no longer existed, having failed in the serious depression of 1867.

The City Hall served the community well for over 60 years. Then, in 1934, in a move that still defies rational explanation, the government demolished it, sold the land on which it stood to the Hongkong and Shanghai Banking Corporation, where the bank was duly erected, and that was that!

Hong Kong lost the centre of its cultural life, yet, surprisingly, there appeared to have been no public outcry at this glaring disregard for public interest. Perhaps the gathering war clouds in Europe, the harbinger of the conflict that would engulf the world in 1939, had obscured all else. One can only lament the loss of this magnificent building, yet another victim of so-called progress.

Sir John Smale has again called attention in the Supreme Court of Hongkong to the prevalence of slavery and kidnapping among the Chinese inhabitants of that Colony. ... The Chief Justice frankly confessed that until a short time previous to the delivery of his address he had no idea that in Hongkong many thousands of human beings of both sexes were held as slaves, and that, in particular, parents and guardians were in the frequent habit of selling their children.

China Mail
30 October 1880

❖ *See also* Hongkong Telegraph, *18 January 1896.*

Signor Cagli's Italian Opera Company inaugurated what promises to be a most successful operatic season, at the Theatre Royal, City Hall, last evening with the production of Verdi's well-known masterpiece 'Il Trovatore'.

China Mail
26 November 1880

❖ *It used to be fashionable to refer to Hong Kong as a 'cultural desert', but, in fact, it never was; a scrubland perhaps, but not a desert.*

The *Government Gazette* is again remarkable for its lack of interesting matter.

China Mail
27 December 1880

1881

From the Editorial:
In the brusque letter which was the signal for the battle dated 19ᵗʰ Sept. 1879, the Governor [Hennessy] asked that the distinction which existed in the opportunities afforded to Europeans and Asiatics of visiting the Museum on all days of the week alike might be discontinued, otherwise he would discontinue the grant. ... The decision of the Secretary of State ... it is that the distinction made between the hours of admission [to the Museum] for Chinese and those for Europeans does not constitute ... a violation of the original conditions as to warrant a suspension of the grant.

China Mail
9 February 1881

❖ *It seems incredible, even for 1881, that there were different visiting hours for Europeans and Chinese at the Museum. Governor Hennessy failed to change this, as the Secretary of State ruled against him.*

China Mail **23 February 1881**	Hongkong Races 1881. Wednesday, Feb. 23 Stewards:- His Excellency Sir John Pope Hennessy, KCMG; His Excellency Major-General Donovan ... The Hon. W. Keswick ... T. Jackson [Manager of Hongkong Bank], F. D. Sassoon ... The Races to-day were only fairly interesting. The weather again was splendid for the sightseers; there was an enormous gathering of all nationalities about the Course, and there is no record of any one who did not enjoy himself well, save and except the stray pick-pocket or two on whom the Police laid their hands. The time was good in almost every race, although there were loud and bitter complaints against the condition of the course.

China Mail
2 April 1881

In view of the fact that the Census will be taken here again ... it may be of interest that we produce the figures of the last ... 1876:

Europeans and Americans	2,767
Goa, Manila, Indians & other of mixed blood	812
Temporary Residents	154
Chinese in the Employ of Europeans, &c	5,879
" Residing in Victoria	84,425
" " in Villages	15,230
" Boat Population in Victoria Harbour	12,404
Chinese Boat Population other than Victoria Harbour	10,341
Vagrants	–
Prisoners	512
Total	132,524

China Mail
14 April 1881

Last night His Majesty the King Kalakaua, of Hawaii, visited the Victoria Lodge and was received with honours due to his exalted rank and high position in Masonry.

Reception for the King of Hawaii: 1881

During the tenure of Sir John Pope Hennessy as Governor of Hongkong, 1877–1882, a number of distinguished dignitaries visited Hong Kong. Among them were several senior Chinese ministers and ambassadors, General Ulysses S. Grant, the hero of the American Civil War, Prince Heinrich of Prussia, and several others. But none could rival the exuberance or the rank of His Majesty King Kalakaua of the Hawaiian Islands, or the Sandwich Islands, as they were sometimes referred to.

King Kalakaua arrived in Hong Kong on 12 April, 1881, and was invited to stay at Government House. A public reception and a banquet were held in his honour, the latter hosted by C. P. Chater (later knighted). The king, a big and imposing man, had created a lasting impression on the Hong Kong public.

In the photograph, the King, in a straw hat, is seated in the centre; on his left, wearing an 'ascot' top hat, is Sir John Pope Hennessy.

It is a pity that it is no longer possible to be sure who the others in the photograph are.

China Mail
14 April 1881

From the Editorial:
As His Excellency the Governor very well puts it, 'there is but little change' in the Estimates for 1882. So far as can be judged ... there is continuous prosperity, in accumulating surplus, the same fixed rate of taxation as before, the same absence of public works of immediate importance, and the same desire to hoard up funds for the benefit of others than the present residents of the Colony. In spite of the fluency with which Governor Hennessy explains his financial schemes, there are many who decline to give him credit for ability as a financier. With plenty of money and no reduction of taxation, there is no credit whatever in storing a surplus.

It is no doubt important to know that 'the princely house of Jardine, Matheson & Co.' contributes so much to the revenue; but the information would never have been offered but for the serene satisfaction with which His Excellency parades his sixteen Chinese who pay so much towards the revenue of the Colony. What may be meant to be inferred from all this talk about Chinese preponderance is somewhat beyond us. If it be meant that we are to have government by the majority, let the Chinaman who pays $3878 a quarter in taxes be at once asked to replace His Excellency in the duties of administering the government.

❖ *Throughout Governor Hennessy's term, the* China Mail, *solidly behind Hong Kong's European establishment, spoke out against his liberal views and his attempts to remove discrimination against the Chinese residents of Hong Kong.*

1882

Another newspaper joins the field — the Hongkong Telegraph.

Hongkong Telegraph
2 March 1882

From the Editorial:
The excitement of the race-week has passed away, leaving the Colony to lapse into its customary comatose condition which will know no change until the birth of a new racing season. For one week in the year the good people of Hongkong are in one continual whirl of excitement; during the remaining fifty one there is hardly a ripple on the waters of our quiet, uneventful existence.

From the Editorial:

As we go to press, the Peninsular and Oriental Steam Navigation Company's mail steamer *Cathay* is leaving the harbour homeward bound, having on board H.E. Sir John Pope Hennessy, K.C.M.G. ... who goes to England on a well-earned holiday. For the past five years Governor Hennessy has worked hard and conscientiously in the best interests of this Colony, and notwithstanding the unceasing opposition ... the undeniable results of his policy conclusively prove that he has worked successfully. ... Governor Hennessy has not been a social success in Hongkong. Although one of the most courteous and well bred gentlemen in existence ... he utterly failed to win favour with the *elite* of our colonial society. His Excellency's ideas of social equality found no responsive echo in the bosoms of the commercial magnates of Hongkong. The Governor's utter indifference to the views or opinions of a self constituted autocracy, whose absurd claims ... sanctioned by social *status* and old custom, to ... exclusive commercial privileges and advantages, were ignored ... and caused a bitter feeling ... against the ruler who was neither to be cajoled or coerced into sanctioning irregularities and abuses. Sir John Pope Hennessy was the very antithesis of his recent predecessors. ... He was no holiday Governor of a type quite common in our local history; no quiet harmless gentleman whose greatest desire was to be left at peace to draw his salary and leave his work in the hands of his subordinates; but a thoroughly earnest and conscientious legislator.

❖ *What a brilliant message of praise for the Governor who was far ahead of his time!* Hongkong Telegraph *was, of course, the complete opposite in its views to the* China Mail*, and the two often exchanged salvos of vitriolic abuse at each other as the next snippet shows.*

From the Editorial:

We have long ago given up the *China Mail* as a hopeless case. It is not a very great disappointment; but still we cannot help feeling a tinge of regret at seeing this venerable and at one time highly respectable ... public organ going from bad to worse. ... As a factor in our local politics the *China Mail* has long since lost, by its spiteful meanness, whatever influence it may have ever possessed. ... It has also lost its popularity as a trustworthy and reliable exponent of public opinion.

Hongkong Telegraph
7 March 1882

Hongkong Telegraph
25 March 1882

**Hongkong Telegraph
30 March 1882**

Mr. Ho Kai, the new Chinese barrister, was formally admitted to practice of the Supreme Court yesterday. … The Chief Justice cordially welcomed the new addition to the Bar, referring in complimentary terms to the creditable manner in which Mr. Ho Kai has passed his several examinations at home.

❖ *Dr Ho Kai was a remarkable person and notable for several accomplishments. He practised law in preference to medicine; became a member of the Legislative Council; brought with him a young English wife from England, and established a hospital in her memory after her death; and was reputed to be the first Chinese in Hong Kong to wear European clothes.*

Ho Kai (何啟), Sir Kai (1859–1914), c.1900
An eminent community leader, physician and barrister, and one of the founders of the Hong Kong University, Dr Ho Kai qualified in medicine at the University of Aberdeen, in Scotland, and was called to the Bar at Lincoln's Inn, London. He married Alice Walkden who had died soon after they arrived in Hong Kong. Deeply affected by this loss, he founded Alice Memorial Hospital, in 1886, in his wife's memory. Ho Kai became an unofficial member of the Legislative Council in 1890, representing the Chinese community, and served on the Council until his death in 1914. He was knighted in 1912. Kai Tak Airport was named after him (Kai) and his partner Au Tak (Tak).

The shrubbery of the Colony is certainly being put to a nice use. A tailor, who was brought up this morning for being found yesterday in unlawful possession of some newly cut shrubs, stated to the magistrate that they were wanted for the purpose of decorating brothels! If this is not a desecration, we should like to know what is.

Hongkong Telegraph
19 April 1882

The two lots of property in Jervois Street, Inland Lots 858 and 859, were sold by Mr. J. M. Guedes by public auction this afternoon, realising, with the four houses, the handsome sum of $33,500 … .

Hongkong Telegraph
12 May 1882

Hair Dressing Saloon: Hongkong Hotel. W.P. Moore begs to inform the Gentlemen of Hongkong and Visitors that he has reduced the price of Hair-Cutting to 50 cents. Having now in his employ three competent Assistants … he guarantees to execute this class of work … with a perfection which cannot be excelled in any part of the world.

Hair-Cutting, 50 cents; Shampooing, 25 cents; Shaving, 25 cents; Trimming Beard, 25 cents. Razors most carefully re-set.

Hongkong Telegraph
12 July 1882

From the Editorial:
Apparently, observes the *Daily News*, the Russians feel towards the Jews as the Roman did to the fair sex, when he said that men could neither live with them nor without them. While the population is excelling itself, if reports be true, in exquisiteness of cruelty, while the Government is bringing out mediaeval decrees, the trading classes are declaring that the expulsion of the Jews means the ruin of business.

Hongkong Telegraph
18 July 1882

It is reported that W. S. Gilbert and Arthur Sullivan, the joint authors of 'Trial by Jury', 'Pinafore' &c., are at work on a new comic opera. It is said that the plot of the new work is most amusing, the principal character being a Lord Chancellor who is in love with one of his own wards, and who is consequently compelled to obtain his own consent to his union with her … .

A very droll idea, and we have little doubt it will be worked out by Gilbert in very droll fashion.

❖ *The opera was named* The Princess Pearl.

Hongkong Telegraph
5 August 1882

1883

Hongkong Telegraph
21 July 1883

From the Editorial:

We regret to hear that the views expressed by Dr. Ho Kai in the name of the Chinese community at the Kennedy Memorial meeting ... have been practically repudiated by his fellow countrymen. Dr. Ho Kai ... had no authority from the Chinese community to pledge them in any way as regards the proposed memorial to Sir Arthur Kennedy [Governor of Hong Kong, 1872–1877] ... The real leaders of Chinese opinion in Hongkong, including Mr. Ho Amei, the past president of the Tung Wah Hospital, and Mr. Lee Tuk Cheong, the present holder of that important position ... have decisively declined to have anything to do with the matter, and moreover their decision has been warmly endorsed by all classes of the native community. ... It is the intention of the Chinese community to show their respect and gratitude for eminent services rendered, alike to living and dead governors of Hongkong, in the persons of Sir John Pope Hennessy and Sir Richard Macdonnell. To the latter the Chinese are mainly indebted for the Tung Wah Hospital, and to the former for all the privileges of citizenship which they at present possess. The Chinese fully recognise the fact that they were appreciated by Sir Arthur Kennedy and his predecessors — as cooks, house-boys and coolies, and they are also quite well aware that socially they were regarded as pariahs until Governor Hennessy broke down the barriers of snobbish conservatism and made Government House free alike to all subjects of Her Majesty of whatever nationality. ... Everybody knows that Governor Hennessy effectually set aside invidious class distinctions, that he abolished flogging and other crying abuses.

❖   *A remarkable editorial which sheds much light on the social conflicts and gaps between the two main communities of Hong Kong at the time. It has been emphasized again and again how Governor Hennessy was far ahead of his time. In the event, the statue of Governor Kennedy was erected in the Botanical Gardens.*

Hongkong Telegraph
18 September 1883

From telegrams by Reuter:

The Croatian revolt is extending to Bosnia.

❖   *Nothing has since changed in the Balkans!*

Statue of Sir Arthur Kennedy, Botanical Gardens, Hong Kong Island, c.1885–90

Sir Arthur Kennedy served as Governor of Hong Kong from 1872 to 1877. A capable and popular governor, he introduced important legislation designed to protect Chinese women and children, a register of births and deaths, and much needed expansion of schools for Chinese children. In recognition, a full-length statue of Kennedy was erected in the Botanical Gardens after his departure in 1877. Like most other statues in Hong Kong, it was removed by the Japanese during their occupation of Hong Kong, 1941–45, and was never recovered.

**Hongkong Telegraph
5 December 1883**

'Prisoner, how old are you?' 'Twenty-two, your honour.' 'Twenty-two? Your papers make out you were born twenty-three years ago.' 'Sir, I was, but I spent one year in prison and I don't count that — it was lost time.'

❖ *Today this would hardly be considered funny. This snippet is included to show how sense of humour has changed with the passage of time.*

1885

**China Mail
9 January 1885**

The annual Belilios Scholarships for St. Joseph's College were awarded this morning. ... Masters J. P. Braga and L. G. Barretto were the recipients of the first year's Scholarships. ... Dr. Eitel, one of the trustees of the Scholarships, then addressed the boys at some length. He said it might appear strange that Mr. Belilios should give these Scholarships to Portuguese. He was not a Portuguese himself, and he was not a member of the Catholic Church. The explanation was this — Mr. Belilios had been nurtured in that spirit of liberty and fair play which disregarded the distinctions of creed and nationality. ...

❖ *What a roundabout way of describing Belilios's persuasion! Dr Eitel surely must have known that Emanuel Rafael Belilios, an opium trader turned philanthropist, was a sephardic Jew, born in Calcutta. J. P. Braga became a prominent printer and later distinguished himself in local politics; Braga Circuit, in Kowloon, is named after him. His many sons and daughters — among them Jack, Hugh, Paul, Anthony, John, and Caroline — had also contributed richly to the quality of life in Hong Kong.*

**China Mail
22 January 1885**

At the next meeting of the Legislative Council, the Government is to be asked if the fort now being constructed this end of the Ly-ee-moon Pass is to be armed with old 40-pounder* guns. ...

For no military officials in possession of a grain of sense, or knowledge ... would think of arming an important marine fort nowadays with old 40-pounders. ... These defences are of great importance to the

---

* Pounder: e.g. 40-pounder, a gun which fires a projectile weighing 40 lbs.

Colony, and as we have to contribute over £55,000 for the cost of construction, we have the right to demand ... the provision of the armament ... in a thoroughly satisfactory manner.

❖ *In fact, the sum contributed by the Legislative Council was £55,625. The Council also specified that 'the armament to be provided ... will be of the best and latest pattern of breech-loading ordnance'. Nothing of the sort! The 40-pounders intended for Lei Yue Mun (present spelling) had been obsolete for nearly 20 years. It is easy to understand the newspaper's anger, shared by the Governor Sir George Bowen who expected 'nothing less than making Hongkong impregnable ...'. In the event, Lei Yue Mun's defensive potential and its immense strategic importance was finally recognized, but not until 1886, and its batteries adequately equipped. See p.68.*

Mr. Wong Afuk, a gentleman of the light-fingered fraternity who has on more than one occasion figured as one of the ornaments of Victoria Gaol, was to-day, on the recommendation of the magistrate before whom he last had the honour of appearing, deprived of the multifarious advantages of residence in a Christian land, and sent to his native place in the Sanon district with strict injunction not to return ... .

China Mail
24 August 1885

❖ *San On (新安), or New Peace County, was a district of Kwangdong province known by this name since AD 1573. It included originally Hong Kong Island, Kowloon, the New Territories, and a portion of the adjoining Chinese mainland. The cession of Hong Kong Island and Kowloon and the lease of the New Territories, reduced San On to a relatively small area of the Mainland. After 1912, with its area considerably enlarged, it reverted to its ancient name of Po On (寶安).*

DEATH: On the 22nd September, at his residence, DHUNJEEBHOY RUTTONJEE, Esq., aged 65 years. Deeply regretted.

China Mail
22 September 1885

❖ *Dhunjeebhoy Ruttonjee Bisney (Bisney Road was named after him) was one of the four Parsee merchants who arrived in Hong Kong in 1841, as soon as it was ceded to Britain, and bought land at the first land auction held in June 1841.*

Sketch of 'Lyeemoon' by Lieutenant T. B. Collinson, Royal Engineers, 1846
Collinson's survey of Hong Kong Island was accompanied by a set of excellent sketches.

Lei Yue Mun Barracks, c.1915

The proposal [made by a number of leading Chinese residents], ... is to form an association on the lines of the General Chamber of Commerce. ... This influential and prosperous body may furnish a very good model ... and we doubt not but that in years to come the new Chinese Chamber of Commerce, if established and judiciously managed, will become a centre of intelligence, of education, and an influence for good, in a municipal and mercantile sense, among the native residents of the Colony.

China Mail
14 October 1885

❖ *The Chinese Chamber of Commerce was formed in 1887. The Hongkong Chamber of Commerce (here referred to as the General Chamber of Commerce) was formed in 1861.*

From a gossip column, recently started, called 'Fragrant Water's Murmur': That it can never be too frequently called to mind that the vast native population of this island is governed by a small number of Britishers, and that firmness is always greatly needed ...

China Mail
14 November 1885

That the peak Tramway will be a well-deserved success ...

That native roughs ought not to be permitted to pass ribald jests upon unprotected females, or level uncivil remarks at the maternal relatives of foreigners passing by ...

❖ *The Chinese have never been known to indulge in what is described in the last paragraph; more likely European seamen, seen frequently drunk, as noted in these snippets.*

1886

An attempt has once more been made after a lapse of many years, to introduce into this Colony the great English game of football. Mr. J. H. Stewart-Lockhart, the Honorary Secretary of the Victoria Recreation Club, with his usual enthusiasm for manly sports, has been working the matter with a view to a match between the Garrison and representatives of other bodies.

Hongkong Daily Press
3 February 1886

Hongkong Daily Press
4 June 1886

The Alice Memorial Hospital, Hongkong; Laying the Foundation Stone. Owing to the benevolence of the London Missionary Society and of private individuals in this colony there is shortly to be opened here a most useful addition to our charitable institutions, in the shape of a hospital which shall be open to all those who have not the means of paying the moderate charges ... in the existing institutions in the Colony. ... The matter for a time dropped out of sight ... until after Dr. Ho Kai was bereft of his wife, whom he had only about two years before brought out of England. Not long after her death Dr. Ho Kai, feeling a great desire to ... perpetuate the memory of his deceased wife, offered to provide the requested building, to be called 'Alice Memorial Hospital' ... .

❖ *The hospital, jointly with the Nethersole Hospital, continued to provide good medical care for the less affluent members of the Hong Kong community.*

China Mail
3 August 1886

There visited the City Hall Museum during the last week 177 Europeans and 2,273 Chinese.

The Museum, the City Hall, Hong Kong Island, c. 1880
A large variety of objects reflecting Hong Kong life and its people is displayed in glass cabinets. The City Hall, designed in the classical style, was built by public subscription and was formally opened on 2 November 1869 by Prince Alfred, Duke of Edinburgh. The City Hall housed a theatre, a museum, a library, and was the centre of many public functions. It was demolished in 1934.

The new Chinese Minister at Washington goes to see 'The Micado' played every night, and applauds it with continually increasing enthusiasm. So far comic operatic art gives the Japanese Minister no chance to get back at him.

❖ *Opera* Turandot, *by Puccini, which gives an equally absurd picture of China, was not performed until 1926.*

From the Editorial:
What is usually termed malarial fever is a disease which for over forty years has contributed largely towards giving a bad reputation to the climate of this Island. The decimation of our soldiers in the early days of the Colony were principally caused by this disease. … The general principle, that fever almost invariably follows the exposure to virgin soil in Hongkong even now, is admitted by nearly every one who has resided here for many years. … Now that Hongkong can boast of a Sanitary Board, a Medical Board, and a Medical Society, it does seem strange that so little notice appears to be taken of what has assumed rather serious dimensions.

❖ *Malaria was a scourge of the Tropics and Subtropics in those days. 'Happy Valley' was particularly bad (was the name a morbid joke?). The disease could not be controlled since neither the causative organism nor its connection with mosquitos had yet been discovered. An obscure doctor, working in Java at the time, suspected that mosquitos carried the disease. It was his idea that led Major Ross of the Indian Army Medical Service to discover the cause and transmission of malaria. See also Victoria Barracks, p.72.*

The Chinese papers of this Colony have constant occasion to remark on the wretched quarelling that goes on in Chinese families between husbands, wives, and concubines. The *Chung-ngoi San-pu* has a leading article on the subject to-day, in which it begins by saying that the blame lies chiefly with the husbands. But the writer seems not to have reflected that the government of a wife and concubines is more than any ordinary man can be expected to carry out successfully.

Victoria Barracks, c.1875

In the first decade after Hong Kong's cession to Britain, living conditions of the garrison were very primitive and unhealthy; there were no proper barracks and most of the troops lived under canvas or in rough matsheds constructed from bamboo. Poor sanitation brought disease and death.

However, by 1848, several barrack blocks and other buildings were completed by local labour employed and directed by the Royal Engineers. The first permanent barracks for troops were the Murray, the Wellington and Stanley barracks.

In the second phase of building, five blocks, known as Victoria Barracks, were completed between 1868 and 1870 on the hills overlooking the Royal Naval Dockyard.

The photograph shows Victoria Barracks at the time of completion, though only four of the five blocks are visible. These barracks were a great improvement on the old ones and they lasted for 100 years. Two lower blocks, on the left, and part of the fourth block, on the right, were still there in 1979 when the army relinquished the area to be taken over by the Hong Kong Government. It has since been converted into a public park.

1887

From the Editorial:
Now that it has been agreed in public meeting to carry out 'the scheme for Park in the Wong-nai-cheong Valley', as a permanent memorial of the Jubilee year of the reign of Her Majesty Queen Victoria, it is perhaps needless to advocate any alternative proposal. … It seems necessary … that some special mark must be set up — a pillar, a gateway, or a statue — anything that will commemorate the event about which the loyalty of our citizens is being stirred … it would be most fitting that such a … memorial should bear an inscription, telling posterity that the Jubilee Year of the Queen … had been celebrated by the formation of the Victoria Park in this little Colony of Hongkong.

❖   *This was the Golden Jubilee of the Queen's accession to the throne, which gave Hong Kong the Queen's Recreation Ground, later renamed Victoria Park, at Causeway Bay.*

China Mail
3 March 1887

THE TEA STEAMERS FOR 1887: The tea season for 1887 is again at hand, and there is as usual a little speculation as to which steamers are to take part in the race home with the first cargo …

❖   *The 'tea races' was the romantic side of the China Trade, first the clippers, then the steamers, racing home (England) with the first crop of tea before its flavour was impaired. The seamy side of this trade was its cargo on the way out — opium; though by 1887 the opium trade was rapidly declining.*

China Mail
5 May 1887

Telegram:
<u>Wimbledon Rifle Meeting.</u> The Queen's Prize was won by Lieutenant Warren, 1ˢᵗ Middlesex.

China Mail
22 July 1887

A prisoner at West Point Police Station committed suicide this morning by hanging himself with the braid of his queue … .

China Mail
23 August 1887

China Mail
5 September 1887

... the Hon. C.P. Chater has issued an invitation to the owners and the Attorneys or Agents of absent owners of marine lots ... to meet him in the City Hall ... for the reclamation of the foreshore.

❖ *The result was a major reclamation which was carried out between 1890 and 1904 and which brought the waterfront to the present Connaught Road, lined with magnificent, colonial-style buildings.*

1888

Hongkong Telegraph
16 March 1888

Messrs. Melchers & Co. inform us that the ... steamer *Preussen*, Capt. C. Pohle, with the German mails from Berlin ... left Singapore for this port at 8 o'clock this morning and is due here on or about the 21st inst. His Excellency the Governor and Lady de Voeux are passengers ... .

❖ *The German firm of Melchers & Co. has a remarkable history of resilience. First established in Hong Kong in 1866, its business was twice disrupted by the two World Wars; the firm is still active in Hong Kong. The Governor Sir William Des Voeux began his duty in Hong Kong in October 1887 and served until May 1891.*

Hongkong Telegraph
6 April 1888

Here is the latest piece of medical enterprise, in the shape of an advertisement from a pushing member of the profession:- 'I undertake to pay one half of the funeral expenses of those of my patients who do not recover their health under my treatment'.

Hongkong Telegraph
17 April 1888

From the Editorial:
In November 1886, when the Hongkong and Kowloon Wharf and Godown Company Limited was first formed, we indicated ... in no uncertain language the prosperous future that, with judicious management, lay before the new enterprise. Events have amply justified our confidence in an undertaking which has completely revolutionised the shipping business of the port ... Up to the present time the Hongkong and Kowloon Wharf and Godown Company has far more than justified its existence as one of the leading industries of the Colony, and its past success and encouraging prospects plainly enough indicate a brilliant future.

Hongkong & Kowloon Wharf and Godown Co., Tsim Sha Tsui, Kowloon, c.1890
The picture shows the main offices of the company with its ornate gate on the seashore of Tsim Sha Tsui. Established in 1886, this successful firm was mainly engaged in loading and unloading freight ships and storage of goods. The buildings were constructed by the Hong Kong firm of Danby & Leigh, Architects.

The latest from the Moon is to the effect that our popular and sympathetic satellite is really inhabited by living beings ... [according to] the experiment of Dr. Bernhard Puegel, who has constructed a solar microscope four times as powerful as the largest known. On submitting to this monstrous microscope the photographic view of the lunar disc ... has attained a diameter of seven metres. The result ... went to show that there are living beings moving about on the moon possessing irregular statures and very different from those of the inhabitants of the earth.

Hongkong Telegraph
5 May 1888

❖   *This surely must be a joke! But, in 1888, there could be many who would take it seriously.*

The Peak Tramways commenced operations this morning, the first car leaving St. John's Place punctually at 8 O'clock, and the succeeding cars being dispatched according to the Co's Time Table. A few passengers,

Hongkong Telegraph
30 May 1888

ladies included, availed themselves of the opportunity to enjoy a ramble over the breezy hills in the morning — an extremely healthy diversion … after the oppressive nights which they have to endure in this season.

Peak Tram Terminus, Garden Road, c.1890
Compared with the present lower terminus, on Garden Road, the one in this photograph is a very modest structure. The Peak Tram was the single most important factor that had allowed the successful residential settlement of the Peak.

In the first decade or so after the acquisition of Hong Kong by Britain, European residential areas were developing along the waterfront of the new city of Victoria, mainly east of the military barracks and to a lesser extent on the adjoining hill slopes. Under the increasing pressure of a large influx of Chinese residents, the European residents moved to the Mid-Levels, always preferring to live among their own kind. By 1880, European residences were moving higher — into the Peak area. There, protected by the infamous European District Reservation Ordinance, they felt safe in their lofty though often foggy and misty elite enclave.

However, the problem was access. Too steep for rickshas, the sedan chair — slow and not very pleasant — seemed to be the only form of transport available, unless one resorted to walking. The problem was brilliantly solved by the construction of the Peak Tram, or as it was often referred to in the past, the funicular railway.

The Peak Tramways began operating on May 30, 1888. It was certainly a considerable achievement for that period and for a small and relatively insignificant place that Hong Kong then was. The Peak Tram has since proved to be safe, efficient and fast. After more than 100 years, its usefulness and popularity remains high, both with visitors and residents.

**Hongkong Telegraph
26 June 1888**

From the Editorial:
Cholera: Another sad death from cholera occurred last night, the latest European victim being a nurse to Mrs. W. G. Brodie, who succumbed after a few hours' illness. After two or three official heads of departments or influential *taipans* have been carried off, we may expect the

Government to recognise that fact, patent to everybody else, that Asiatic Cholera of a virulent type is sweeping through the colony with deadly effect — but not till then. An obscure teacher of music, a blue-jacket or two, or a humble nurse girl, apparently count for little with the official powers that be. What are the unofficial members of the Sanitary Board about that they do not arise in their indignation and protest against this sham being kept up any longer?

❖ *Epidemics of cholera occurred in Hong Kong regularly, usually during summer time, right up until World War II. Ironically, the Japanese who brought so much suffering during their occupation of Hong Kong, managed to control and eradicate cholera in Hong Kong by ruthlessly enforcing inoculations, and by forcibly 'repatriating' local people to the Chinese mainland and thus reducing Hong Kong's population.*

The present Emperor of China when he was a boy, had eighty nurses, twenty-five fanners, twenty-five bearers of his palanquin, ten umbrella-holders, thirty physicians and surgeons, seven chief and twenty-three inferior cooks, fifty waiters and messengers … and other attendants to the number of over four hundred. His spiritual welfare was looked after by a corps of seventy-five astrologers, sixteen tutors, all of high rank, and sixty priests.

Hongkong Telegraph
25 July 1888

❖ *This needs no comment!*

From the Editorial:
Our readers were informed yesterday that the much debated and strongly opposed European District Reservation Ordinance has obtained Her Majesty's sanction and is now one of the standing laws of the colony.

Hongkong Telegraph
31 July 1888

❖ *There are still people who insist that there has never been a law restricting Chinese residing in certain areas, e.g. the Peak. This snippet definitely proves that an ordinance to that effect was passed, opposed mainly by the Chinese members of the Legislative Council. Although never officially rescinded, this plainly discriminating ordinance was gradually abandoned, and certainly not applied by the 1930s. A similar ordinance was passed for the 'Peak Area' of Cheung Chau (Island) in 1919.*

Hongkong Telegraph
31 August 1888

The Jews in Jerusalem have increased since 1880 from 5,000 to 30,000. Thousands of refugees from Russia have lately fled to the City of David. Hongkong can spare from the serried ranks of the brokering fraternity, without greatly feeling the loss, a powerful contingent of the ancient race to assist in the rebuilding of the temple.

Hongkong Telegraph
27 September 1888

It is rumoured that Messrs. Butterfield & Swire, whose energy and enterprise in all branches of commerce have become a byword in the Far East, intend shortly erecting at Quarry Bay a patent slip of considerable dimensions and capacity ... If this is not the commencement of the long threatened opposition to the Hongkong and Whampoa Dock Co., it looks very much like it.

1889

Hongkong Telegraph
17 January 1889

We learn that a telegram has been received here from Hamburg announcing the death of Mr. Blackhead, an old Hongkong resident and founder of the well-known local firm of Blackhead & Co. The deceased gentleman had long since retired from active business, having left Hongkong some seventeen years ago.

❖   *His German name was Schwartzcopf, anglicized to 'Blackhead'; the firm was established in Hong Kong in 1860. 'Blackhead Point' in Tsim Sha Tsui, Kowloon, is where the firm's godowns once stood. See Tsim Sha Tsui Bay, p.13.*

Hongkong Telegraph
19 January 1889

A big batch of beggars were up before the Magistrate to-day. There were all sorts, from the lady with no eye-balls to the extensively-diseased individual. ... The police caught them in one cast of their net in Hollywood Road yesterday besieging a Parsee shop because it was distribution day. Three very old people were let off and carried in blankets outside for fear they should drop in pieces; the others — most of whom had already been deported a few hundred times — were ordered to be sent back again. The Court was then disinfected and locked up to prevent them coming back.

Sir William Des Voeux (1834–1909)

Des Voeux, descended from a French Protestant (Huguenot) family, was appointed Governor of Hong Kong in 1887, after a distinguished colonial service in British Guyana, Fiji, and Newfoundland. His appointment in Hong Kong followed an interregnum of almost two years, during which time Hong Kong had no governor but was administered by the next senior officer.

Almost immediately his attention was occupied by a large reclamation scheme of the Central District advanced by C. P. Chater, a wealthy merchant born in India of Armenian origin. This was the second large land reclamation, and like the first one (1868–73) was not wholly supported. Des Voeux threw his full support behind Chater's scheme, thus ensuring its success. The reclamation began in 1890 and was completed in 1904. The waterfront now moved ahead and the old praya was now inland. It was renamed, deservedly, Des Voeux Road.

Sir William Des Voeux took active interest in the Sanitary Board, education and other important areas of government. Perhaps the only unfavourable comment which may be made of his administration is his support of the exclusive European residence on the Peak.

He was a gentle, courteous man whose gracious manners had made him popular with his subjects. Frail health hampered his efforts. The

governorship of Hong Kong was his last appointment. He retired in 1891, well remembered for his courtly, polite manner and his quiet, even temperament.

From the Editorial:

We reported in our issue yesterday that the local Share Market was in a state of intense excitement in consequence of the sudden development of another of these sensational 'booms' … The new 'corner' has been established in connection with the scrip of the Hongkong Rope Manufacturing Company Limited … what actually is this 'corner' in the Rope Co.'s shares? In plain English it is a combination … *to obtain money under false pretences.* These shares, it is as certain as anything can be, are not worth one half the rate at present quoted.

Hongkong Telegraph
13 February 1889

❖ *Clearly, Hong Kong's stock market's booms are as old as Hong Kong itself. Actually, notwithstanding the* Telegraph's *prognostication, the Rope Co. proved to be a highly successful enterprise, and those who bought its shares must have done very well!*

**Hongkong Telegraph
13 March 1889**

It appears that the Foreign Ministers at Peking specially requested to be allowed to personally congratulate the Emperor on the occasion of his marriage. In reply they received an invitation to dinner at the Foreign Office, when a few trifling presents were to be distributed among them. The 'Son of Heaven', it would thus appear, is not yet visible to barbarian diplomats.

The peace in Hongkong is not very often disturbed by clan fights. … However, the Punti and Chinchew elements got at loggerheads this week, the bone of contention being a chair-stand in Caine Road, the possession of which was disputed between coolies of different clans. Accordingly, a grand field day was organised for yesterday afternoon, and although a few police were patrolling the locality, the battle continued briskly for some time.

**Hongkong Telegraph
21 March 1889**

Intimation:
One box of Clarke's B41 pills is warranted to cure all discharges from the Urinary Organs, in either sex (acquired or constitutional), Gravel, and pains in the Back. Guaranteed free from Mercury. Sold in boxes, 4s 6d each, by all Chemists.

❖   *What a nice-sounding word, 'intimation', instead of 'notice'.*

**Hongkong Telegraph
3 April 1889**

From the Editorial:
The discussion on The Praya Reclamation Bill at the meeting of the Legislative Council … shows plainly both the strength and character of the so-called opposition to this great measure … Mr. Ryrie raised … objection on behalf of some of the marine lot-holders, who … allege that their particular lots will be depreciated by the reclamation. Considering that the scheme was unanimously agreed to by the lot-holders, that not a single voice was raised against it when it was decided at a public meeting to finally accept the proposals of the Government, frivolous objections of this sort come rather late in the day.

❖   *The reclamation went ahead the following year and was completed in 1904. See Central Praya Reclamation, p.206.*

Sir Robert Hart: 'Although the somewhat original form, from a European point of view, in which the Empress of China has been pleased to confer nobility upon Sir Robert Hart may provoke a smile, there is no doubt that the ennobling of three generations of his ancestors is an honour of no small magnitude. … Sir Robert Hart has long been a most able, valuable, and valued servant of the Chinese Government; and to his talent and skill China owes, not only the establishment of a most efficient Customs Service, but also, in no small degree, her satisfactory and peaceful relations with Foreign Powers.'

❖ *There is no doubt that Sir Robert Hart, who had served the Chinese Government as Inspector-General of the Customs for 45 years (1863–1908), was an exceptionally capable organizer who by his high integrity won the respect and confidence of the Chinese. It must be remembered, however, that placing the Chinese Imperial Maritime Customs under foreign control (by the Treaties of Tientsin and Peking), must have been repugnant and deeply humiliating to the Chinese.*

**Hongkong Telegraph
12 April 1889**

Old Chinese Customs Station Ma Wan Island, c.1930

From the records of the Chinese Imperial Maritime Customs, we learn that a Customs Station on Ma Wan Island (also known as Kap Shui Mun) was one of four Chinese customs houses located in the vicinity of Hong Kong (the other three were on Cheung Chau, Junk Island and Mirs Bay).

In 1887, they came under the management of the Kowloon Customs Commission under foreign inspectorate. Following the lease of the New Territories to Britain, in 1898, these stations were allowed to remain for a period, but all ceased activity at midnight of 4 October, 1899. Since Hong Kong was made a free port, the stations ceased functioning and eventually were run down.

For some years past there have been two plaques, near the Ma Wan Rural Committee premises, commemorating the customs station. Because of these plaques, it has been widely assumed that not a trace was left of the old station.

This is incorrect. The photograph reproduced here shows what is undoubtedly the remains of the original station.

Around 1960, this large building was reused and considerably altered by the Asia Vacuum Flask Factory, but after the factory had closed down the building gradually fell into ruin.

During a survey of the island by the author in 1993, it was discovered that the west gable wall, the only remaining part of the original building, was still standing.

It is a relic of an important historical house and it is now preserved as a monument.

**Hongkong Telegraph
3 May 1889**

From the Editorial:
We published the other day the results of the Cambridge Local Examinations in which it was shown that the Diocesan Home and Orphanage stood highest on the list of successful candidates presented, all its four pupils having passed. The Public School contingent, with three successful candidates out of seven, coming next, and the Central School showing the ghastly picture of as many failures as there were pupils for examination ... .

❖ *Very poor show by the British school! Cambridge Examinations, Junior and Senior, were roughly equivalent to the later O and A levels, and were practised right up until the 1940s. The Central School was later the Central British School and still later the King George the Fifth (KG5).*

**Hongkong Telegraph
7 June 1889**

Telegram:
The Chamber of the Exchequer at Lisbon, with the approval of the Government, has decided to consider the expediency of subsidising a line of tea steamers to run between Macao and the ports of Portugal.

From the Editorial:
The telegram which we publish in another column [see above] has only three drawbacks. In the first place Macao papers are generally that which the Psalmist said in his haste men were; in the second place there is neither the *cha* [tea] nor the credit in Macao, and, in the third, neither the money, the market, or the steamers, in Portugal ... .

**Hongkong Telegraph
4 July 1889**

Wonders of China will never cease. The *Shih Pao* now tells us that the bamboos in Tientsin are putting forth 'white flowers, the shape of which is like a tuft of woman's hair'; and this has never been known to occur before.

**Hongkong Telegraph
24 July 1889**

<u>Heavy Loss to the Hongkong and Shanghai Bank</u>. A telegram was received by the manager of the Hongkong and Shanghai Bank yesterday stating that the Lyons branch had sustained a loss of $330,000. Details are not yet made public. The quotation for Banks declined gradually from 6 to 10 points during the day.

❖   *It is difficult to assess the loss in the present context, but a factor of 500 is probably near enough. If so, the loss in present time terms would be about 150 million.*

Hongkong and Shanghai Bank, c.1885

Hong Kong's remarkable progress as a successful entrepôt has been firmly rooted in trade and commerce. It is, therefore, an odd fact that the banks were slow in setting up their offices in Hong Kong. Before they did, the trading firms were forced to act as their own bankers, shippers, and insurance agents. Once Hong Kong's trading position was seen to be stable, banks followed the traders, but not until the 1860s.

The Hongkong and Shanghai Bank commenced business in Hong Kong in 1865, after several other banks were already operating in the colony. Today, regarded as one of the biggest banks in the world, it had a peculiar start, for it seems to have owed its inception to a wild speculative boom which occurred at the time in Bombay! (See also *Hongkong Telegraph*, 20 March 1908.)

The photograph shows the bank's headquarters in Hong Kong, which was built in 1886, replacing its first home — Wardley House. The present remarkable, if controversial, building is its fourth headquarters; all stood at No. 1 Queen's Road Central.

1890

**Hongkong Telegraph
4 January 1890**

Not content with defiling the harbour of Hongkong by depositing junk-loads of rubbish in it, two men were arrested this morning while in the act of throwing a couple of buckets of 'sanitary' produce into … [the] harbour. We think Mr. Woodhouse, who tried the case … was far too lenient in fining the culprits one dollar each, with the option of seven days in 'limbo'.

❖ *Clearly, the pollution of the harbour, of which Hong Kong today is very conscious, began more than a century ago, and brought at the time an equally strong responses from the media.*

**Hongkong Telegraph
7 January 1890**

The Praya Reclamation will soon be begun. The first contract will be signed to-morrow, in respect to the section between the old P & O Wharf and Wilmot Street — a space about 782 feet broad. Then, in about a month, work will probably be commenced on the portion between Murray Pier and Ice-House Street, a distance of some 1,200 feet. … There is some talk of having a big banquet to inaugurate the work.

❖ *It took 14 years to complete the reclamation. The Duke of Connaught who laid the foundation stone at the start of the reclamation, opened the completed new waterfront, which was named after him — Connaught Road.*

**Hongkong Telegraph
21 March 1890**

From the Editorial:
We infinitely regret that Mr. Francis Fleming, in the capacity of Acting Governor, has so foolishly blasted his official career in this Colony by a glaring want of tact and discretion for which there is no excuse. … It has been publicly announced that the arrangements made for the Duke of Connaught to formally lay the foundation stone of the Praya Reclamation with Masonic ceremonial have been cancelled because — Mr. Francis Fleming is a Roman Catholic and cannot participate in any ceremonial which is … antagonistic to his religious beliefs!

… We are sorry for Mr. Fleming because his career in this colony is practically finished. … Considering that the Duke of Connaught is an enthusiastic Mason of high rank, and that the Hon. C. P. Chater, the originator of the Praya Reclamation scheme, is the District Grand Master of English Freemasonry in Hongkong and South China, the appropriateness of the inauguration … with Masonic honours must be clearly apparent and it had so been arranged. …

❖   *Mr Fleming may have been unreasonably stubborn in this case, but it is difficult to agree with the* Hongkong Telegraph *that the inauguration 'with Masonic honours must be clearly apparent' simply because both the Duke of Connaught and Mr Chater were prominent Masons. In any case the foundation stone was laid by the Duke of Connaught (it is at present in the Chater Gardens), though it is uncertain whether with or without Masonic honours. As for Mr Fleming, he did not ruin his career. He was a very popular Colonial Secretary, was awarded a C.M.G. (Companion of the (Most Distinguished) Order of St Michael and St George) and managed to have a street, in Wan Chai, named after him.*

Visit of the Duke of Connaught to Hong Kong, April 1890
The Duke has just landed at Blake Pier (its matshed roof is seen on the right) and is walking towards the official sedan chair. He is wearing black uniform; on his right is the Governor, Sir William Des Voeux, wearing white uniform and plumed hat. A guard of honour is lined up and there is a large gathering of invited guests to welcome the royal visitors. During his visit, the Duke laid the foundation stone of the new major praya reclamation, which would be completed in 1904. The stone is still extant and can be seen in the Chater Garden, in Central, Hong Kong.

Hongkong Telegraph
25 March 1890

From the Editorial Address to Duke of Connaught:
Arthur William Patrick Albert, Duke of Connaught and Stratherne, will not be the first of the Hanoverian brood who has taken flight as far as Hongkong, we are afraid that he will not be the last. ... We endure our monarchial system of Government without much complaint because it is such an ... invisible system but when scions of the Dutch dynasty come around visiting us, and showing what perishable articles they are ... we — the community — rise and vigorously protest. ... let us conclude with our own little amended Address:-

To Arthur of Connaught: We are glad to see you, since you are passing, and we think you are not the worst of your family, by any means. We do not regard you as a very useful public servant, but you do as a figure-head, and we hope you will keep your place. Come and see our Colony, but pay your own bills, like anybody else, and don't expect us to go into hysterics over you. Tell your Mother [the Queen] how you found us, and mention that this idea of doubling the Military contribution is unjust. Now enjoy yourself, and let us go on with our work.

❖ *The* Hongkong Telegraph, *having castigated just four days ago (see snippet of 21 March) the Acting Governor, Mr Fleming, for refusing to sanction Masonic ritual at the foundation stone laying of the Praya Reclamation, now publishes this very ill-mannered 'Address' to the Duke of Connaught.*

Hongkong Telegraph
2 April 1890

Anent the Stock Exchange mooted some time ago, we learn on good authority that certain well known brokers ... visited the Officer Administering the Government with a view of getting the affair carried through. This was certainly a step in the right direction, and if the majority of the respectable brokers possess any *esprit de corps* an Exchange should be an established institution before very long. A considerable proportion of the so-called share-brokers now ... carrying on a very doubtful business under the verandahs of the Hongkong Hotel, are nothing more nor less than an irresponsible and unreliable rabble of 'jobbers' of the worst kind, and such a dangerous element would not exist in this Colony if the share business were conducted under proper regulations.

❖ *It seems that moving the Exchange from under the verandahs of the Hongkong Hotel into a prestigious building of the official Stock Exchange, did not ensure the conduct of the business under proper regulations. The notorious scandals of the more recent years indicate that the 'rabble' is still in the business.*

The Prince's and Queen's Buildings and Statue of Sir Thomas Jackson, c.1910
These two buildings were built on land reclaimed between 1890 and 1904 in
the large Praya Reclamation Scheme in the Central District, which advanced
the waterfront from the present Des Voeux Road to Connaught Road. The
reclamation was not without problems; money nearly ran out in 1893, and
storms had slowed down the work.

Nevertheless, when the reclamation was completed, in 1904, 65 acres of
land had been reclaimed, of which about half was available for building
development, and the rest for roads and open spaces. The cost exceeded $3
million.

The statue of Sir Thomas Jackson is seen facing the Hongkong Bank, the
destiny of which he guided for nearly three decades. He became chief manager
of the bank in 1876 when its fortunes were not flourishing and he left it in 1902
'firmly established as the premier Bank in the Far East' (*Hongkong Telegraph*,
24 February 1906).

The statue was unveiled on 24 February 1906 by the Governor, Sir Matthew
Nathan, at a colourful ceremony with flags of all nations; even the crescent
and star, we are told, was displayed. The statue was lost during the War but
later recovered and replaced at the Statue Square, but for some strange reason
is no longer facing the bank but the Legislative Council Building.

Hongkong Telegraph **12 April 1890**	<u>To Let, Furnished</u>: From 1st June, a HOUSE, vicinity of Caine Road, ten minutes from Club. Rent $65 per month. Apply to … .

Hongkong Telegraph
17 April 1890

There was recently a sharp conflict between the revenue cruiser *Kulu* and some salt smugglers near Whampoa. The cruiser opened fire upon the smugglers, who replied and made a desperate struggle to prevent capture, and save their cargo, but the contrabandists, being outnumbered, had to give up the battle after a struggle of about half an hour, leaving all their salt to the revenue cruiser's people. Some 20,000 catties of salt were seized. But the smugglers themselves managed to escape.

❖ *Salt was an ancient monopoly controlled by China.*

Hongkong Telegraph
24 April 1890

THE ELECTRIC LIGHTING OF HONGKONG: The electric lighting of the main streets of Hongkong will in all probability be completed by October … placed along Queen's Road and the Praya at intervals of 150 yards, and we guarantee that people will be able to see where they are going then.

Hongkong Telegraph
8 May1890

Mr. Thomas Jackson, the popular Chief Manager of the Hongkong & Shanghai Banking Corporation, arrived here from London by yesterday's English mail, and once more assumes direction of the bank's affairs.

❖ *For the benefit of our young people, who may perhaps know little of the old ways of transportation, Thomas Jackson, a big man, did not arrive in Hong Kong in an envelope, by mail, but on a mail steamer.*

Hongkong Telegraph
15 May 1890

A professional foot-binder named Wong Achap was this morning … sentenced by Mr. Robinson to six months' hard labour and to be put into the stocks for three hours at a time … for hacking at his widowed mother's head with a chopper.

Punishment by Stocks, Hong Kong, c.1910
Sitting between two Indian policemen, a sergeant and a constable, the prisoner is undergoing public punishment by stocks. In front of him is a placard, probably listing his offences. The 'stocks' is a wooden frame with holes for offender's feet (in this case), or for feet and hands. This humiliating, but relatively harmless, form of punishment was popular in the West in the Middle Ages, but apparently still practised in the twentieth century Hong Kong!

The entire absence of sanitary arrangements in Chinese towns and villages being well known ... there is no isolation of infectious diseases, and no attention is paid to causes of death unless there is a supposition of violence. ... But speaking generally, Chinese towns enjoy immunity from these dangerous outbreaks almost as complete as that of well-drained European communities. ... The healthiness of Chinese cities has been ingeniously attributed to the universal habit of fanning, a practice which is said to keep the atmosphere in constant circulation ... but so far as contaminated water supply is concerned, we believe the real secret of immunity from its evil effects to lie in the universal custom of boiling all water intended for drinking ... the Chinese never drink cold water. In the matter of ablutions ... the Chinese enjoy facilities ... far in advance of anything within reach of the poorer classes of our own ... land. Every little hamlet in China has a shop where hot water can be bought for a trifling sum at any hour of the day or night.

Hongkong Telegraph
29 May 1890

Hongkong Telegraph
3 June 1890

On the 30th ulto., the police arrested a Chinese man … charging him with being in possession of illicit opium. After some detention in the Police Station the Opium Farmer was satisfied that the opium found had been regularly obtained and desired to withdraw the charges.

❖   *By this time, opium was a monopoly, sold to the highest bidder, who would then be designated as the Opium Farmer.*

Hongkong Telegraph
7 June 1890

In a library in Paris, said to be the largest in the world, is a Chinese chart of the heavens, in which 1,460 stars are to be found to be correctly placed according to the scientists of the present day. The chart was made in 600 B.C.

Hongkong Telegraph
11 June 1890

The question of overcrowding in Victoria will be wrestled with the Sanitary Board meeting to-morrow.

❖   *As a matter of fact, the total population of Hong Kong Island and Kowloon, in 1890, was around 200,000; the New Territories had not yet been leased.*

Hongkong Telegraph
13 June 1890

A Munich firm has made a carriage which is propelled by gas generated from benzine or analogous material. The motor, which is not visible from outside, is placed in the rear of a three-wheeled carriage … and the benzine used in its propulsion is carried in a closed copper receptacle … from which it passes, drop by drop, to the generator. … A speed of about ten miles an hour can be obtained.

❖   *Actually, the earliest petrol-engine cars were: a three-wheeled Benz built in 1885 and a four-wheeled Daimler of 1886.*

An Austrian photographer named Varens has succeeded in producing a certain range of colours, running from ruby red to light orange. … scientific men who have followed his experiments predict that all colours are obtainable, and that a revolution in camera work is at hand.

❖   *Not a bad prediction. Although colour process was said to have been invented in 1904 (by the Lumiere brothers), it did not achieve wide use until 1930s when Kodak introduced colour photography, first as a transparency film.*

DEATH OF A NOTABLE CHINESE. Another link binding the old Canton of ante-treaty times with the Hongkong and China of today was snapped asunder the other week, when Mr. Ng Chi-sing, better known as Howqua, passed over ... at the comparatively early age of 56 years. Mr. Ng was the son of that historical character Houqua, who more than half a century ago was the principal member of the unique corporation in Canton known as the Co-Hong, through whom the whole of the foreign trade was transacted in the old Factory days when the East India Company was still a power in the land, and Hongkong was *terra incognita*.

Hongkong Telegraph
26 June 1890

The brutal manner in which pigs are shipped to and landed in Hongkong from ports in Hainan; packed in baskets and stacked tier upon tier in the holds of steamers, was again brought to the notice of the Magistrate at the Police Court this morning.

❖ *This certainly has not changed much, but now seldom reaches the courts.*

Transporting Livestock, Hong Kong Island, c.1910
Pigs packed in rattan baskets, probably on the way to a market. The method of carrying pigs in baskets, in which the animal can hardly move, may be simple, but is clearly cruel and should be condemned.

Transporting Livestock, Hong Kong, c.1950
Forty years later but the method unfortunately has not changed.

**Hongkong Telegraph
28 June 1890**

Belgrade, May 30th: A number of Christians at Kossovo, Old Servia, have been massacred by Mohammedans.

❖   *A hundred years later, and the picture has only slightly changed: the roles have been reversed.*

Boa Vista Hotel, Macao, c.1920
The grand old hotel, boasting of a 'history of more than a century of Portuguese hospitality', Boa Vista, or Bela Vista, is located just above the sea shore commanding a superb view. Its elegant, old colonial style made it very popular with residents and visitors alike, especially those anxious to exchange the luxury of modern hotels for the leisurely atmosphere of a bygone era.

**Hongkong Telegraph
2 July 1890**

Intimation:
THE BOA VISTA BISHOP'S BAY. MACAO.
This House, situated on the Coast in one of the best and healthiest parts of Macao and commanding an admirable view facing the South, will be OPENED as a HOTEL on the 1st July next.
    Every comfort will be provided for visitors with excellent cuisine and choice Wines.
    Hot, Cold, Shower and Sea Water Baths. Large and well-Ventilated Dining, Billiard, and Reading Rooms, and well supplied Bar.
Mrs. Maria B. Dos Remedios, Proprietress   Macao, 28th June 1890.

❖ *The 'Boa Vista', or 'Bela Vista' as it is better known, was much loved by Hong Kong visitors for more than 100 years. In contrast to modern hotels, it was old-fashioned but comfortable. It was recently renovated and probably lost much of its old colour and atmosphere.*

Sir, Will you permit me through your columns to draw the attention of the authorities to the disgraceful state of the Peak Road. ... From the Albany upwards, the road has been torn open for the purpose of laying pipes, but no progress is being made. ... All the morning building materials are being carried up to the Peak by ... coolies who never think of going out of their way when a chair is coming down the exceedingly narrow roadway. ... the police are conspicuous by their absence, frequent collisions and great danger of being severely bruised are the results. ... It appears, however, that the road has been opened up before the pipes were ready to be laid, and, you, Mr. Editor, are perhaps in a position to inform me who is responsible for this very foolish manner of carrying out the public works of the colony?

Hongkong Telegraph
4 July 1890

Editor's Reply:
The Public Works department is supposed to have direction and carrying out of the matters referred to, but where the Surveyor General's responsibility begins and ends is a conundrum we are quite unable to expound. Our correspondent doubtless remembers that we once very narrowly escaped being legally victimised for publishing the truth about the shady methods of the Public Works department. ... [It] requires to be either entirely abolished, and its duties placed in the hands of an elected Municipal Council, or subjected to a thoroughly practical reform in every branch. ...

❖ *The Peak Road referred to is the present Old Peak Road. The Public Works Department has changed its name but, sadly, not its reputation.*

HONGKONG GOLF CLUB. The first golf match ever played in Hongkong took place on Saturday on the links at Happy Valley between teams of the Club chosen by the Captain (Commander Rumsey) and the Secretary (Mr. Mitchell-Innes).

Hongkong Telegraph
7 July 1890

❖ *See the photograph of the club on p.94.*

Hongkong Golf Club, Race Course, Happy Valley, Hong Kong Island, c.1895–1900
This small but handsome building of the Hongkong Golf Club, proudly displaying its flag, was located on the grounds of the Race Course at Happy Valley. Unlike other sporting activities in Hong Kong, golf seems to have had a relatively late start, around 1888. The club was inaugurated in 1889 and given accommodation by the Jockey Club in the basement of the Grand Stand until 1895, when the building shown in the photograph was erected. Sadly, it was destroyed in the tragic Race Course fire of 1918.

Hongkong Telegraph
10 July 1890

NATIVE OPIUM IN CHINA. Our Shanghai … contemporary translates from the *Hu Pao* of July 2nd the following circular which the Grand Council of State at Peking has addressed to each province of the Empire …

'On the 2nd June the Tsung-li Yamen and the Board of Revenue memorialised the Throne recommending the issue of orders for reports on *likin* on native opium with a view to reform in the system of collection. It was observed that native opium was now one of the principal productions of the soil of China, and that the time had come for the consideration of the increase of the *likin*. … The justice of the suggestion is evident when attention is given to enormous drain on the wealth of China for the purchase of foreign opium which has existed for so long. Of late the quantity grown in China is increasing from day to day; the profits are great, and the practice has spread to such an extent that it is now impossible to stop it. Should it ... be found to be practicable to arrive at a system of dealing with the question in such a manner that a large revenue may be derived by the Government of China from the actual state of the case, China will both recover profits ... and have the control of the whole traffic greatly in her hands.'

❖ *Likin was a tax on foreign opium collected by China. In this emotionally charged issue of opium trade, it is often forgotten that China was not entirely blameless. Once it began to grow its own opium in significant amount, China seemed to be more concerned with making profit than the welfare of the people. The official explanation was, as this announcement shows, since the habit cannot be stopped, China might as well profit by it.*

Sir, Has the Small Birds Protection Ordinance become a dead letter in this colony? This morning, and for several mornings ... I have noticed several small Portuguese lads armed with butterfly nets and bird cages, each containing one or more small birds, which I presume have just been captured. This morning I counted no less than eight birds in one cage. Surely if this kind of thing is allowed to go on unchecked we shall soon have no small birds in the colony. ... I remain Yours, etc. ...

Hongkong Telegraph **12 July 1890**

Dr. Amelia B. Edwards, the eminent authoress, says: 'The franchise is something which I don't want, but which I really think I ought to have'. Strange to say, these are Amelia's sentiments on the breeches question also. She doesn't want the 'pants' but still, yes, she thinks she decidedly ought to have 'em. And so think we.

Hongkong Telegraph **19 July 1890**

Telegram:
The general Act of the Anti-Slavery Conference has been signed by all the Powers represented except Holland, who has been allowed six months delay.

Hongkong Telegraph **21 July 1890**

❖ *A disgraceful record for human species which had waited until the end of the 19th century to totally abolish one of the most terrible abuses of humanity.*

Hongkong Telegraph
22 July 1890

The Peking correspondent of the *Shanghai Mercury* writes: ... An Imperial Decree was issued ... To the Board of Defence and the Board of Revenue in connection with the fund to be provided by the eighteen provinces for building railways. The issue of a large foreign loan for the same purpose has also been sanctioned. ... almost all the Treaty Powers have been busy tendering advice and, directly or indirectly, profess to assist the Imperial Government with reference to the big State loan of Tls.* 30,000,000 since the edict ... was issued, but it remains to be seen who will be successful.

Hongkong Telegraph
24 July 1890

On the 25th ultimo, Mr. J. W. Scott, secretary of the Deccan brewery at Dapuri, fell into a vat of beer. The liquor, which was worth Rs. [rupees] 4,000, was afterwards poured away.

Hongkong Telegraph
28 July 1890

The Government has decided to increase the Military Contribution of the Crown Colonies where an inadequate amount is payable at present. Ceylon and the Mauritius are under consideration, but the increase is demanded of the Straits and Hongkong.

Hongkong Telegraph
30 July 1890

The Stewards of the Hongkong Jockey Club have agreed to the proposed extension of the Race-course, with the requisite alterations, and if the Government will only do the needful as far as the 'sinews of war' are concerned, some very extensive and desirable improvements in the Happy Valley will be effected by this time next year, and the claims of everybody who has any actual claim to consideration thoroughly satisfied.

Hongkong Telegraph
31 July 1890

ALFRED S. DYER, the social purity crank who spends his time in raving about opium divans, brothels and the 'British India Government in alliance with hell' writes to a London contemporary as follows:- 'The Viceroy Li [Hung-chang] spoke in strong terms to me of the moral and material evils of opium trade, and if the foreign import were prohibited, they would at once turn their efforts ... to put down the home growth.

---

* Tael: a trade weight measured in fine silver, generally 583.3 grains (from the Malay *tahil*).

But, he asked, would not the demand for a prohibition treaty with Great Britain bring on a third opium war'. We ... cannot refrain from telling Dyer plainly that he is an infamous liar, and an impertinent and vicious scandal-monger. Li Hung-chang is far too astute a statesman to either give away his policy or confide State secrets to a fanatic of the Dyer type. Neither is he likely to have made the slightest reference to the possibility of 'a third opium war with Great Britain'.

❖ *The subject of 'opium trade' certainly stirred up passions, even as late as 1890. But a possibility of a Third Opium War? Most unlikely; by 1890 the opium trade had shrunk to a small fraction of its former volume. By the way, this Dyer has nothing to do with J. Dyer Ball, the famous Sinologist, Hong Kong's civil servant, and the author of 'Things Chinese'.*

Race Course, Happy Valley, Hong Kong Island, c.1895–1900
Race Day at the Happy Valley. Hong Kong's racing community views this 'sport of kings' as an important social occasion; men and ladies are fashionably dressed. The Grandstand, now considerably enlarged, is dressed in flags. In this members' enclosure few Chinese can be seen, but this would be strongly reversed in later years. Racing in Hong Kong began around 1846. From the start, the management relied entirely on 'gentlemen jockeys' — men of other occupations who rode for pleasure. Their size and weight did not apparently prevent them from competing at the races, and it was not uncommon for these amateur jockeys to weigh as much as 180 lbs. or stand six feet tall. This tradition continued well into the 1960s, when the gentlemen jockeys were finally replaced by professional riders. The Race Course's proximity to the cemetery evoked many unfavourable comments in the early days (the cemetery was there first, preceding the Race Course by about a year); today this unseemly proximity has long been accepted as normal.

Hongkong Telegraph
1 August 1890

The discoveries made by Stanley, according to that first-class bushwalker's account, show that the Nile is the longest river in the world and at least 4,100 miles in length.

❖   *Actually 4,149 miles.*

Hongkong Telegraph
6 August 1890

News has been received in Shanghai from Tientsin that the course of the yellow River at its mouth has shifted, and that junks which were sent with materials for mending the embankments are now high and dry, two miles from the recent channel of the river.

❖   *Speaking of rivers, the Nile is the longest river in the world (see snippet above); the Yangtze comes fifth, with 3,100 miles long; and the Yellow River is the eighth – 2,700 miles.*

Hongkong Telegraph
12 August 1890

The Chicago Chief of Police has stopped the sale of cigarettes to boys under 16 years of age. That might be done here, too, with good effect.

❖   *It is interesting to note that, 100 years ago, girls were deemed so unlikely to smoke, that they are not mentioned.*

Hongkong Telegraph
30 August 1890

The scandalous wharf arrangements to the west of Central Market, whence the Chinese Yaumati launches start, have long been a disgrace to the Colony. The rapidly developing passenger traffic between Hongkong and Hunghom, Yaumati, and Chinese Kowloon makes it imperative that some sort of system and proper wharfage arrangement should be made, at the Hongkong end at any rate, for the safety of the travelling public. …

Hongkong Telegraph
8 September 1890

It is asserted that the habit of opium-smoking is being introduced into Great Britain, not in the nature of an evil custom, but under the advice of some medical men to their patients. There has arisen as a consequence a demand that the medical societies shall deal promptly with any physician who may be found to have prescribed such a vice as a remedy.

Man Mo Temple: Hollywood Road, c.1900

The temple today is richly renovated and is popular with both local people and visitors. Inside are splendid temple decorations, rich embroideries, temple vessels and figures.

It was built in the early 1840s, when the Chinese population of Tai Ping Shan, as the district was called, was rapidly increasing. The temple is noteworthy in that two gods, of very different influence, are worshipped in it — Man Cheong, the god of civil virtues, and Kwan Ti, the patron of martial skills. Sitting side by side in the main hall alcove, the former holds a writing brush in his hand while the latter holds a sword. In worshipping them in the same temple, perhaps the Chinese attempt to reconcile the two different principles and to attest that both can serve the common good.

Although ancestor worship remains the cornerstone of Chinese religious beliefs, as evidenced by the imposing ancestral halls in the clan-dominated districts of the New Territories, temples take over this important role in the urban environment where clan cohesion no longer exists. Temples provide spiritual comfort of a general nature that cuts across the clans. Many deities are worshipped, often more than one in a temple; most had been famous heroes or sages of great valour and virtue, who became endowed with miraculous powers. The commonest deities honoured in temples are: Tin Hau, queen of heaven and patron goddess of sailors and fishermen; Pak Tai, emperor of the north, a Taoist saint or the famous emperor of the Wei dynasty (AD 4th century); Hung Shing, a virtuous official of the Tang dynasty; Che Kung, great general of the Sung dynasty; Hau Wong, a famous official loyal to the Sung emperor; and Kuan Yin, a female divinity, an embodiment of all womanly virtues.

Hongkong Telegraph
23 September 1890

The elephant owners in Kinta, Perak, having lately combined to raise the already exorbitant rates of elephant hire, the Chinese all over the district are beginning to use wheelbarrows to take their stores to the mines. Many elephants have been thrown out of work and the owners are now trying to sell them, but cannot find purchasers.

Hongkong Telegraph
29 September 1890

We are informed that the 'Mexican mail' steamer *Amigo* left the Macao roads* yesterday at 12.30 p.m., for somewhere in Mexico, with 481 Chinese coolies in the steerage and two cabin passengers.

❖ *The notorious 'coolie trade' was largely the result of the discovery of goldfields in California in the 1850s. Large numbers of labourers (coolies) were recruited in Hong Kong and Macao and shiploads of them sent to America, often under appalling conditions.*

Hongkong Telegraph
17 October 1890

TRADE marks were known in ancient Babylon; China had them as early as 1,000 B.C.; they were authorised in England in 1,300; Guttenberg, the inventor of printing, is said to have had a law suit over his trademark.

The long-distance telephone is now in successful operation between Boston and Washington. Conversation is carried on over this great distance with ease.

❖ *Internal telephone communication in Hong Kong was installed in 1881.*

Hongkong Telegraph
18 October 1890

If preliminaries can be satisfactorily arranged, we understand that a roller skating rink will be one of the features of Hongkong during the coming winter. This healthful … amusement would most certainly receive general patronage, and as the promoter is a gentleman who has had extensive experience in the business … we doubt not that the Hongkong Skating Rink will prove one of the most popular places of resort in the colony. Full particulars will be announced shortly.

---

* 'Roads' here is used as a protected place near shore (not a harbour) where ships can ride at anchor.

This day and month the electric lighting service will be inaugurated here. The wires — some eleven miles altogether — are already in position, and all that is now required us to put up the lamps.

Hongkong Telegraph
1 November 1890

❖ *In the event, street lighting on Hong Kong Island started in December 1890 by the Hong Kong Electric Co. A year later, some 600 homes were supplied with electricity. Kowloon was provided with electric lighting a decade later, by the China Light & Power Co.*

Wickham, W. H., the First Manager of the Hong Kong Electric Co., c.1890
The photograph is said to have been taken by Wickham himself. He was born in England, in 1858, and came to Hong Kong in 1888 to take charge of the newly-formed company, inaugurated in 1889. This he accomplished with such success that by December 1890 Hong Kong had its first electric street lighting. Wickham retired in 1910 after an exemplary service, and continued as Company's consulting engineer and expert advisor in London, England.

THE GINSENG PLANT. Proposals have been made to America to cultivate the ginseng plant ... used in Chinese medical practice, for exportation to the 'Middle Kingdom'. ... There is no other plant, not even ... the poppy, which yields opium, of which it can be truly said that it is worth its weight in gold, as is the ginseng of Korea.

Hongkong Telegraph
8 November 1890

The Dutch merchants became aware ... that the precious plant grew abundantly ... in Massachusetts. The root was shipped ... to Amsterdam and London, where cargoes were sold to the East India Company at a profit of 500 per cent. The American ginseng broke the market for a time, but the price rallied after a while, and since then a steady stream of ginseng has been exported to China from the Ohio and Mississippi valleys, where it is found in limitless quantities.

❖ *Americans, eager to get into the lucrative China trade, concentrated on the export of ginseng to China, largely because they could only get minimal quantities of opium (from Turkey), the bulk of which (from India) was cornered by the British firms.*

**Hongkong Telegraph
10 November 1890**

OUR PUBLIC WORKS: THE CENTRAL MARKET. In submitting my report ... on the Central Market, I stated that I had ... estimated this building approximately at $235,000. The detailed drawings have now been prepared. The progress of excavation has also allowed a more careful study of the foundations which prove to be of a less favourable nature than I was led to anticipate. With a view of meeting this contingency ... I find it advisable to increase the estimate to $270,000 which will, I trust, prove sufficient to complete the market ready for occupation.

❖   *The building was completed in 1895. The present Central Market is not the original building, though standing on the original site.*

Central Market, Des Voeux Road, Hong Kong Island, c.1900
When the market was opened, in 1895, it stood on the Praya (later renamed Des Voeux Road, after the reclamation had advanced the Praya seawards). Handsomely designed, in red brick with graceful arches and a central tower, the market served the local community for over thirty years until replaced, in 1937, by a more modern building.

TELEGRAM FROM NEW ORLEANS. Considerable excitement has been caused here owing to the murder of the Police by some Italians belonging to the Secret Society called Muffia Society. The citizens are furious and demand that no more immigrant Italian paupers, brigands, and convicts be allowed to land. The Mayor has received a threatening letter from the Muffia Society.

❖   *An interesting note on the early Mafia; only the spelling has changed.*

A curious example of Chinese etiquette is given in the latest *Peking Gazette*, which says:- The Viceroy at Canton forwards an application from General Hsieh Hung-chang … to alter his name to Hsieh Te-lung. In a letter … from his home in Hunan, the general has been informed that the family register contains the name of a remote ancestor, which is identical with his own, and in conformity with the rule which forbids that the surname of any member of a former generation should be employed by his descendants he now asks sanction for the proposed change of designation. The (request) Granted by Rescript.

**Hongkong Telegraph
11 November 1890**

It will come as a startler to many that an omnibus company has been formed amongst some enterprising Chinese, who will soon run two-horse buses from Wanchai to West Point; the line being along Queen's Road East and Central and down the Praya and Bonham Strand. Horses and vehicles will arrive within the next two months, and the Hongkong Bus Co. will be *un fait accompli* in the spring of 1891.

**Hongkong Telegraph
12 November 1890**

Several local sportsmen are ranging the country around Castle Peak Bay in pursuit of a tiger which has made its appearance there, and is carrying off cattle …

❖   *By this time, the local tiger had already become an endangered species, making only a rare appearance. In spite of this, it was ruthlessly hunted down and all but disappeared by the 1930s.*

**Hongkong Telegraph
15 November 1890**

Under instructions from the Secretary of State for the Colonies, it is notified in Saturday's Gazette that any public servant indulging in the practice of gambling, or visiting Chinese Kowloon for the purpose of gambling, is liable to dismissal from the public service.

**Hongkong Telegraph
17 November 1890**

Hongkong Telegraph
19 November 1890

Telegram:
DOCTOR KOCH AND CONSUMPTION. Doctor Koch of Berlin claims the discovery of a cure for consumption by injection of certain lymph. The German scientists believe in its success.

❖ *'Consumption' is the old name for lung tuberculosis. Koch did discover the bacterium causing tuberculosis, but as for cure, the claim was premature. The injection of 'lymph' was an attempt to immunize against the disease. The first successful drug treatment of tuberculosis was not discovered until 1950s.*

Hongkong Telegraph
20 November 1890

If, for a space of time, the columns of the *Telegraph* lack their wonted vigour we ask the indulgence of our readers, for owing to the unfortunate and altogether unexpected issue of a suit in the troubled … sea of law, the *Telegraph* has temporarily lost the services of the pen which for years has made it the most interesting and popular journal in the Far East.

❖ *The Editor was later convicted and jailed!*

A writer in *Harpers Magazine*, on the utilization of petroleum, says that this natural product, which at the present time has an immense consumption, was known in China at least 2,000 years ago. Professor J. S. Newbury is of opinion … that thirty centuries may have elapsed since is was brought to the earth's surface in the course of boring wells for salt, and he adds that … it was even then used by the Chinese for lighting purposes as well as for medicine.

❖ *China never ceases to amaze one with its number of 'firsts', such as gun-powder, paper, compass, etc.*

Hongkong Telegraph
1 December 1890

A native paper states that the arrest of the notorious pirate Wu, for whom a reward of $5,000 was offered, was effected by Chinese officers acting with the foreign police of Hongkong.

The Hongkong Electric Company Ld. Commenced the illumination of the streets of Hongkong at 6 o'clock this evening. The light is beautifully bright and as steady as that reflected by old 'Sol' himself.

❖ *Certainly a milestone for Hong Kong. The first street lighting, by gas, was installed in Hong Kong in 1864, now to be replaced by electric lighting. Today, it is difficult for us to imagine what life was like without electric*

Lin Fa Kung Temple, Tai Hang, Hong Kong Island, c.1870
It is not known when the Lin Fa Kung (meaning Lotus Flower Palace) was built, but it is probably several centuries old. One of the tablets inside the temple gives the third year of Emperor Tung Chi (1864) as the date of renovation; this was probably the date when it was converted from a small pavilion into a temple.

The temple's principal deity is Kuan Yin, Taoist female divinity and an embodiment of all womanly virtues, but the temple is regarded as Buddhist. This apparent contradiction may be explained by the fact that Kuan Yin was originally a Buddhist deity and a male, later adopted and 'converted' to a female one by the Taoist followers.

The front half of the temple is in the original octagonal shape — remnant of the 1864 conversion — resembling a lotus flower, a Buddhist emblem. Brick, stone, and timber were used for the construction of the temple, while the ceiling is supported by a system of arches. The internal decoration is simple but elegant. The temple is well worth a visit for its unique features.

This early photograph shows the temple standing in complete isolation. Before land reclamation, it stood close to the seashore. Today it is surrounded by massive housing development and stands well inland.

lights, or even earlier — without gas-light — illumination provided only by candle-light. But wait! All is not right, as the next snippet shows.

Last night at about 10 o'clock the electric light gave the first indication that, although its radiance is as brilliant as if it came direct from heaven it is not beyond a partial eclipse. The cause however, was an accident, and in no way detracts from the value of the light. ... All necessary repairs ... have been affected ... and to-night the light will be as powerful as ever.

Hongkong Telegraph
4 December 1890

**Hongkong Telegraph
5 December 1890**

The large sum of $233,572, representing this colony's military contribution to the Imperial Government for the current year, has been solemnly passed in the Legislative Council by the official majority of one, notwithstanding the unanimous opposition of the unofficial members and in the teeth of an adverse and indignant public opinion. … the official members … are not to blame for this latest War Office raid on the local Exchequer; they are mere automatons at the beck and call of the Governor, who is under the thumb of the Secretary of State for the Colonies. … Until we have a properly constructed legislative body … elected by popular suffrage and independent of the official vote, we may talk and protest as much as we please, but we will have to submit and 'pay up' just the same … .

❖   *An important reminder that the clamour for popular suffrage in Hong Kong began long ago, and was not a phenomenon of the 1980s.*

**Hongkong Telegraph
10 December 1890**

From Memorial submitted to the Throne by the Viceroy of Yunnan:
The Governor of Yunnan and the Governor General of the Yun Kwei provinces, report the completion of a Telegraph line from the provincial capital, Ch'u Hsiung-fu to Teng Yueh. … — a distance of 1,600 odd miles. The work was begun … in the spring of 1888, and was completed by the fifth moon in 1889. Memorialists dwell on the difficulties of the undertaking, the line running among high mountains and thick forests, the party suffering from the sun by day and the fear of wolves and tigers by night. … Sometimes in a day's march of 30 miles, they would not meet a living being. Another danger was from crossing three rivers which obstructed their path, from the waters of which rise pestilential vapours which if breathed by a man … are often fatal. The party lost more than ten of their number in this way. Memorialists hand a list of recommendations for promotion, for the Imperial notice. …

**Hongkong Telegraph
23 December 1890**

Two earring snatchers who were caught yesterday whilst practising their profession in Lyndhurst Terrace were sentenced at the Police Court this morning, by Mr. Wise, to the well-merited term of five months' imprisonment. They likewise receive a dozen strokes across the breech on the first and last day of their pilgrimage.

❖   *Earring snatching, which has now almost disappeared, was still common in as late as the 1930s. Not a day passed when house-surgeons on duty at the hospital were not repairing ear lobes of unfortunate ladies, torn in the process of earring snatching.*

Performance of the 'Gondoliers', Hong Kong, 1891
The photograph, unfortunately of poor quality, shows the stage setting for the performance of Gilbert and Sullivan's light opera, the 'Gondoliers', probably at the Theatre Royal in the City Hall.

A large number of residents assembled at the City Hall this afternoon for the purpose of receiving the proposals of the Jubilee Committee of Hongkong [for Hongkong's 50th anniversary] … three days rejoicing … the 22nd, 23rd and 24th January, 1891 … a subscription ball, a meeting of the Legislative Council to draw up a telegram for transmission to the Queen, a salute of 50 guns from the men-of-war … and the batteries, a review of the military naval and volunteer forces … at which the Governor will attend … a performance of 'The Gondoliers' by the Amateur Dramatic Club … pony races under the auspices of the Jockey Club, athletic sports, etc. … The report of the Committee was adopted with acclamation … .

Hongkong Telegraph
30 December 1890

Within the last few days the trustees of the British Museum have become possessed of a Chinese bank note, which was issued from the Imperial Mint just 300 years before the circulation of the first paper money in Europe. … It is impossible to deny that they were acquainted with the art of printing many centuries before the days of Gutenberg. According to native records, the art of printing was in use in China in 593 A.D., but does not appear to have been employed in the preparation of bank notes until the ninth century …

❖   *Another 'first' for China!*

1891

**Hongkong Telegraph
7 January 1891**

The lamentations of Jeremiah were as nought compared with those that are being secretly vented in Hongkong to-day — for news of another defeat has come to hand. Mr. Arthur K. Travers is in receipt of a telegram stating that 'Colombo beat Hongkong by 10 wickets'. Singapore won by 170 runs and now Colombo by 10 wickets! What can it be — the whisky or the weather?

❖   *Or both? Most British overseas possessions readily adopted the 'home sports'; indeed, many still practise them, long after becoming independent.*

Cricketers at the Hongkong Cricket Club, c.1895

Cricket, as we all know, is an essentially English game, which is said to have been played since the 16th century. Like Mary's lamb in the nursery rhyme, wherever the British go, cricket was sure to follow.

In the days of the empire, the colonies took up the game eagerly, and to this day teams from the West Indies, the Indian subcontinent, Australia and New Zealand excel at the game. For some reason, the game never appealed to the Chinese. And so in Hongkong, the game was played by expatriate Europeans, the local Portuguese, the Indians and the Eurasians

with only rare participation of the Chinese.

In 1851, the Hongkong Cricket Club was opened in the heart of the Central District, soon followed by one in Kowloon. In this photograph, a group of cricketers are posing in front of the pavilion of the Hongkong Cricket Club. Alas, none of the men can be identified.

The game was usually played on Saturday afternoons, and there was something very reassuring in the sight of a leisurely game of cricket played on the green lawn of the club in the heart of a busy commercial city.

The Hongkong Cricket Club remained in the Central District until the 1970s, when it was finally moved to Wong Nai Chung Gap Road. It is noteworthy that the vacated site was not redeveloped, but converted into Chater Gardens.

For committing an offence against public decency on the Praya yesterday, a miserable, half-starved coolie was fined a dollar, with the alternative of seven days' retirement, by the dispenser of British justice at the Magistracy to-day. The frequency of these cases shows the necessity for public latrines of which there are next to none in Hongkong.

Hongkong Telegraph
13 February 1891

It is reported that the Japanese military authorities intend to increase the army to 100,000 men — the increase to be made during the next two years. This is in consequence of instructions issued by the Emperor to Count Oyama, Minister of War.

❖ *One wonders how much attention was given to this seemingly harmless announcement? Yet, within the next 20 years Japan took Formosa from China, Port Arthur from Russia, the whole of Korea from Koreans, and had become the strongest military power in the Far East.*

From the Editorial:
THE GOVERNOR. For some days past it has been an open secret that Sir W. DES VOEUX, on account of … ill health … has determined to leave Hongkong for good and to resign the governorship. … however much we deplore the untenable position taken by the Governor … on the Military Contribution 'squeeze' … we cannot but admire the sturdy and independent attitude he has invariably assumed on all public questions with which he had to deal.

Hongkong Telegraph
20 April 1891

❖ *Des Voeux left Hong Kong in May 1891; he was Governor of Hong Kong since 1883, but cannot be credited with any significant achievement.*

From the Editorial:
Until the passing of the drastic Ordinance recently, this colony was afflicted with a craze for gambling such as has no parallel in local history. … universal among the Chinese … (is) the mania for *fan-tan, po-tsz* and *pai-kau*. … whatever gambling goes on is now conducted secretly and with fear and trembling. But it still goes on! … The opium vice … is one of the largest sources of revenue locally. … Then why not tax gambling? It has been tried in this Colony before, between 1867 and 1872, and the revenue gained amounted to over a million dollars, which built the Tung-Wa Hospital and went a long way to paying for Tytam Waterworks. … Everyone was satisfied with the system … but it wouldn't

Hongkong Telegraph
12 June 1891

do. ... Downing Street was compelled to bow before the storm of missionary drivel.

❖   *The Editorial is right. Where is the logic of freely allowing manufacture and consumption of opium but outlawing gambling?*

**Hongkong Telegraph
1 July 1891**

Among the hawkers and sneak thieves and petty offenders in the Police Court to-day were two nobles, Victorino Torres and Basillio de la Cruz, who were fined a ducat each for fighting on the Praya. The quarrel was as to who had the purest Lusitanian blood and the highest standing among the aristocracy.

A Singapore contemporary says that golfing attracts considerable crowds of natives who wonder at the new fad of the *orang puteh* (white men) in hitting little balls into a hole only to take them out again and then hit them into another. That's about what it amounts to, when you come to think of it.

❖   *This may well apply to all sporting activities, unless one is brought up to enjoy them and the achievements which follow. One may equally ask what is the point of hitting a ball over a net only to have it hit back at one?*

**Hongkong Telegraph
4 July 1891**

That harbinger of peace and goodwill, Mr. John Swire, the head of the firm of Butterfield and Swire, is to pay the Far East another visit next month. It is a noteworthy fact that this eminent gentleman's visits to the East, although few and far between, invariably result in the removal of all unnecessary friction connected with the extensive commercial ramification of his firm.

**Hongkong Telegraph
11 September 1891**

Rumours were in circulation ... that agents of the Chinese secret societies ... were busy in this colony buying arms and endeavouring to enlist the services of foreign adventurers ... From what we have been able to gather, half-a-dozen men left here on Wednesday for Shanghai, but whose ultimate destination is said to be further up the Yangsze. ...

**Hongkong Telegraph
29 October 1891**

Young Shanghai: — Is my cigar offensive? HK Trader: — Oh No; I've lived too long on Praya Central.

Tobacco smoking is growing rapidly. … The Empress of Austria, the Szarina [of Russia], the Queen of Italy and the Queen of Portugal are all addicted to cigarette smoking. The former is said to smoke nearly two dozen a day.

Music as an aid to cooking is provided for by a *chef* in Berlin. He has composed a 'Boiled Egg Polka', with this notice on the title page: 'To boil the eggs, place them in boiling water, and play the polka in allegro moderato time, taking them out at the last bar. They will then be found to be boiled to a nicety.'

Marine Police Headquarters Kowloon, c.1890
The building in the centre of the photograph was built in 1884 and was the headquarters of the Water Police, later named Marine Police. It stands on a well-wooded hill close to the Star Ferry in Kowloon. It is of fine construction with arched verandahs on the ground floor and a colonnade above — a good example of Victorian colonial architecture. Originally two storeys high, a third was added to the building in the early 1920s.

A round signal tower stands to the left of the headquarters, with a large hollow copper ball suspended above the tower. A time signal was given at 12 noon (this was changed to 1 pm in 1904) by dropping the ball, and the ships in the harbour would check their chronometers against this time ball manoeuvre. This time ball was moved, in 1907, to the newly built Signal Tower on Blackhead Point, where the time signal could be better observed. The Marine Police Signal Tower was renovated in 1981, and now, renamed The Round House, houses a small maritime museum.

The three-storey building, with arched windows, on the extreme right, is an army barrack, long since gone. A wide stretch of land in front of the beach has been reclaimed, the shoreline straightened, and the present Salisbury Road constructed on it.

1892

**Hongkong Telegraph
21 January 1892**

The annual revenue of the Government of India from opium some thirty years ago was about $42,500,000, and after a gradual decrease it was last year about $15,000,000.

❖   *A staggering amount by the present standard.*

**Hongkong Telegraph
1 February 1892**

The *Peak Pioneer and Magazine Gap and Mount Austin Advertiser* says that in a half gale that visited Cloudland (The Peak) recently the chair coolies' matshed was blown away, and so was 'Mountain Lodge' the dilapidated official summer abode of the Governors of Hongkong, and that when the police were sent to recover the remains scattered about the hills, they could not distinguish which was which.

❖   *The sedan-chair coolies' shed was never rebuilt, but the Peak Cafe was built on its site in 1900, and still extant.*

Mountain Lodge, The Peak, 1874

Mountain Lodge, The Peak, c.1910

The first Mountain Lodge (left photograph), the governor's summer residence on the Peak, was built in 1867 on the site of the Army Sanatorium, purchased by the Government from the Ministry of Defence. It proved, however, unpopular and after it had been damaged by the typhoon in 1874 (when the photograph was taken) it was not rebuilt. Eventually, what was left of it was demolished in 1897. It seems that from around 1891, the governors used rented premises on the Peak, called 'The Cliffs', during the stifling summer months. The construction of the new

Mountain Lodge (right photograph) on the Peak began in 1900 and was completed in 1902. It stood on the site above the previous Mountain Lodge, and was described as 'the largest and handsomest building on the Peak'. Its first occupants were the Governor Sir Henry Blake and Lady Blake. The Mountain Lodge, badly damaged in the World War II, was demolished in 1946; whether in the post-war spirit of equality or for purely economic restraints, it was never rebuilt. Later, in the 1970s, a handsome public pavilion was erected on its foundations.

From the Editorial:
The Chinese have always constituted the industrial class of the eastern Hemisphere. ... As new lands have been opened ... there has been an insatiable demand for labour. ... China has been the only country which could meet this demand. ... the imperfections of the Chinese coolie traffic became more glaring as the traffic grew. ... ignorance and poverty combined are the greatest enemies of freedom. ... 'coolie broker' ... tells strange tales of a land outside of the Middle Kingdom ... where a day's pay, instead of twenty or thirty *cash*, is so many cents; where no mandarin lives to 'squeeze' them; where the workman lives off the fat of the land. ... they have taken passage, food and advance of wages ... they are taken away to a plantation, or a mine, or a railway and told to work off their debts. ... Mr. Henry Varley an Exeter Hall philanthropist ... was greatly struck with the resemblance between the coolie traffic and the ... slave trade.

❖   *The similarity is apt. The infamy of this coolie trade has been commented upon previously. Although not actually slaves, their conditions of transportation were very similar to those of the African slave trade.*

**Hongkong Telegraph
9 March 1892**

A 'MANDARIN' from Canton patronized the Hongkong Trading Company this morning, and signified that he would be graciously pleased to look at some silk goods. The whole staff of courteous attendants hastened to execute his Excellency's wish, and while showing him their gorgeous stocks of silk goods somebody noticed that the noble lord has executed the 'sleeve trick' with a bale of silk, stowing away $20 worth of material in the copious folds of his robe. He was promptly escorted to the *Yameen* of the magistrate, who remanded the case until Monday.

**Hongkong Telegraph
15 March 1892**

All the schools in the colony have closed their doors! They are not bankrupt, nor have any of their 'leading men' skipped the colony — they are not directors of huge concerns ... No, none of these horrors is the cause of the shutters being put up. It is a far simpler and more easily rectified affair — simply an epidemic of *la grippe** and mumps.

**Hongkong Telegraph
6 April 1892**

---

* *La grippe* (French) used in the past for 'influenza'.

**Hongkong Telegraph
9 May 1892**

Telegrams:

May Day went off quietly throughout Spain, none of the expected violent demonstrations occurring.

In the cathedral of Chartres [France] a dynamite bomb was found to-day.

In St. Martin's Church, Liege [Belgium] bombs were planted; all the windows … were destroyed.

In Bologne [Italy] many of the shops were looted.

In Troyes [France] the circus was set on fire.

In Buda-Pesth [Hungary] a large factory was burned down.

In Seville [Spain] a bomb was thrown into St. Vincent's church; the priest was killed.

❖ *Is it really so different from today? Only the name of the perpetrators. Today we call them terrorists, in 1892 they were called anarchists.*

Queen's Road Central, Central District, Hong Kong Island, c.1880
View looking east. The Clock Tower, erected by public subscription in 1863, stands at the junction with Pedder Street. Solid, colonial-style buildings with arched pillars line both sides of the street. At the far end, on the right, is the English Club, the predecessor of the Hong Kong Club, while on the left, partly concealed by trees, are the early Post Office and the Court House. Several sedan chairs are parked on the street. An air of lazy tranquillity prevails in the city centre destined to become, in years to come, a bustling commercial district.

CAPTURE OF 'NAMOA' PIRATE. We are reliably informed that a notorious pirate chief named Chun Shek ... who is alleged to have been one of the pirates who looted the Douglas Co's steamer *Namoa* has been captured by the Canton authorities.

❖ *A photograph, which is reputed to depict the execution (beheading) of the pirates involved in the attack on Namoa, has appeared in a number of publications, but the photograph is perhaps too gruesome to be included here.*

It will probably interest Mr. Lo Hok-pang, late compradore* in this colony, a 'don' in select Chinese circles ... to know that his bogus banks in Bonham Strand are still nailed up, and that his creditors are yearning for his return and settlement.

Hongkong Telegraph
24 May 1892

Hongkong has an unenviable notoriety amounting we believe to an unbeaten record, in the history of swindles and mysterious disappearances. Considering the size of the place ... and its population, which scarcely reached four figures ... it is simply appalling to contemplate the number of big swindles and fatal financial crashes, the millions of dollars stolen by downright ... thieves and forgerers, or by mealy-mouthed land sharks. ... There is no need to rehearse the long list of 'absent friends' ... three kinds — first, the deliberate thief ... second, the criminal optimist, who steals to gamble, confident of squaring up soon; third, the utterly incapable idiot, who throws away everybody's money in a perfectly lawful way without seeming to know what he is doing. ... A little inspection shows that these headings pretty well cover all the big crashes of the present generation in Hongkong.

Hongkong Telegraph
2 June 1892

In England they stand for office; in the United States they run; and in both countries they lie more or less.

Hongkong Telegraph
16 June 1892

---

* Compradore: a Chinese or Eurasian steward responsible for management of native staff and surveillance over local procedures and transactions (from Portuguese *comprar*, to buy).

Rock Engraving: Big Wave Bay

Although the date of the photograph is relatively recent, the rock engraving depicted on it is believed to be ancient.

Eight sites are known in Hong Kong territory where similar engravings occur. Most are cut into vertical rock surfaces, close to the coastline overlooking the sea. They are all deeply eroded from long exposure to the weather.

The finest of these engravings is the one shown on this photograph, located on Hong Kong Island, overlooking the popular beach of Big Wave Bay. Surprisingly, most of the engravings have been discovered only in the past 30 or 40 years; this one in 1970, by B. Haigh, a police officer. Its pattern is still clear and very striking, especially a number of pairs of concentric circles, possibly representing animal faces.

Although the exact age and origins of engravings remain a mystery, their antiquity is without doubt. Probably they were carved several thousand years ago by the early pre-Chinese, seafarers of this area and were intended as magical symbols propitiating the powers of the sea.

I like to regard them as the early forms of shrines by which the early pre-literate man communed with the forces of nature.

This fascinating ancient relic should not be missed. A path has been constructed by the Hong Kong Government so that the public can approach the engraving safely.

The best time to view it is early in the morning, when the sun shines obliquely from the east.

***Hongkong Telegraph
6 July 1892***

From the Editorial:
BANKS. In the Share Report of Mr. JOHN SULLIVAN, the well-known Shanghai broker ... we find the following:- 'There has been a complete collapse in Hongkong and Shanghai Bank shares, attributable to forced sales, it is with difficulty that shares can be placed at the present low prices ... .' One thing is certain — namely that the barefaced 'ring' of unscrupulous monopolists and schemers who for many years past have generally manipulated the affairs of the great Hongkong and Shanghai Banking Corporation for their own advantage ... is on

its last legs. ... The Directors of the ... Bank ... conspired to smash the *Hongkong Telegraph*, because that Journal had fearlessly exposed impudent shams and did not hesitate to openly declare the truth.

From the Editorial:
THE CHINESE MEDICAL COLLEGE.
The speech of His Excellency Sir William Robinson, Governor of Hongkong ... contained two promises — the first, that within two or three years he would put the finances of the Colony into a satisfactory state; and the second, that as soon as that was ... well established, he would allow the Unofficial Members of the Legislative Council, if they wished, to vote $40,000 as an endowment to the College of Medicine for Chinese in Hongkong ... .

❖ *The Hongkong College of Medicine, as it was officially called, was founded in 1887; it was the forerunner of the future University of Hong Kong. The college s most famous graduate was Dr Sun Yat-sen, the founder and the first president of the Chinese Republic.*

Hongkong Telegraph
27 July 1892

The Chinese money-changers, the shroffs* of the leading foreign and Chinese hongs, the hotels and stores, &c., have boycotted the notes of the Chartered Mercantile Bank since yesterday afternoon, and refuse to accept them as legal tender. As the other Banks of the colony accept Chartered Mercantile notes without hesitation, we can only regard this as another scare caused by idle gossip. So far as we can ascertain the Chartered Mercantile Bank is perfectly sound ... .

❖ *The Chartered Mercantile Bank was the first of the banks to open in Hong Kong. It did not fail, but its Hong Kong branch was wound up shortly afterwards.*

Hongkong Telegraph
6 October 1892

Our contemporary the *Sydney Bulletin* says that the Chinese still plentifully sneak into Australia. Their side-entrance is now Tasmania which province has only a Chinese poll-tax, but not limiting provision that restricts the number of Chinese passengers to a proportion per tonnage.

Hongkong Telegraph
27 October 1892

---

* Shroff: (Anglo-Ind.) a banker or money-changer in India and the Orient.

An American citizen named William Gerke figured in the Hall of Justice this morning and answered to the charge of being a vagrant, as alleged by a Sikh constable who took him in charge. ... Defendant proved to the satisfaction of Mr. Wodehouse that he was earning $28 *per mensum* (per month) by teaching four Portuguese clerks shorthand, so he was allowed to go on his way rejoicing.

❖ *Not all Westerners in Hong Kong at the time were traders and rich!*

Hongkong Telegraph
17 December 1892

A leading Japanese newspaper complains that the good manners of the Japanese have been ruined by the importation of Western civilization.

1893

Hongkong Telegraph
12 January 1893

Sam Ping Lee, a Chinese lawyer of New York, who is president of the Chinese Equal Rights Club, said to-day in an interview that the Chinese in this country do not intend to comply with the Act of Congress requiring them to register and deposit their photograph with the local collectors of internal revenue ... under penalty of expulsion from the country. The Chinese have combined to engage counsel, and will contest the constitutionality of the Act.

Hongkong Telegraph
30 January 1893

In the crowded state of the Harbour, it is somewhat surprising and highly creditable that the 'Star' ferry launches hardly ever meet with accidents while threading their way at full speed between Pedder's Wharf and Kowloon, even in the thickest and heaviest weather. Yesterday morning, however, the 'Morning Star' and 'Evening Star' met bows-on in mid-stream, the latter being rather badly though not dangerously damaged.

❖ *The remarkable skill of the Star Ferry coxswains has been the subject of frequent comments; accidents are, indeed, very rare. On one occasion, when the coxswains went on strike, the brought-in substitutes could hardly cope with the job.*

Star Ferries, Hong Kong Harbour, c.1910
Cross-harbour passenger ferry service was started around 1880 by the
enterprising Parsee businessman, Daorobjee Naorobjee. This uniquely efficient
and cheaply-priced service became known as the Star Ferry Company. The
early ferries were relatively small, carrying only about 100 passengers. Two
such ferries, the Evening Star and the Northern Star, are depicted in the
photograph. They were not, however, of the earliest type, but described by the
company as the 'Second Generation' ferries.

The enterprise ... and perseverance of the famous 'Taikoo' hong have
long been a byword throughout the Far East, and notwithstanding the
huge business Messrs. Butterfield and Swire already control, they are still
going rapidly ahead. The Taikoo Sugar Refinery is one of the largest
individual refineries in the world, but it isn't nearly big enough for B &
S. The huge works at Quarry Bay are to be greatly enlarged and we learn
that Messrs. John Swire and Son of London have arranged contracts
for machinery which ... will enable the Refinery to turn out four
thousand tons of refined sugar per week. Only think of it! The buildings
for this additional plant are already under construction. ... In the very
near future there will be quite a large township at Quarry Bay. Bravo,
Tosh! Gang forward!

Hongkong Telegraph
30 January 1893

❖ *A remarkable prediction about 'a township at Quarry Bay', but even
the* Hongkong Telegraph, *in its obvious enthusiasm, could not have foreseen
the immense size of the present Taikoo Shing! See Tai Koo Sugar Refinery,
p.120.*

Tai Koo Sugar Refinery, Quarry Bay, Hong Kong Island, c.1899
Extensive installations testify to the scale of this enterprise. Built by Butterfield
& Swire, one of the biggest and best-known of the Hong Kong traders, the
Sugar Refinery was one of the most important and lasting of the local Swire
industries. Tai Koo (太古 'great and ancient') was the Chinese name chosen by
the founder, John Samuel Swire, for Butterfield & Swire when it was first formed,
around 1870.

**Hongkong Telegraph
14 February 1893**

To-day being the feast of Saint Valentine, the Portuguese have obtained
permission to thump drums and blow whistles and make exhibitions of
themselves all over the colony.

**Hongkong Telegraph
16 February 1893**

Quaint Items of Interest:
The glowworm lays luminous eggs.
More than a third of Great Britain is owned by members of the House
of Lords.

From the Editorial:
TAXATION AND REPRESENTATION. The moral of recent events in Hongkong is that taxation does not always imply representation — that, in fact, it never has done so at all in this part of the world. The reason is not far to seek; the principle of representative Government is based on the right to revolution — if the people cannot obtain a hearing, they can refuse to pay taxes. That is the root of the matter. ... Of course the right of revolution does not become a right until it succeeds; prior to that point it is sedition and rascality. In Hongkong it has not yet developed — not more than half a dozen men in the Colony have the courage of their opinions and ... they are too weak to do anything unaided. ... Hardly a man but says the existing non-representational system is a scandal and a crying shame; yet no one will rise and strike the first blow. What fools these mortals be! ...

Hongkong Telegraph
7 March 1893

❖ *The last part of this statement sounds close to sedition and incitement. However, let it not be said that Hong Kong never wanted representational government prior to 1984. This editorial, more than a hundred years ago, speaks for itself.*

THE RATEPAYERS MEETING. A special meeting of ratepayers interested in the formation of an Association to protect public interests was held in the City hall. ... There was a fairly large attendance ... Resolution to create the 'Hongkong Association' — ... what was needed in Hongkong was either a Municipal Council or a preponderance of unofficials in the Legislative Council, men whom they could trust (Applause). The Colony had had enough of this second-hand business of electing the *Taipan* of this or that Hong to the Legislative, no matter what his capacity. The time has come when we in Hongkong should insist on having, as all other Colonies have, in Australia, in South Africa, in Canada and elsewhere — a voice in the management of our own affairs (Applause).

Hongkong Telegraph
15 May 1893

❖ *A hundred years later we, too, can applaud this.*

A woman's definition of tiffin is that it is 'a base insult to breakfast and a premeditated insult to dinner'.

Hongkong Telegraph
16 June 1893

❖ *'Tiffin' is pretty well obsolete. A very colonial synonym for 'lunch', it was still used in the 1930s and 40s.*

Paddies and Buffaloes

Somewhere in the New Territories, sometime in the past. This scene can no longer be seen, except on the mainland side of the border. Under the impact of massive urbanization, the farming of rice in the New Territories has ceased completely, only limited vegetable cultivation and flower growing can still be seen.

Rice paddies and buffaloes are a happy combination and is typical of southern China, and, indeed, of Southeast Asia. The sluggish but powerful buffalo can easily pull the plough through the sticky and muddy paddies, while the animal loves to wallow in the wet paddies.

This seemingly gentle creature is not as gentle as it appears. It can be dangerous, especially to strangers to whom it has a strong objection. But to those it knows, it is docile and gentle, and it is common to see village children riding on its back in full control of the animal. With the disappearance of rice farming, the buffalo too has gone, though one is encountered occasionally, being kept as a pet by the village.

Hongkong Telegraph
27 June 1893

A correspondent writes to enquire if we are aware of the existence of any special arrangements between the Acting Post-master General and an hotel-keeper named Bohn — with regard to the Post-office launch. ... Does the Post-master know that Mr. Bohn is in the habit of using the Post-office launch when engaged on his business as a hotel runner? ... not the first time complaints have been made ... It must be remembered that the Government launches of this Colony are maintained by the tax-payers and the tax-payers have a decided objection to their property being prostituted. Legitimate business has to be protected and when it comes to pass that the Post-office launch … is made the vehicle of a public-house runner, it is high time that the tap was turned on. The Acting Post-master should at once investigate this matter.

❖   *It must be said that Hong Kong newspapers, from the early days of the colony, have been very strict watch-dogs of the uses and abuses of Government property and the rights of tax-payers.*

Is fishing by the aid of dynamite permissible in Hongkong harbour: It is a brutal practice and ought to be prohibited. Every morning, when the tide serves, Kowloon Bay is crowded with Chinese sampans engaged in this deadly method of supplying the fish-market, greatly to the annoyance and inconvenience of residents in the vicinity.

***Hongkong Telegraph
1 July 1893***

❖   *One can hardly sympathize with residents who are merely subjected to annoyance and inconvenience! Fishing with dynamite is effective but highly dangerous. It was certainly prohibited during the last 70 years or more, mainly because it killed a lot of young fish and thus depleted the source. It also resulted in many maiming accidents — mostly hands being blown off by premature explosions.*

Last night Inspector Bremner made a raid on a gambling-house at 16, Nullah Lane, Wanchai. When he arrived on the scene of operations he found the staircase blocked … so he went into the next house … climbed over to the gambling-house roof, and promptly tumbled through, falling into the middle of the *po-tse* party like a thunderbolt. … He managed, with the aid of his constables, to arrest thirteen out of about twenty revellers, the rest escaping by two ladders out of the back window. The prisoners were duly brought before the magistrate to-day — fined $2 each.

***Hongkong Telegraph
24 July 1893***

❖   *Limited gambling under licence was allowed in 1867–1870, mainly as an experiment in controlled gambling. It was deemed a failure and was discontinued on 1 January 1871.*

Hongkong Club, Statue Square, Central District, Hong Kong Island, c.1896–97
The English are a 'club' people, that is, they like to belong to a club. It is, therefore, not surprising that soon after Hong Kong was ceded to Britain, the English Club was opened in 1845, at the corner of Queen's Road Central and Wyndham Street; it was later renamed the Hongkong Club (see photograph on p. 38). In 1897, the club moved into its newly completed building, seen in this photograph in the final stages of construction, still unoccupied and with scaffolding at the back. It was a distinguished four-storey, colonial-style building with three bell towers perfectly proportioned and harmonious with the rest of the building. The exterior, with an elegant porch, arched verandahs, and fluted columns, had a noble and imposing appearance. The interior was spacious and consistent with the style outside; the columns, the high ceilings, and the mouldings on the walls reflected the grace and leisure of former times. The club's exclusive membership has been the subject of many comments in the past. Chinese were not admitted as members until some years after World War II, and it was said that while this was in force, no ruling governor joined the club in a symbolic gesture of protest. Aptly described in the past as the 'citadel of the colonial establishment', it had in later years relaxed its rules of exclusive membership. The club was demolished in 1981 to be replaced by a large modern building, not without a bitter opposition by the conservationists. The South China Morning Post wrote on the occasion: '… the almighty dollar has triumphed yet again and the cause of conservation has been sacrificed on the altar of expediency and greed'.

It would interest rate-payers and the public generally ... what is intended to be done with that splendid piece of reclaimed land extending from Murray Pier to Pedder's Wharf. A very large sum of money has been spent on this reclamation, and ... it seems a great pity ... that it should be allowed to lie fallow. It has been reported that the members of the Hongkong Club are desirous of changing their present habitat and of erecting a palatial club-house ... if the required ground is obtainable on ... reasonable terms. ... If put up to auction, it is hardly likely that any local land speculators would care to compete — money is so tight — so that the Club would in all probability secure the lot at a fractional advance on the upset price ...

Hongkong Telegraph
26 July 1893

❖   *The promoters of this major Central Praya Reclamation had not the slightest intention of allowing this land to 'lie fallow'. Between 1897 and 1904, splendid buildings in grand style were erected on the reclaimed land. The Hongkong Club was one of them, the new 'palatial club-house' being completed in 1897.*

A Stanley fisherman whose wife was found dead with marks about her neck yesterday, was brought before Mr. Wodehouse charged with causing her death. He said he had been rubbing her neck with ginger to revive her. He was remanded.

Hongkong Telegraph
17 October 1893

It is stated from Peking that the birthday celebrations of the Empress Dowager ... cost the Imperial Treasury taels 420,000. And yet starvation is rampant in many of the provinces of the Empire.

Hongkong Telegraph
28 November 1893

❖   *Poverty and starvation have never stopped those in power from indulging in expensive festivities or conducting an expensive war.*

The Shanghai morning paper says it was not the soldier who did the recent decapitation who died of consequent fright and remorse, but the assistant to the regular executioner, who was present as a student in the art of decollation.

Hongkong Telegraph
6 December 1893

❖   *How does one practise decollation (apparently a synonym for decapitation) as a student?*

A bad ricksha accident occurred this morning in Lyndhurst Terrace. A European, in a private ricksha … was foolish enough to go at a brisk pace down Old Bailey Street. … Naturally, in trying to turn along Lyndhurst Terrace the vehicle turned over, and the occupant was picked up … and taken to the Central Station close by. Thence he was taken home, and is believed to be doing well. After a few more such affairs, people will perhaps learn that the common … ricksha is no use for either mountaineering, steeplechasing, or parachute performances.

Hong Kong Rickshaw, c.1890

The vehicle's full name, used in the early days, is jinrickshaw, *jin* deriving from *jen-man*, indicating that manpower is used. It is not an ancient contraption, and said to have been invented, and first used, in Japan in the 1870s. It then found its way into the Treaty Ports of China — ports where foreigners were allowed to live and trade — then to Hong Kong and finally into inland cities of China. In Hong Kong it became very popular and continued to be used right up to the Second World War.

With the sedan chair, the two vehicles dominated Hongkong transportation in the early days, the rickshaw ruling over the level area and the sedan chair the hilly parts. After the advent of the rickshaw, a horse-drawn vehicle never gained a firm foothold in Hong Kong.

The life of a rickshaw coolie was a hard one. Continuous running soon affected their health and they were seldom able to continue after the age of 45 or 50. However, it was the running, not the weight of the rickshaw which was harmful, for the vehicle was so constructed, and its weight so well balanced, that the pulling was easy. A rickshaw coolie often had an apprentice, usually a boy, who ran behind the rickshaw and helped when a slope was encountered; one is shown in this photograph.

The post-war period brought the gradual decline of the rickshaw, and today only a few of them are seen near the Star Ferry, used only by tourists and for very short runs.

No new licences have been issued for a number of years.

1894

The following appeared in a recent Transatlantic publication:- 'Subscribers paying in advance will be entitled to a first-class obituary notice in case of death'. Good!

Hongkong Telegraph
4 January 1894

We hear that there is going to be a big jamboree at Government House [Chinese New Year's Eve] … to which all the leading Chinese residents in the Colony will be invited. The leading Chinese, as far as we know, detest Government House functions. … As is well known … they would be much more at home drinking afternoon tea … with the representative of Britain's majesty than in a reception room filled with Hongkong's *elite*. … It is strange that the so-called Protector of Chinese … or some other obsequious toady, has never explained this to His Excellency. …

Hongkong Telegraph
5 January 1894

❖ *The* Hongkong Telegraph *assumes too much. It was well known that the 'leading Chinese residents' enjoyed Government House garden parties (generally held to mark the Sovereign's birthday), and felt slighted when not invited.*

It is officially notified that the firing of crackers will be permitted (to Chinese only) from 4 p.m. to-day until 4 p.m. on Wednesday the 7th inst. The firing of bombs is strictly prohibited.

Hongkong Telegraph
5 February 1894

As Governor Robinson seems to be making no effort to keep his word about prohibiting the steam launch traffic to the gambling halls of Chinese Kowloon and Sam-sui-po, the natives seem to be under the impression that, in common justice, there will be no interference with similar establishments on this side. That fond illusion was roughly dispelled this morning at the police court, where some thirty Chinese were fined various sums aggregating over $200 for contraventions of the Gambling Ordinance.

❖ *The* Telegraph's *constant reference to the local Chinese residents as 'natives' is inappropriate, reprehensible, and irritating.*

**Hongkong Telegraph
3 March 1894**

It was in a Hongkong school that the following conversation took place:- Is your father Eurasian? No, Sir. Is he a Parsee? No. A Jew? No. Then what is he? A broker, sir.

**Hongkong Telegraph
22 March 1894**

The *Anti-Opium News* declares that the serious damage recently inflicted upon the Indian opium crop is an answer to the prayers of an aged member of the Society of Friends, who during the late three days' prayer meeting at Exeter Hall, several times publicly prayed that the crop might be blasted.

**Hongkong Telegraph
9 May 1894**

A fatal disease, somewhat similar in its effects to the 'black fever', which has carried off thousands of natives of Canton during the past month … made its appearance among the Chinese residents in the Taipingshan [west Mid-levels] district … since Saturday.

❖　*A very ominous announcement. The disease was, of course, plague, making its first, but not the last, appearance in Hong Kong. Its arrival was expected. It had appeared in North China several years before, and the epidemic was gradually moving south. The following months would be dominated by the news of plague, which claimed many lives, but also made Hong Kong famous; of this later …*

**Hongkong Telegraph
10 May 1894**

Froms the Editorial:
THE BLACK PLAGUE. Without being desirous of sounding an unnecessary note of alarm … duty compels us to direct public attention to a report of the proceedings occurring at this afternoon's Sanitary Board meeting … an impending epidemic of deadly disease … the 'black plague' … .

**Hongkong Telegraph
12 May 1894**

Theatre-goers have a treat in store to-night when the Potter-Belew Company, assisted by local amateurs, will produce 'She stoops to conquer' in the Theatre Royal. Almost every available seat has been already secured.

❖　*In the midst of a disaster, the show goes on …*

Temporary Plague Hospital, Kennedy Town, Hong Kong Island, 1894
The year 1894 would be long remembered in Hong Kong's history as the year when the plague epidemic had first struck the colony with dreadful ferocity. It was not unexpected. Plague had been present in the northern and western parts of China for many years. It was only a matter of time before it would spread to the southern areas. Then, in May 1894, the whole southern coast of China, including Kwangtung, Kwangsi, and Fukien became infected. Inevitably, the disease had soon spread to Hong Kong.

The spread of the infection was so rapid that Hong Kong's medical facilities were strained to the utmost and could barely cope with the disease. The photograph shows one of the plague hospitals hastily converted from a glass works factory. The appalling conditions in this 'Glass Works Hospital', as it became known, can be seen: desperately sick victims of plague lying on the floor or on thin rattan mats. To make matters worse, many of the measures adopted to combat the epidemic, according to the Western concepts of medicine, conflicted with the Chinese ideas and customs, resulting in further difficulties.

Hongkong has been declared an infected port, and vessels coming from there must undergo fifteen days quarantine as long as the proclamation is in force.

Hongkong Telegraph
19 May 1894

**Hongkong Telegraph
23 May 1894**

From the Editorial:

... never, perhaps, the sentiments of the Government and the *Telegraph* been more in accord than in the determined ... stand which His Excellency has taken in regard to the petulant, ignorant and nonsensical revolt of a section of the Chinese community against the absolutely necessary sanitary precautions taken for stamping out the plague ... protest against the house-to-house visits of the Sanitary authorities, claiming that the sacred privacy of ... domestic life was being violated. ... Rumours of fiendish doings of foreign doctors were put in circulation.

❖ *There is no doubt that drastic measures were necessary to control the epidemic, infected articles had to be burned and lime freely used to disinfect residential premises where plague cases occurred. But the attitude of the Chinese residents, if not helpful, was at least understandable.*

**Hongkong Telegraph
12 June 1894**

THE PLAGUE IN HONGKONG. Queer phases of the plague come to light every day. In the ... exodus from Hongkong, the average coolie has formed the opinion that the steamboats have a bad *fung-suey* and he accordingly takes his departure by junk. ... The disease has not yet reached Macao. The Holy City is so thoroughly cleaned and disinfected that it looks as if it would pass through the fire unscathed.

**Hongkong Telegraph
18 June 1894**

THE PLAGUE IN HONGKONG. AN IMPORTANT DISCOVERY. ... with the outbreak of the bubonic plague in Hongkong, a number of high-class scientists are flocking to these plague-stricken shores to study the mysterious disease and arrive at a clear understanding as to the circumstances which led to such fatal results. ... Dr. Kitasato of Tokyo ... Dr. Yersin of the Pasteur Institute in Saigon ... discovered presence of bacilli ... a very important discovery, as it rests all doubts ... [whether] this loathsome disease [is] being diffused by bacilli. This interesting point having been definitely settled, there is now reason for hope that the day is not very far distant when the bubonic plague can be treated with ... success.

❖ *Of the various aspects of Hong Kong's renown, the discovery of the cause of plague ranks as one of the world-wide fame. The bacillus causing the dreaded disease was discovered, if not by Hong Kong's own scientists, in Hong Kong's laboratories. This was an essential step towards the discovery of a successful treatment, which was made in due course.*

THE PLAGUE IN HONGKONG ... the plague has wrought havoc among the members of the more respectable of the native mercantile community, thousands of whom have fled these shores regardless of vast consignments of piece goods, coal, kerosene oil and other foreign products. ... The result can but prove disastrous in the extreme, for the banks will assuredly become very chary about advancing on outward shipments, while wholesale exporters will restrict their transactions to cash customers.

Hongkong Telegraph
1 July 1894

THE KOREAN IMBROGLIO ... reported that the Emperor of China had decided to send ambassadors to Korea to endeavour to settle affairs with the Japanese Minister, as he did not wish to go to war with Japan. But the Empress-Dowager and the Grand Council do not like China to 'lose face', and they are therefore of opinion that war should be declared.

Hongkong Telegraph
11 July 1894

THEATRE ROYAL, CITY HALL HONGKONG; THE BLACK PLAGUE.
THE HONGKONG MINSTREL TROUPE WILL GIVE TWO FIRST-CLASS ENTERTAINMENTS.
For the benefit of those SOLDIERS AND POLICE who have been, and those who are still engaged upon work in connection with the PLAGUE.

Hongkong Telegraph
9 August 1894

THE CHINA — JAPAN WAR. Twenty thousand Japanese troops have landed in Korea and are converging on Seoul in order to meet the Chinese troops advancing from the North.

❖ *The dispute between China and Japan over Korea arose when the two Powers supported the opposing parties in a rebellion in Korea. Both China and Japan sent troops there and the war between them broke out on 1 August 1894. It was a short war and a quick victory for Japan. Peace was concluded in February 1895, with Japan acquiring Formosa, the Pescadores, and part of Liaotung Peninsula.*

Hongkong Telegraph
13 August 1894

**Friend of China
23 August 1894**

The plague scare is now fairly at an end, — and it is to be hoped for all times. The streets … are just as crowded now-a-days … as ever. … many of our leading Chinese citizens, who virtually constitute the backbone of the Colony's commerce and who fled these shores when the loathsome bubonic disease was claiming scores of victims daily, are now … flitting about from hong to hong endeavouring … to make up for lost time.

The plague, as far as Hongkong is concerned, has been practically stamped out. … deaths from the outbreak [May 9th] up to August 22nd, numbered 2,484 …

❖   *Alas, the fervent wish for the disease to end 'for all times' was not to be fulfilled. Plague revisited Hong Kong on many occasions hence.*

Plague in Hong Kong, 1894
The photograph shows members of the Hong Kong Sanitary Department, assisted by the police and volunteers from the local garrison, carrying out disinfection of the street and houses, probably in Tai Ping Shan (Mid-Levels), one of the worst affected areas. Infected articles are piled up on the street and burned. The first, and the deadliest, outbreak of plague epidemic in Hong Kong, in May 1894, was probably one of the darkest events in Hong Kong's history. The epidemic lasted 4 months and when it subsided, at least 2,500 people had died from it (Hong Kong's population at the time was about 250,000). Plague continued to affect Hong Kong periodically until the 1920s.

Queen's College, which was closed about two months ago owing to the plague, reopened this morning. There was a very large attendance of old and new pupils.

Hongkong Telegraph
3 September 1894

Queen's College, Junction of Aberdeen Street and Hollywood Road, Hong Kong Island, c.1900
Established in 1889, Queen's College replaced the earlier Government Central School, located near by on Gough Street. The initial object of the college was to offer western subjects to students of all nationalities; however, after 1903, it admitted mainly Chinese students. The college premises on Aberdeen Street, shown in this photograph, were destroyed during the Second World War. After being temporarily housed (in 1947) on Kennedy Road, the college moved in 1950 into the new building in Causeway Bay.

THE TYPHOON. SIXTY LIVES LOST.
It is somewhat remarkable that on the twentieth anniversary of the ever-to-be-remembered disastrous typhoon of 1874 … this colony of Hongkong should to-day have been placed in the same devastating danger of two decades ago.

Hongkong Telegraph
25 September 1894

❖ *It was a curious coincidence that this, very severe, typhoon occurred on the precise 20th anniversary of a disastrous typhoon of 1874. On this occasion, the Royal Observatory — usually very efficient with typhoon warnings — was less so, and little warning was given until quite late. This was not the end: a mere 10 days later, on 5 October, another severe typhoon struck Hong Kong causing much damage and loss of lives.*

Hongkong Telegraph
5 November 1894

Hongkong is one of the British colonies which must regard with the utmost interest any developments of importance in the Pacific. Its importance could, says the London *Times*, hardly fail to grow with the gradual opening of China to the outer world, and it was fully prepared in 1869 to take its share of the benefit accruing from the diversion of trade through the new route of the Suez Canal. ...

Hongkong Telegraph
17 November 1894

A messenger from a local business house was sent to the Post Office this forenoon to purchase fifty two-cent and twenty five-cent stamps, and tendered a ten dollar note in payment. ... The note was refused, the stamps not delivered — why? — because the Post Office had no change available. Perhaps the Government will enquire into this matter!

Hong Kong's Postage Stamp (2½ times the actual size)
The 2-cent stamp depicted here differed in colour and watermark in different issues, which were in circulation from 1862 to 1900. A more precise dating of this stamp cannot be given from a black-and-white photograph. Hong Kong issued its first stamps in 1862 with the portrait of Queen Victoria on them.

At a special parade of the Garrison troops at 11 a.m. on Wednesday, His Excellency the Governor will convey to the military the thanks of the community for their services during the recent epidemic of bubonic plague.

Hongkong Telegraph
3 December 1894

❖ *The military readily responded to the disaster affecting the community. In this epidemic, the serving men of the garrison took an active part in fighting the spread of the disease. At least seven servicemen caught the disease and died, and some 300 medals were issued to the men in recognition of their good work.*

The King of Spain is learning to ride a bicycle, with the assistance of two attendants.

Hongkong Telegraph
8 December 1894

Telegram:
LI HUNG-CHANG. Li Hung-chang has only been nominally stripped of other ranks and decoration, but he still retains full Viceregal power.

Hongkong Telegraph
11 December 1894

❖ *Li Hung-Chang, Chinese elder statesman and adviser to the Empress Dowager, was stripped of his honours following China's defeat by the Japanese in Korea. The honours were later restored.*

Minister Li Hung-Chang (1823–1901)
This photograph was taken probably during his visit to England, c.1896. Chinese elder statesman and advisor to the Empress Dowager Tz'u Hsi, Li Hung-chang was a very popular personality in international circles. His career embraced important positions culminating in the post of Viceroy of Kwangtung Province. See also *Viceroy Li Hung-chang Visiting Hong Kong*, p.175.

1895

**Hongkong Telegraph
14 January 1895**

The Allahabad *Pioneer* says that a couple of months further delay in the coining of the new British dollar at the Bombay mint is due to indecision on the part of the authorities as to whether Britannia shall be represented standing up or sitting down. Why not give the lady a chair, and have done with the matter!

**Hongkong Telegraph
29 January 1895**

The latest thing in the way of disasters, of which this Colony has, unfortunately, experienced a very unwelcome plethora in recent times, is an epidemic of shocking outrages perpetrated by gangs ... of cold-blooded ruffians. ... During the months of October and November last year ... three gang robberies were committed in Winglok Street and Praya West, the robbers' victims being tied together by their *queues* while their houses were looted. ...

❖ *Five robbers were subsequently arrested; two of them were found guilty of murder, sentenced to death and duly executed in Victoria Gaol.*

**Hongkong Telegraph
15 February 1895**

An article from the pen of Mr. R. W. Egerton Eastwick, the late Sheriff of Singapore, contains the following in reference to Chinese as colonists:- 'As a citizen the Chinese is a very desirable acquisition in a Colony, seeing that he is a careful, methodical, patient and persistent toiler, a keen and sagacious trader, and a peace-loving man. In addition to this, his conduct as a son, a husband, and a father is most exemplary, and deserves the greatest praise. In this respect he sets a noble example to people of other nationalities.'

**Hongkong Telegraph
20 February 1895**

Hongkong Jockey Club Race: Meeting 1895.
The Hongkong annual race Meeting was commenced this afternoon under most favourable circumstances — in fact, the weather was glorious. ... The race-course was in excellent condition. ... The crowd was orderly and well-behaved. ... For picturesque beauty the Happy Valley is probably the prettiest race-course in the world.

❖ *There follows list of races and 'tips for to-morrow'.*

Wong Nai Chung Village, Happy Valley, Hong Kong Island, c.1875
The charming, neat village at the head of Happy Valley had been inhabited long
before the British occupation of Hong Kong. This fine photograph shows well the
symmetrical layout and the authentic traditional Chinese style of the buildings.
The early beginning of racing, in 1846, and the construction of the Race Course
in front of the village, must have created problems for the peaceful little village.
The final straw was the severe typhoon, in August 1923, which caused flooding
and massive damage to the village; it was abandoned after that.

A railroad between Kowloon and Canton cannot be expected to make
its own way, but if the way is made it should soon pay for it. Likewise a
West River Steamboat Company would not be expected to *make* its own
way, but if the way was made for it there can be no shadow of a doubt
whatever that it would pay for it 'hand over fist'.

❖ *The way* was *made for the railway which opened in 1911.*

Hongkong Telegraph
7 March 1895

From the Editorial:
The [new sanitary] bye-laws contain thirty-one clauses and are intended
to provide an efficient means of protecting the city from the spread of
fatal diseases. ... While they [the population] have shown sufficient
confidence in the integrity ... of the British Government to settle in
large numbers in Victoria and have here located great wealth in fixed
investments, yet they never feel perfectly sure of their future rights and

Hongkong Telegraph
27 March 1895

naturally always view with some distrust changes. ... [they] view with alarm the new Sanitary Bye-Laws. ... if the efforts of the Sanitary Board receive proper support ... Hongkong ... will never have again to chronicle such a disastrous epoque as that of the 'plague year' 1894.

❖   *This, of course, was wishful thinking; plague continued to affect Hong Kong in the next few decades though less severely than in the first epidemic of 1894.*

THE STRIKE: ... From some of the leading merchants we learn that it will probably be some time before the strike ends ... since it is rumoured the coolie Lodging-House proprietors and the Chinese Guilds have already put up $40,000 and are willing to put up more to maintain the coolies in idleness.

❖   *It may surprise the readers to learn that labour strikes in Hong Kong are not new. One of the earliest occurred in 1844, when Governor Davis introduced a poll-tax. Most of the strikes had been in protest against strict or unfair laws. In this case — against the sanitary bye-law allowing the authorities to inspect poor lodging-houses.*

Hongkong Telegraph 30 March 1895

The conduct of the two belligerents in the present [Sino-Japanese] war may be ... summed up by stating that the Japanese have done better than even their best friends expected ... the Chinese have done less than might have been anticipated, and ... the corruption and incompetence of officers generally is found to be deeper seated than even the best informed thought to be the case.

Hongkong Telegraph 9 April 1895

From the Editorial:
ARE WE SAFE? The home Government propose to spend a very considerable sum of money in improving the naval establishments in Hongkong ... but where are the docks to be constructed so that they shall be out of range of enemy's guns in time of war? ... The whole range of hills on the mainland is Chinese territory ... the entire south of the island of Hongkong is undefended ... the time has come either for us to think seriously of extending our boundaries ... or make up our minds to forfeit our claim to the title of the 'Malta and Gibraltar of the East'.

❖   *One can see where this is leading to! The first hint of the soon-to-come: the Lease of the New Territories in 1898.*

BUYING THE FLEET. We have it on good authority that the report is based on facts. A Chinese boat carrying a mandarin went off to the [HMS] Centurion and offered to buy her, the [HMS] Spartan, the [HMS] Edgar, the [HMS] Gibraltar and the [HMS] Aeolus. Not only this, but they offered to take them as they stood — Admiral, officers and crews. The Chinese left very ill at ease, not because they believed the fleet was not on the market, but for the reason that they felt they had not been able to offer money enough to secure it.

Hongkong Telegraph
10 April 1895

❖ *One is naturally suspicious of a newspaper report which begins with 'We have it on good authority …'. An amusing story but probably untrue; perhaps an April Fool's joke?*

A report is … going around Canton that a revolution against the Manchu dynasty is nearly ripe, and that the rebels will rise on Friday. Many of the leading Chinese are said to be coming to Hongkong. Our informant, who has just returned from Canton, says that yesterday he saw a notice over a shop in Canton city which read 'Chief Office of the Revolution'.

Hongkong Telegraph
17 April 1895

❖ *Another 'tall story'?*

Canton, c.1885–90
A panoramic view of Canton City. A mass of tightly packed similar dwellings creates a flat uniform appearance except for the one prominent feature, the famous Flower Pagoda. Its top appears damaged and there are signs of neglect. However, it would be repaired and restored in later years, and become a great attraction for locals and visitors alike.

**Hongkong Telegraph
18 April 1895**

THE CHINA-JAPAN WAR TREATY OF PEACE SIGNED.
Peace has been signed. The *Times'* Shanghai correspondent states that
the terms are the independence of Korea, the retention by Japan of the
conquered places, also the territory east of the Liao River, the permanent
cession of Formosa, the payment of a war indemnity of 100,000,000 yen,
and an offensive and defensive alliance between the two countries.

❖   *Poor China, rich in ancient culture but not in modern technology,
with its backward imperial rule, is paying heavily for its technological
weakness: first Hong Kong, in 1841, and now Formosa (Taiwan). Also
significant is the fact that, while England, France, Germany and other
Powers offered their congratulations to Japan, Russia remained silent ...
anticipating she may be the next victim?*

**Hongkong Telegraph
4 May 1895**

THE CONSTITUTION OF HONGKONG. The petition of the
inhabitants of Hongkong for an amendment of the constitution ... in
the direction of representative government ... was presented to the
House of Commons on Thursday [21st March]. ... Its [Hongkong]
situation at the mouth of the Canton river gives it peculiar facilities
for trade with China, and its population is either military and naval, or
commercial. These are not ... the populations in which self-governing
institutions have been found to flourish. In Hongkong ... a very large
majority of the population is composed of Chinese, who are totally
unaccustomed to the responsibilities of self-government. ... That it
should be proposed to restrict the electoral franchise to the 800 British
voters seems scarcely a possible proposition. ...

❖   *It has been repeatedly shown in these notes that the idea of an
electoral franchise for Hong Kong is not new. In the above statement,
however, the* Telegraph, *usually progressive in its policy, appears to be
against the idea.*

**Hongkong Telegraph
17 July 1895**

It is a disgrace to the Government of Hongkong that in this harbour,
with its enormous shipping and its busy steam-launch traffic, that there
should be only one wharf. The scene at the so-called New Pedder's
Wharf every evening is most discreditable ...

Pedder's Wharf, Hong Kong Waterfront, Hong Kong Island, c.1880

Pedder's Wharf, Rebuilt and Renamed Blake Pier, Hong Kong Waterfront, c.1900

An early photograph, on the left, shows the original Pedder's Wharf, one of the oldest piers on Hong Kong Island, named after the first Harbour Master, Lieutenant William Pedder, R.N. The wharf is a crude wooden structure and is located opposite the early, 3-storey, Hong Kong Hotel (previously Dent & Co.'s premises), on the left. Across Pedder Street, premises of Jardine, Matheson & Co. can be seen on the right.

The photograph on the right shows the same wharf, rebuilt after the start of the Praya Reclamation, in 1890, as a more substantial structure, with landing stairs on either side and moved slightly west, directly opposite Pedder Street. In 1900, it was renamed Blake Pier, after the Governor Sir Henry Blake, and an entrance pavilion was added, as seen in the photograph on the right. The premises of Jardine, Matheson Co. are still on the right, and the rebuilt and renovated, now 6-storey, Hong Kong Hotel is on the left.

The Clock Tower, at the top of Pedder Street, built in 1863 by public subscription, can be seen in both photographs.

Several complaints have reached this office of the poor physique of many of the ricksha and chair coolies who are granted licences in Hongkong. Coolies taken along Queen's Road to go to Quarry Bay, or even to Bay View, refuse to carry their passengers further than Jardine's Sugar works and demand their fares. In the same way many of the chair coolies are unable to carry a medium-sized man from Queen's Road to the Albany Gardens. If the Police could see to it that none but able-bodied men are licensed these annoyances would cease.

Hongkong Telegraph
4 November 1895

Hongkong Telegraph
25 November 1895

A Chinese Chamber of Commerce, an institution that has long been needed and should prove to great benefit to our thrifty and busy Chinese fellow-citizens, will be opened in New Street about the middle of January 1896.

❖ *For those unaware, New Street is in the Sai Ying Pun District, Hong Kong Island; it joins Queen's Road West and Po Yan Street, and is close to the Tung Wah Hospital.*

Hongkong Telegraph
30 November 1895

It is worthy of note that the meaning of the English text of the Liaotung Convention [Sino-Japanese Peace Treaty] is to rule in the event of any differences arising respecting the interpretation of the Chinese or Japanese texts.

❖ *Is it not strange to bring in the English language, totally unrelated to either the Chinese or the Japanese languages, to mediate in possible disputes between two texts of related languages?*

1896

Hongkong Telegraph
8 January 1896

From the Editorial:
A SERIOUS BLUNDER. His Excellency the Governor [John Pope-Hennessy] has, of his own authority and without legislative sanction, suspended the operation of the *Light and Pass Ordinance*. He has committed an offence … against constitutional law. JAMES II lost his throne for the same offence. … When His Excellency determined, and rightly determined, that the … [Ordinance] ought not to be in force, it was his duty to have called the Legislative Council together and either to have repealed the law or amended it, or suspended it. …

❖ *The Ordinance in question, which stipulated that Hong Kong Chinese citizens should carry a pass after dark, was particularly repellent to the Chinese, but repeated petitions to abolish it were refused. Governor Pope-Hennessy, a reformer, would continue to single-handedly cancel laws which he considered either unfair or discriminatory. Bringing the matter to the Legislative Council, with its European majority, would have been a useless gesture.*

THE PO LEUNG KUK SOCIETY. LAYING DOWN THE FOUNDATION STONE.

Hongkong Telegraph
18 January 1896

This afternoon a very interesting ceremony was performed by his Excellency the Governor, who ... formally laid the foundation stone of a new home for women and girls to be built by the Po Leung Kuk on ground placed at its disposal by the Trustees of the Tung Wah Hospital ... for the temporary accommodation of the destitute women and girls who had been rescued or might be rescued from the terrible fate that was intended for them. ...

❖ *The reference here is to young women, later called 'mui tsai', who were effectively sold as bonded servants to other families. Although not actually slaves, their fate was often not much better. That organization, Po Leung Kuk, has continued to do excellent work.*

Po Leung Kuk, Opening of the Premises, Western District, Hong Kong Island, 1896
This important photograph shows the opening ceremony of the Po Leung Kuk premises. In the centre are Dr Ho Kai, prominent doctor and barrister, and Stewart Lockhart, the Colonial Secretary, who are surrounded by a gathering of prominent members of the Chinese community. Both Ho Kai and Stewart Lockhart had played vital roles in promoting Po Leung Kuk (literally 'protecting the innocent'), a charitable organization, founded in 1878, with the purpose of protecting Chinese women and children from exploitation.

**Hongkong Telegraph
5 March 1896**

Blue-jackets* on leave last night made things 'hum' in the western part of town, and as a result several who had shipped too much 'FIRE WATER' ... were charged at the Magistracy this morning with stealing a gold ring from a Chinese shop. The property was returned, and they were handed over to their own officers, as it was believed that the ring had been appropriated more as a lark than as intentional dishonesty.

**Hongkong Telegraph
20 March 1896**

There are between two and three hundred thousand Chinese living here. ... We profess to desire to attract men to bring their families here and to become British subjects. Yet no attempt has ever been made to legislate for them ... to investigate ... upon what conditions ... they may cease to be Chinese and become naturalized. ... A Chinese woman has no assured status ... before the Courts of the Colony, and it is an open question whether Chinese marriages are marriages in the eye of the law ... and whether children born of such marriages are legitimate.

Chinese Wedding, New Territories, c.1963
A simple wedding procession is making its way through the countryside with the bridal chair carried behind. Completely secluded from prying eyes as the custom dictates, and with much ceremony, the bride is being carried to the bridegroom's house.

---

* Blue-jackets: name sometimes given to British sailors.

We learn from Canton that anonymous proclamations have been posted about the city offering rewards for foreigners heads. The life of Mr. Barton, of the Customs Service, is fixed ... at $500, the Commissioner of Customs Service and the Harbour Master are thought, apparently, to be worth double that amount each, and any ordinary *fan kwai** at any sum ranging from $50 to $150 a piece.

Hongkong Telegraph
1 April 1896

A few days ago a Chinese shop-keeper of Wanchai had a horrible experience. Some two months ago one of his *fokis*** was taken to Kennedy-town suffering from plague, and ... was reckoned as Death by his friends, and his goods and chattels were disposed of ... After nearly two months in hospital the patient was discharged as cured, and at once made his way to his old haunts. On his appearance consternation was general. One old lady went into hysterics and the man's step-mother actually fainted. It was not until one man, brave as a lion ... carefully felt him to see that he wasn't a ghost, that those present could be persuaded that it was not the dear departed's spirit which had returned. ... Once assured that it was 'O.K.' there was great rejoicing ... and feasting and all was 'merry as a marriage bell'.

Hongkong Telegraph
9 April 1896

THE OLYMPIC GAMES. The revival of the Olympic Games has been an occasion for great enthusiasm in Athens. The races were run in the presence of the Royal Family and enormous crowds of people. Everything went off smoothly and pleasantly, but, unfortunately, the Greeks were not successful in the games.

Hongkong Telegraph
14 May 1896

❖ *A splendid revival of the ancient custom, which has become an outstanding success today. On that first Olympic Games 'of the modern era', Americans won most of the events. When a Greek was at last successful, it was at, of all the games in the world, lawn-tennis!*

---

* *Fan kwai* (番鬼): foreign devil.
** *Foki* (伙記): minor staff, usually a shop assistant or a waiter.

Hongkong Telegraph
28 May 1896

UNVEILING THE QUEEN'S STATUE. To-day, May 28th, the day officially appointed for the celebration of the seventy-seventh anniversary of the birth of Her Most Gracious majesty Queen Victoria, whose reign over the vast Empire of Great Britain has now been extended almost to three score years, will long be remembered in this most loyal of colonies as the occasion upon which was formally unveiled the statue of our most beneficent ruler erected by the citizens of Hongkong in commemoration of the completion of the Jubilee of her reign. ...

❖   *The statue was installed at the centre of the Statue Square and in due course was surrounded by statues of other royal personages. After capturing Hong Kong in 1941, the Japanese shipped all the statues, to be melted down, no doubt. After the war, only Queen Victoria's statue was recovered; it was returned to Hong Kong and reinstalled in the present Victoria Park at Causeway Bay.*

The Unveiling of Queen Victoria's Statue, Statue Square, Central District, Hong Kong Island, 28 May 1896
Troops are drawn on parade and a roofed pavilion was specially erected for important guests. The bronze statue of the seated Queen is enclosed in a handsome ornate stone pavilion. A large crowd of spectators is watching the ceremony. Although cast in 1887, the golden jubilee of the Queen's reign, the statue was not installed until 1896, on the Queen's official, 77th, birthday.

AS OTHERS SEE US: Over the initials R. Y. an occasional correspondent of the *Kobe Chronicle* airs his knowledge of our fair 'Isle of Fragrant Streams'* in the following manner:- 'The changes effected in Hongkong during the last eight years are remarkable. The town has mounted up to the Peak on one side, while on the other, land has been reclaimed from the sea, whereon some magnificent buildings — for the English Club among them — are being erected. The expansion is perhaps most noticeable at Kowloon. Eight years ago there were, besides the barracks, only half a dozen residences. ... To-day there are fine broad roads with trees along each side and terraces of comfortable houses. ... For all the growling and grumbling of Hongkong merchants that business was never so bad as during the last few years, it is clear that, if the percentage of profits has diminished, the volume of trade has increased.

Hongkong Telegraph
11 July 1896

The Chinese Detective who was shot on Sunday last while in pursuit of a criminal was buried on Wednesday with due honours, all the members of the Police Force not on duty taking part in the funeral procession. It was a very proper mark of respect to be paid to a man killed in the performance of his duty.

Two daring [American] navigators, Captain Frank Charles and his brother, are preparing to cross the Atlantic in a boat 20 feet long and 6 feet beam. They are to advertise an American dentifrice.

Hongkong Telegraph
17 July 1896

This morning an old widow was charged before Captain Hastings with cruelly beating and abusing a little slave-girl. The girl bore traces of several beatings.

❖ *As mentioned earlier, these girls were known as 'mui tsai'; they were purchased or 'adopted' for child servitude. The practice was evil and was condemned by many Chinese, while the Po Leung Kuk, the Chinese charitable organization, did its best to alleviate the results of this evil (see 18 January 1896, p.143). In spite of this, the practice continued, illegally, into the 20th century.*

Hongkong Telegraph
5 August 1896

---

* Actually, 'Fragrant Harbour' — the accepted meaning of 'Hong Kong'.

Hongkong Telegraph
7 September 1896

The Chinese have taken kindly to the bicycle and it is no uncommon sight to see two or three gaily disporting themselves on 'foot rickshas' around the Queen's statue.

Hongkong Telegraph
21 September 1896

PROBABLE STRIKE OF NIGHT-SOIL COOLIES: It is rumoured that owing to the Sanitary Board having given notice ... to the night-soil carriers that ... they must procure licenses and buckets approved by the Board, the whole of the night-soil coolies, being perfectly free agents, will go out on strike.

❖ *There was, of course, no modern plumbing, no flush-toilet system. In large sections of the city, night-soil — a euphemism for domestic sewage — was left on the street, outside the premises, to be collected by the night-soil coolies very early in the morning. Even as late as the 1930s, large sections of the city remained dependent on this form of disposal. In this case, the night-soil coolies did go on strike.*

NOTICE TO NIGHTMEN: 'Each nightman who furnishes his name and address will be registered and a pair of buckets will be presented to him on Monday, 21st instant, at the same time as moon-cakes are given to him by the conservancy contractor. ... Registration is free.'

❖ *Buckets and moon-cakes at the same time; to sweeten the unsavoury job?*

Hongkong Telegraph
14 October 1896

Hongkongites have just reason to be proud of possessing the only company in the British army clothed in silk, which distinction is enjoyed by the local Chinese Company of Sappers, their 'full dress' being composed of that material.

❖ *The unit referred to is probably the Hongkong Company of Submarine Miners, which began enlisting local Chinese in 1891.*

Hongkong Telegraph
4 November 1896

It may interest some of our readers to hear that the hairy variety of large house spider found in Hongkong is decidedly poisonous. Though the bite would probably not affect human beings more than that of a centipede, the effects would be far from pleasant, as a mynah [a bird] which was bitten by one in Kowloon recently, only survived a few minutes. ... The culprit has been preserved in glycerine, and will be sent to Calcutta Museum for identification.

Street Physician (Apothecary), Hong Kong, pre-1911
Street apothecaries (the word is seldom used today), or sellers of medicines, are common in China. They also frequently act as physicians and surgeons. The placard behind the man in the photograph, with his stall of remedies, offers cures of such diverse ailments as dysentery, leprosy, tuberculosis, as well as resetting broken bones.

Hongkong Telegraph
7 November 1896

THE DOCK OF HONGKONG. Hongkong has every reason to be proud of its dockyards, which will bear comparison with many European docks, and undoubtedly surpass any to be found in other Eastern colonies. Starting in 1866 with the modest little Lamont Dock at Aberdeen, Hongkong can now boast of six docks and two patent slips, while the rumours of proposed additions have for some months past been rife in the Colony. ...

Aberdeen Docks, Hong Kong Island, c.1920s
Built by John Lamont, in the 1850s, the first dock was known as the Lamont Dock and proved highly successful. In the early 1860s, Lamont added another dock to his enterprise, the Hope Dock, but before the latter was finished, both docks were bought, in 1865, by the large and very successful firm, the Hong Kong and Whampoa Dock Co. of Hung Hom, Kowloon.

Hongkong Telegraph
17 November 1896

We hear that the leading Chinese merchants and shopkeepers doing business in the colony have attached their 'chops' to a memorial to the Secretary of State for the Colonies urging ... to use his influence in the matter of ... the law providing for the regulation of brothels, which it is said, was very unwisely repealed a year or two ago. ...

❖   *The status of brothels changed from legal to illegal several times, and was finally made permanently illegal, in the 1930s, by Governor Peel.*

The flourishing suburb of Kowloon is becoming quite a cyclists' resort, every afternoon several journeying across by the Star Ferry, taking their machines with them to enjoy a spin on the good flat roads in preference to hill-climbing in Hongkong.

Hongkong Telegraph
19 December 1896

Kowloon, Tsim Sha Tsui, c.1905
This interesting photograph, taken probably from the Signal Hill (Blackhead Point), shows several colonial-style residential buildings in the foreground. On the right, the road stretching along the shoreline is Des Voeux Road, later renamed Chatham Road, and the road across is Granville Road. The long-shaped building in the distance is the Knutsford Terrace and further, on the hill, is the Observatory, built in 1884. On the right, the spire of Rosary Church can be seen and beyond, on the far right, the Gun Hill with the army barracks.

**Hongkong Telegraph
22 December 1896**

If war should break out between Spain and the United States there would speedily be an American squadron at Manilla. No successful resistance could be offered and the Spanish flag would have to give place there to the Stars and Stripes. ...

❖ *Correct prediction. The war between the two countries broke out in 1898, mainly because of Cuba — at that time a Spanish colony. The United States did acquire Philippines, according to some historical accounts for 20 million dollars!*

1897

**Hongkong Telegraph
5 January 1897**

Who wrote 'Rule Britannia'? ... 'the political hymn of this country', as Southeby called it, seems likely to pass from generation to generation with its authorship still a matter for controversy. Originally forming part of a masque written conjointly by James Thomson and David Mallet, and produced at Maidenhead in 1740, it has baffled the critics to determine to whom credit is due for its composition. ...

❖ *We thought it was well established that the music of 'Rule Britannia' was composed by Thomas Arne (1710–78), but perhaps this was not known in 1897.*

**Hongkong Telegraph
19 March 1897**

If paint counts for anything then certainly great progress is being made with the *Tamar*. Not only has the completed portion of her roof been painted, but it is now covered with canvas.

**Hongkong Telegraph
3 April 1897**

Dr. Sun Yat-sen, author of 'Kidnapped in London', and Dr. James Cantlie were to give a lecture on 'Things Chinese', illustrated by lantern slides and Chinese curios, on the 11th ultimo, at St. Martin's Town Hall, London; the proceeds to be devoted to the Special Fund of £100,000 now being raised in aid of Charing Cross Hospital.

❖ *Dr Cantlie was instrumental in rescuing Dr Sun when the latter was kidnapped by the Chinese government agents in London and secreted in the Chinese Embassy. If sent back to China, he would have certainly been executed.*

HMS *Tamar*, Hong Kong Harbour, c.1910
The photograph presents the bows (front view) of this handsome ship with the female figurehead, dressed in flowing robes, carved in wood; her origin is uncertain though a biblical connection has been suggested. Of all the Royal Navy ships connected with Hong Kong, HMS *Tamar* has had undoubtedly the longest and the closest association. Naval records list six ships of this name succeeding each other since 1777. It was the last *Tamar*, an iron-screw troopship of some 4,600 tons, launched in 1863, which had made Hong Kong her final home. She arrived in Hong Kong in 1897 as the base ship, first anchored in the harbour, but after 1913 moored alongside the Naval Dockyard where she became a familiar feature. She was scuttled on 12 December 1941, during the Japanese attack on Hong Kong, to avoid capture, and was commemorated after the war in the name 'HMS *Tamar*', given to the naval base, the dockyard, and the headquarters of the British Forces.

Hongkong Telegraph
26 April 1897

PIRATES ON THE WEST RIVER: For generations the West River has earned for itself a bad name on account of piracy. ... The latest victim was a high military mandarin, one Colonel Tin, Commander of Samkong, who was travelling ... with his wife, family, concubines and servants, when they were set upon by a fleet of piratical craft, whose occupants severely handled one of the concubines, and looted the mandarin's boat of all the valuables.

Hongkong Telegraph
29 May 1897

The Military Authorities have, after prolonged negotiations, purchased the Mount Austin Hotel from Messrs. J. D. Humphreys and Son for the sum of £100,000 sterling. The negotiations were conducted in Hongkong and not in England as had been rumoured ... sold to the Military Authorities for a sanatorium for the troops.

The Peak, Hong Kong Island, c.1920s
View towards south-west. Fine residential houses dot the picturesque Peak scene. In the foreground is the former Mount Austin Hotel. Built around 1890, with every expectation of success, this venture did not succeed. It was sold, in 1897, to the army and converted into quarters for troops.

Hongkong Telegraph
9 June 1897

Preparations for the celebration of the Diamond Jubilee are being vigorously pushed forward. ...

A number of European residents in various parts have arranged for illuminations in gas, and the front of the Club Germania has already been fitted with gas jets in the shape of a large crown and the imperial star — also the figures '1837' and '1897'. It is reported that there is a regular boom in fancy lanterns, and, given the fine weather, the display should be a remarkably fine one.

JUBILEE CELEBRATIONS: … His Excellency the Governor will lay foundation stone of the Hospital for Women and Children … proceed to Jardines Wharf … convey them to Sulphur Channel, past Kennedy Town. The company will then be enabled to view from the steamer the laying of the commemoration stone for Victoria Road by His Excellency.

Hongkong Telegraph
21 June 1897

❖ *On 22 June 1897, Hong Kong, together with the rest of the British Empire, celebrated the Diamond Jubilee of Queen Victoria's reign. Two foundation stones were laid on that day to mark the start of two projects, both bearing Her Majesty's name. One was placed at the western end of Hong Kong Island, at what would become the start of the new Victoria Road; a similar one for the Victoria Hospital for Women and Children, on Barker Road. Both stones are still extant, though the first one had to be relocated.*

Victoria Hospital for Women and Children, Barker Road, The Peak, Hong Kong Island, 1903
The foundation stone of this hospital was laid by the Governor, Sir William Robinson, on 22 June 1897, marking the Diamond Jubilee (60 years) of Queen Victoria's reign. The photograph shows the hospital decorated with flags at its completion in 1903. The foundation stone still stands at the original site though the hospital was demolished many years ago.

**Hongkong Telegraph
21 July 1897**

We hear that owing to the whole of the Detective Force having been cleared out ... there is a feeling of uneasiness among the better class of Chinese who, not unnaturally, fear that the criminal classes of the mainland will consider the present a favourable time for swooping down on us like hungry hawks seeking their evening meal. ... It may be that the criminal classes will find the police better prepared to protect lives and property of the residents than they anticipate, but ... the fact remains that there is just now quite a considerable exodus of the wives and families of well-to-do Chinese, many of them going to Canton and others to Macao.

❖   *It was a bad period for the Hong Kong Police. Several detectives were dismissed including Detective Inspector W. Quincey, after 27 years of service (the only Chinese Inspector, featured in the photograph on p. 36) Among the reasons were bribery and gross neglect of duty.*

**Hongkong Telegraph
8 October 1897**

Now that the weather is really growing cooler and a walk can be taken without having to depend on the services of ricksha or chair coolies, a stroll ... through Yau-ma-ti to Kowloon City will repay anyone valiant enough to brave the terrors of the Yau-ma-ti streets. Once clear of this village, the road runs through paddy-fields and gardens, the former being at the present time in the height of their beauty. ... the road winds up over bare and rugged hills, which are a great contrast to the fertile valleys below. ... [the road] skirts the Chinese cemetery ... until the bamboo boundary fence, dividing British from Chinese territory, is reached. Kowloon City, well worth a visit, is within easy reach. ... Along the boundary fence, in the paddy fields, a few snipe and an occasional wild duck are to be seen.

❖   *The passage is interesting for what we have lost: paddy fields at Yau Ma Tei, bare and rugged hills, a bamboo fence and perhaps a snipe or a wild duck or two at Boundary Street!*

**Hongkong Telegraph
27 October 1897**

The inconsiderate eagerness of the Wyndham Street flower sellers is a great nuisance to those ladies who prefer to buy their own flowers rather than trust to the artistic sense of their Chinese 'boys' for a suitable selection. The appearance of a lady in the vicinity is a sign for a general scramble of all the flower vendors ...

Boundary Between the Chinese and British Territories, Kowloon, c.1896–1900

One of the matshed posts constructed along the bamboo fence which served as the boundary between the Chinese and the British Kowloon, and which ran along the later Boundary Street over the east Kowloon Peninsula.

Wyndham Street, Central District, Hong Kong Island, c.1900–05

An early photograph showing the bottom of Wyndham Street where it joins Queen's Road. The entrance on the right leads into the offices of Hong Kong Electric Co. Flowers and wreaths had been sold there for many years earning the street its nickname of 'Flower Street'. In 1928, however, the flower stalls were moved to the portion of D'Aguilar Street above Wellington Street, with the 'Flower Street' name attached, to the new location.

**Hongkong Telegraph
4 December 1897**

Although the cold weather has set in, yet a few mosquitoes are still to be found … and, as the low temperature drives them to the house and sharpens their appetite … they are regarded as anything but welcome visitors. However, our tame entomologist has found [that] a small quantity of vermouth placed in a wine glass in the middle of the room will attract all the mosquitoes and, as they do not recognise the paralysing effects of the liquor until too late, their debauch ends by an involuntary bath and death.

**Hongkong Telegraph
31 December 1897**

There has been a good deal of trouble over the stoppage of rice exports. The law of China prohibits the exportation of rice to any foreign country, presumably for the fear of famine. … Some years ago the Viceroy of Kwangtung made an exception for the benefit of Chinese living in Hongkong and Macao on the express understanding that they must not send it abroad. The export allowed to Hongkong is 500,000 piculs* per annum, Macao about half that. It is not that China is the only food-producing country in the world, but simply that the Chinese, like the European, wants what he used to have at home. To a meat-eating barbarian, all rice is rice, but to the rice-eating races there are marvellous differences, as clearly definable as brands of tobacco or spirits.

1898

**Hongkong Telegraph
13 January 1898**

MUSEUM: The chief addition to the museum during the year … were a crocodile's skull from Borneo, two cobras killed at the Peak, three other snakes, a scorpion and two broad-tailed lizards caught on the island and a 'wire snake' [*tit sin she*] caught in Canton.

**Hongkong Telegraph
18 January 1898**

In the annual Chinese Customs Returns, the number of foreign firms in the various treaty ports of China is given, Great Britain comes first with 363 out of total 672. As compared with 1895, the total increase to date has been 69. … The German houses have increased from 92 to

---

* Picul: (Malay) weight measure in the East, varies from 130–140 lbs.

99, the Japanese from 34 to 79, the American from 31 to 40, and the Russian from 13 to 14. The French total shows a decrease of two … and there have also been decreases in the case of Portugal, Spain, Italy and Holland. The total foreign population at the treaty ports at the end of last year was 10,855 against 9,755 at the end of 1895.

Mr. WONG YUK-CHO recently published in Hongkong a phonetic system of writing Chinese words, intended to supplant the ideographic system, like the Japanese *kana* and the Korean *unmun*. … While cordially sympathising with all who wish to lift a heavy load from the Chinese race in the struggle for intellectual emancipation, by simplifying the reading and writing of the language, we regret to find that there is absolutely no chance of success, as far as we can see. …

By the ideograph … the Throne is upheld; art and religion, the classics and the moral teachings of sages survive.

**Hongkong Telegraph
22 February 1898**

❖   *It is interesting to learn that the recent 'pinyin' was not the first attempt to simplify the Chinese written language, and that a hundred years ago such a move was initiated in Hong Kong.*

Some people in Hongkong are getting terribly excited over the question of Post Office site. … Hongkong is such a wonderfully compact place that no part of it is further than a stone's throw from any other part, and what difference would a few yards make? Hongkong residents forget how fortunate they are in having every place so near. It is unique. No city in the world contains so much in such narrow space.

**Hongkong Telegraph
5 March 1898**

❖   *The Post Office was built at the corner of Pedder Street and Connaught Road, and what a magnificent building it was! Alas, like many others of its vintage, it was demolished in 1976.*

Speaking of the present condition of trade generally in Hongkong, some leading businessmen informed a *Telegraph* reporter that things are very slow and that money seems to be very scarce. At one time April was a brisk month … but the present month is quoted as being the slowest in the past ten years. … It is understood that the plague is in considerable degree answerable for many people leaving Hongkong.

**Hongkong Telegraph
28 April 1898**

❖   *As mentioned previously, plague had made many unwelcome returns to Hong Kong since the initial epidemic of 1894.*

Hongkong Telegraph
31 May 1898

THE BRITISH FLAG HOISTED AT WEI-HAI-WEI.
The British flag was hoisted at Wei-hai-wei on the 24th inst., Queen's birthday. ... Captain Kinghall then addressed the people present and read his authority for proclaiming the lease of Wei-hai-wei and a declaration that the place was a British property. ...

❖ *Wei Hai Wei, now spelled Weihai, is a port in Shandong Province of China. It was leased (not ceded) to Britain 1898-1930, during which time it was a naval and coaling station.*

Ceremonial Gathering, Wei Hai Wei, China, c.1901–05
In the photograph, J. H. S. Lockhart, in full dress uniform, as the Civil Commissioner of Wei Hai Wei, is conducting some sort of official ceremony in the presence of a large gathering of Chinese notables and other guests. The flagpole, with a young scout standing at attention, suggests that a flag had been raised. Lockhart was appointed Civil Commissioner of Wei Hai Wei in 1901 after a distinguished career in the British Civil Service, most of it spent in Hong Kong. He remained in Wei Hai Wei until his retirement in 1921.

Hongkong Telegraph
13 June 1898

THE KOWLOON HINTERLAND LEASED TO GREAT BRITAIN:
China has leased to Great Britain 200 square miles of territory around Hongkong, including the mainland behind Kowloon to a line joining

Mirs Bay and Deep Bay, besides the waters of these Bays and the Island of Lantao.

❖   *What is extraordinary in this event is that Britain had to fight two unpopular wars with China to obtain Hong Kong and Kowloon, but managed to lease far greater territory with the minimum of fuss and diplomacy!*

Sir William Robinson, late Governor of Hongkong, has expressed the following view ... regarding the extension of Hongkong:- 'The Kowloon arrangement' he said, 'is an admirable one, and will be of great benefit to the Chinese as well as the European inhabitants of Hongkong. ... We must, however, have European management. Kowloon City, which has hitherto been a nest of gamblers and robbers, will now be cleansed and properly policed, to the great advantage of Victoria.'

Hongkong Telegraph
18 July 1898

❖   *The jurisdiction over Kowloon City, however, remained unresolved for the next 100 years, allowing it to be reduced to crime-ridden slums. See also the* Hongkong Telegraph, *11 November 1901, p.185, and Kowloon Walled City, p.186.*

Since the Declaration of Independence the United States has had six wars, not counting the little differences with the Indians. These were the War of the Revolution, the War of 1812, the War with the Barbary States, the Mexican War, and the War for the Union. The present war with Spain makes the sixth.

Hongkong Telegraph
3 August 1898

We understand that on Saturday, at Kam Tin Hu, when they saw the Hon. J. H. Stewart-Lockhart's party approach, the Chinese beat gongs and shouted 'ta' and 'foreign devils'. About a thousand of the villagers responded and shut the gates. The Hon. J. H. Stewart-Lockhart gave orders to bring up two Maxim guns and seventy blue-jackets, and on the arrival of his force the villagers were given ten minutes to open the gates. The demand was promptly complied with.

Hongkong Telegraph
22 August 1898

❖   *Contrary to popular belief, the takeover of the then New Territories was anything but peaceful. The villagers organised local militia and a full-scale battle developed at Tai Po, in which many villagers lost their lives. The official takeover did not take place until April 1899.*

Sir William Robinson with Members of the Legislative Council, c.1897

The Legislative and Executive Councils of Hong Kong were set up in 1843 by the Hong Kong Charter and began to function in early 1844, the former to pass laws and ordinances, the latter to advise the governor on administrative matters. The two councils, modified and expanded over the years, still have essentially the same functions today.

In the photograph, the governor, Sir William Robinson, is in the centre in dark uniform and plumed hat. He governed Hongkong from 1891 to 1898 and proved to be an experienced and capable man who had made a substantial contribution to Hong Kong. On the governor's right is General Black (in white uniform) and next to the general is J. Stewart Lockhart, the colonial secretary. Dr Ho Kai, a distinguished barrister and community worker, is behind and between the governor and the general. C. P. Chater, another great Hong Kong personality, is on the governor's left.

During Robinson's period in office, plague epidemic struck Hong Kong for the first time. His efforts to introduce drastic measures to combat the epidemic, however, met with strong resistance from the tradition-oriented Chinese community.

In 1896, important reforms were carried out within the two councils, when the Legco membership was increased, and for the first time two unofficial members were appointed to the Executive Council. The Legco now had three Chinese members, but the governor was still opposed to any Chinese on the Executive Council.

Sir William Robinson left Hong Kong in 1898, just before the lease of the New Territories, which he had actively secured, was to take place. In spite of his achievements, it must be noted that Robinson Road in the Mid-Levels is not named after him, but after Sir Hercules Robinson who governed Hong Kong from 1854 to 1859.

A Chinese living near Shanghai has been interviewed, and among other things says, concerning the 'barbarian' Europeans:- 'They certainly do not know how to amuse themselves. You never see them enjoy themselves by sitting quietly upon their ancestors' graves. They jump around and kick balls. ... Again, you will find them making long tramps into the country; but that is probably a religious duty, for when they tramp they wave sticks in the air, nobody knows why. They have no sense of dignity, for they may be found walking with women. They even sit down at the same table with women, and the latter are served first.'

Hongkong Telegraph
15 September 1898

... If, as we most earnestly hope will prove to be the case, the long projected Kowloon-Canton Railway is at last to be constructed, then there can be no possible doubt that a great future lies before our hitherto somewhat despised suburb and those persons possessing property in the peninsula are to be congratulated upon the rosy prospects now opening up before them.

Hongkong Telegraph
19 September 1898

HONGKONG'S NEW GOVERNOR: It is not every day that a colony gets a new Governor and in Hongkong such a happening is marked with a red letter. Sir Henry Blake, G.C.M.G., was lately appointed to represent Her Majesty in Hongkong and to-day, accompanied by Lady Blake and Miss Blake, he landed in the colony where his new sphere of labour lies.

Hongkong Telegraph
25 November 1898

'Glenealy' one of the prettiest spots in Hongkong is to be given up to the ruthless hands of the builder. ... The west side ... is privately owned ground, and the owners have decided to utilise their property by building upon it. The ground has hitherto been kept in order by the Government, being planted with palms and ferns, and probably many may have been under the impression that it was Government land.

❖ *The ugly words 'developer' and 'development' had not yet crept into the vocabulary of the media; instead they are 'builder' and 'utilise'. See Glenealy, p.164.*

Hongkong Telegraph
12 December 1898

Glenealy, Mid-Levels, Hong Kong Island, c.1910
The steep path surrounded by lush tropical vegetation leads from Robinson Road above to Wyndham Street below. A picturesque 'glen' (narrow valley), it was known at first as Elliot's Vale, after Captain Charles Elliot of the First Opium War, the man chiefly responsible for the acquisition of Hong Kong for Britain. But the name did not survive, and when a house called 'Glenealy' was built on top, the path took the name, at first Glenealy Ravine and later simply Glenealy. It has lost much of its early charm, but a few pleasant spots can still be found for a leisurely stroll.

Hongkong Telegraph
27 December 1898

Regulations for the traffic on Kennedy Road in place of those previously existing, are published in the *Gazette*. The chief change is that rickshas, bicycles, or other similar machines, and perambulators are to be allowed on the road but are cautioned to go around the bends at a moderate pace.

❖   *The blessed past, when perambulators (today's 'prams') were part of the traffic!*

1899

A SAD STORY: Many people will remember James Josiah Jones, who arrived in Hongkong some little time ago from England. The day after his arrival he wrote … to his people at home:- 'I have just arrived in Hongkong; it is a wonderful and wicked place. What grieves the heart most is to see a vehicle, called a ricksha. It's downright horrible cruelty; they are nothing more than beasts of burden. … When I landed, about twenty of these poor fellows crowded around me … each one begging … me to patronize him. … I scorned the idea of being drawn through the streets by a fellow man. I told them all how sorry I was for the degradation they had to suffer.'
Two weeks after James Josiah Jones appeared at the Police Court to answer three charges:-
1. Battering six ricksha coolies, 2. Refusing to pay legal ricksha fare of ten cents, 3. Damaging two rickshas. The next letter James Josiah Jones wrote to his friends at home concerning ricksha coolies we dare not publish.

Hongkong Telegraph
5 January 1899

The question of the water supply of the Colony … is daily becoming more serious and to which the earnest attention of the Government should be turned without delay. … On the 1ˢᵗ January 1898, the storage at Tytam and Pokfulam amounted to 424,050,000 gallons, or roughly sufficient for 134 days of consumption with an estimated population of 198,000. … According to these figures it is evident that a dry season may very easily bring us face to face with a water famine.

Owing to the scarcity of water, the supply in the public mains in Kowloon Peninsula will be turned off from 6 p.m. to 6 a.m. until further notice.

❖   *Even after several more large reservoirs had been constructed (Shek Pik, Plover Cove), the water shortage persisted. At one period, in 1966/67, the water was turned on for 4 hours every 4 days! Only after the High Island Reservoir had been built, and water continuously piped from China, did the shortage stop.*

Hongkong Telegraph
9 January 1899

Pok Fu Lam Reservoir, Pok Fu Lam, Hong Kong Island, c.1910
The earliest of the water reservoirs in Hong Kong, Pok Fu Lam Reservoir, with the capacity of 2 million gallons, was constructed in 1863 on the southern aspect of Hong Kong Island. It was extended in 1871 (66 million gallons). Across the channel, Lamma Island can be seen, with no obvious signs of habitation.

Hongkong Telegraph
14 January 1899

THE SMOKE NUISANCE: ... a letter to the *Times* ... that a society should be formed for obtaining the enforcement of the law against smoke nuisance. ... It is high time that something of the same sort was done in Hongkong. The City of Victoria is becoming dreadfully smoky. Factories are multiplying. Steamers and steam launches are vomiting the blackest smoke all day and all night and steps ought to be taken without delay to make them consume in some fashion their own smoke.

Hongkong Telegraph
26 January 1899

RESERVATION OF AN HISTORICAL SPOT. SUNG WONG T'OI. Last year the Legislative Council, on a motion of the Hon. Dr. Ho Kai, passed a resolution in favour of the reservation ... at British Kowloon known as Sung Wong T'oi or Sung Wong T'ong; and at the Council meeting yesterday ... first reading passed ... Dr. Eitel [writes] in the *History of Hongkong* ... 'As to the history of Hongkong previous to the rise of the Tatsing Dynasty [AD 1644] very little is known. There is, however ... an ancient rock-inscription, on a large loose lying granite boulder ... close to the village of Matauchung, directly west of Kowloon city. This inscription consisting of three Chinese characters [宋王臺 Sung Wong Toi, *lit.* 'Hall of a King of the Sung'] arranged horizontally. ... The Chinese Government believe it to be a genuine inscription, about 600 years old.'

Sung Wong Toi Rock, c.1920

Among local traditions, one of the richest and most enduring relates to the end of the Sung (now spelled Song) dynasty (AD 960–1279) and the flight south of its last two boy emperors pursued by Mongol invaders. The princes are believed to have rested briefly on the site of the Sung Wong Toi Hill in Kowloon Bay.

The original boulder, shown in this photograph, was for many years an important historic relic much esteemed and protected by the local people. The boulder has three large characters engraved upon it which have been interpreted as 'Terrace of the Sung King', and stood prominently on top of a hill above Kowloon Bay. During the Japanese occupation of Hong Kong, 1942–45, this boulder became dislodged while the hill was being levelled for an extension of Kai Tak Airport.

The part of the boulder displaying the three characters, about one-third its original size, survived the blasting operations, and after the war, was rescued and placed in a small park especially constructed for it close to the original site.

Local historians believe that the characters were cut during the Yuan dynasty, 1271–1368, long after the Sung dynasty had fallen and after the imperial visits.

**Hongkong Telegraph
11 March 1899**

TO SAVE THE ELEPHANT: A practical method of discouraging the trade in ivory would be efficacious if it were only adopted generally. It is simply that we should all forego the use of ivory, and have our knife handles, etc., made of xylonite, or one of the good forms of celluloid. The 40,000 elephants annually destroyed for manufacturing purposes have their long wise lives sacrificed mainly in the service of billiard players. This is quite unnecessary, as xylonite billiard balls are now made as truly and are as pleasant to play with as those of ivory.

❖ *It took fully a hundred years to stop the ivory trade; one can only hope it is not too late for the elephant.*

**Hongkong Telegraph
10 April 1899**

At last we have the long expected report of the Hon. J. H. STEWART LOCKHART upon the new territory ... the physical features of the country, its water supply, soil, products, industries, population, form of government, revenue, means of communication, etc., are all dealt with ... We are glad to see that the question of Chinese jurisdiction in Kowloon City is still under negotiation ...

❖ *It was a very thorough, substantive report on the newly leased 'hinterland', later to be referred to as the New Territories, accompanied by photographs. Stewart Lockhart, the Colonial Secretary at the time, was an extremely capable administrator who later served as the Commissioner of the Chinese port of Wei Hai Wei, leased to Britain (see p.160).*

**Hongkong Telegraph
13 April 1899**

DR. CLARK'S ANNUAL REPORT: ...The domestic buildings of the city of Victoria number 7,438 (excluding of barracks and Police Stations) of which 530 are European dwellings, while there are also some 120 houses in European occupation in the Hill district [the Peak]. The various villages over the Island contain 31 European dwellings and 1,600 Chinese dwellings, while in Kowloon there are 93 European dwellings and 1,850 Chinese dwellings, exclusive of the Barracks for the Hongkong Regiment and 72 small houses used by this Regiment as married quarters.

**Hongkong Telegraph
17 April 1899**

THE KOWLOON HINTERLAND. BRITISH TROOPS ATTACKED. As was anticipated, there has been trouble between the Chinese and British forces in the preliminary steps ... for the establishment of British jurisdiction in the Kowloon hinterland. Yesterday Captain Berger left with a company of the Hongkong Regiment for Taipohu, in Mirs Bay, to pave the way for the ceremony of the hoisting of the British flag … On arrival at Taipohu it was found that the Chinese had prepared a warm reception for the troops, and they were fired upon, but luckily without any disastrous result. … On the news being received, three more companies of the Hongkong Regiment … were dispatched … to the scene of the disturbance. This morning it was decided that in view of the unforseen hostility … to the hoisting of the flag, it would be as well to abandon Monday's ceremony …

❖ *The flag was hoisted but without a ceremony. The takeover was not peaceful; there was fighting opposing the British takeover of the New Territories (the Kowloon Hinterland), though the British news tried to play down the scale of the fighting. Incidentally, the Hongkong Regiment mentioned here was* not *the Hong Kong Volunteers, but a local regiment composed of Indians recruited in India.*

Sir Henry Blake, Governor of Hong Kong, Addressing Chinese Functionaries and Leaders of the Chinese Communities in the New Territories, August 1899
The Governor, in formal ceremonial dress, is seen addressing his audience in a hastily constructed matshed. Although the lease of the New Territories to Britain was to run from July 1898, the effective takeover did not take place until April 1899, and this not without some armed resistance by the local militia. In August 1899, the Governor toured the New Territories where he met local leaders, no doubt with the object of reassuring them of the Government's good intentions — the event depicted in the photograph. Sir Henry Blake served as Governor of Hong Kong from 1898 to 1903.

**Hongkong Telegraph
20 April 1899**

THE KOWLOON SCHOOL. His Excellency the Governor ... has announced that schools would be established in all the villages of the new territory. ... It is pleasant thus to observe the fatherly care exercised by our Government for the welfare of its Chinese subjects, but it must not be forgotten that the Government owes an equal debt of duty to our own children. It is the children of British parents to whom it will be entrusted the task of carrying on the government and maintaining the integrity of the empire in the future. ... Why, then, should the children of European parents resident in Kowloon be denied the privileges which are extended to the poorest of the Chinese? Can it be, as some facetious writers have suggested, that Hongkong is indeed a dependency of China, run by Chinese for the Chinese, and that the British are merely regarded as alien interlopers whose claims to consideration are nil?

❖   *This amazing outburst shows firstly that the* Telegraph *has changed, in the last few years, from a thoughtful, progressive and liberal paper to a staunchly colonial and imperialistic one; perhaps a change in the editorial staff? Secondly, British children in Hong Kong have never been denied good primary and secondary education, while the parents often chose to send them to school in England.*

**Hongkong Telegraph
26 May 1899**

It is a peculiar fact that despite the flourishing condition of Hongkong and decayed state of Macao, the latter settlement far surpasses us in the matter of rickshas and ricksha coolies. True, the vehicles are somewhat dilapidated ... but they are roomy and comfortable. ... Here the coolie is insolent and moves at a snail's pace; there he is obliging. ... The Macao coolie takes an eight mile run as a matter of course, takes you up hill and down dale and at the finish accepts his fare without demanding four times the amount to which he is entitled.

**Hongkong Telegraph
6 June 1899**

AFFORESTATION: In the report of the Superintendent of the Botanical and Afforestation Department ... is given a table showing the statistics of trees planted during 1898. In all 33,923 trees of various species were planted and were distributed over the Colony. ... It will be noted that, despite the large amount of planting work undertaken by the Department during last year, not a single tree has been planted in Kowloon.

❖ *It should be noted that at the time of the British acquisition of Hong Kong, the hills of the island were very bare and largely devoid of trees.*

Cannot some sort of supervision be exercised by the police over the prostitutes who roam the streets at night? Take a walk down Queen's Road after dinner and the chances are you will be accosted by some of these women between the Clock Tower and the Central Fire Station. Take a walk eastwards as far as the Naval Hospital and matters are nearly as bad; loose women appear to swarm about the streets and are a source of annoyance to respectable male pedestrians.

Hongkong Telegraph
7 June 1899

Interesting experiments were carried out at Lyeemun Pass by ... the Royal Engineers. ... Military reasons prevent us from giving a detailed account ... but we don't think we shall be giving our enemies much information by stating that the experiments are in connection with the ... defence of the harbour by means of the Brennan torpedo.

Hongkong Telegraph
16 June 1899

❖ *This highly secret torpedo was invented by an Irishman (later turned Australian), Louis Brennan, and was installed in a number of British naval bases, including Hong Kong. The machinery for the torpedo was installed at Lyeemun (now Lei Yue Mun), but it is not clear whether the torpedo itself was ever installed, let alone fired.*

The scale of crown rents to be paid on land in the 'New Territories' is published in the *Gazette*. The rents range from 66 cents to $3.20 per acre per annum.

Hongkong Telegraph
17 July 1899

'Worried' suggests that as our legislators are anxious to increase the revenue of the Colony they might tax pianos, when situated in the business quarter ... and played all the afternoon. He assures us that ... he has been driven nearly frantic ... by the musical efforts of a neighbour.

Hongkong Telegraph
8 August 1899

❖ *The piano has been described as 'the most patient domestic animal'.*

Hongkong Telegraph
18 August 1899

THE TUNG WAH HOSPITAL: In view of the increased population of the Colony and the Hinterland, the Directors of the Tung Wah Hospital ... have decided to erect a new building as an extension on a site opposite the present hospital. ... In this building it is proposed to set aside a special apartment for midwifery, which is urgently needed. ... His Excellency the Governor has kindly subscribed $50 ...

Hongkong Telegraph
31 August 1899

The Tropical Diseases Expedition ... has discovered that malaria is spread by means of a particular variety of mosquito.

❖ *The discovery of the 'anopheles' type of mosquito as the carrier of malaria, was absolutely crucial in the control of the disease.*

Hongkong Telegraph
29 September 1899

Last evening on the Praya ... a water-pipe burst and for a considerable time a huge spout of water ascended even higher than the theatre building, which sparkled and scintillated in the light of the electric lamps like myriads of diamonds. Hundreds of spectators witnessed the spectacle with great interest and seemed to be much disappointed when the defect was remedied.

❖ *A burst pipe is still a common occurrence, but we seem to have lost the knack of enjoying such a spectacle.*

Hongkong Telegraph
9 October 1899

Messrs Lane Crawford & Co. have now in stock a large number of phonographs, which they are disposing of at very popular prices. The phonograph appears to have caught on in Hongkong so intending purchasers of these very amusing instruments should hurry to obtain them before the stock is exhausted.

❖ *For those born in the 20th century, a phonograph is a gramophone or a record player.*

Hongkong Telegraph
12 October 1899

A perusal of the reports of the Hongkong Legislative Council meetings cannot but serve to impress the reader with the great pains so frequently taken to draft a reply to a question in such a manner that while it cannot be said that the query remains unanswered yet the information required is skilfully withheld.

Hong Kong Waterfront (The Praya), Central District, Hong Kong Island, c.1890

Prominent in the foreground is the Pedder's Wharf, the principal jetty in the Central District for many years. It would move forward after the next major praya reclamation, of 1890–1904, and be renamed Blake Pier after the Governor, Sir Henry Blake. The corner building on the left is the premises of Jardine, Matheson & Co. Next to it, a 3-storey building with a flagpole housed a German trading firm of Stoltecroft & Hirst. The next, 4-storey building with a flag, is the Peninsular & Oriental shipping company, recently moved there from a site further west. The Lane, Crawford & Co.'s small, 2-storey building is standing beside it with the firm's name clearly seen on the signboard. The two buildings next are the Union Insurance Company and the Douglas Lapraik & Co., a shipping firm.

A Committee is just now at work on a report upon the most vital question of the disposal of the night-soil of Hongkong. At present the whole of it is carried away to Canton and used by the silk growers. … Why … should it not be made use of in the New Territories for fertilising the land upon which our Military Authorities hope to see our food stuffs produced?

Hongkong Telegraph
31 October 1899

❖   *An interesting revelation: the destination of our night-soil! One would have thought that Canton, with its much larger population than Hong Kong, would have enough of its own excreta to meet the demands of the silk growers.*

Hongkong Telegraph
17 November 1899

THE TRIAD SOCIETY: The trials of two members of the Triad Society this morning were chiefly interesting for the history that was disclosed of the original formation and reason of the formation of the society. ... It would seem that the aim of the society is to upset the Tsing Dynasty, which in 1644 upset the Ming Dynasty, and once more to restore the power of the latter.

Hongkong Telegraph
29 December 1899

In the present transitory stage of Hongkong, when the business portion of the town is being shifted bodily to the Reclamation, one cannot expect the new roads to be in first rate order, but still ... the Authorities might at least make an effort to render them as safe as possible. Take the portion of Pedder Street ... from the Hongkong Hotel to the sea front ... we have seen rickshas capsize there, to the discomfort and danger of the occupant.

❖ *The reclamation referred to here pushed the waterfront from the present Des Voeux Road to Connaught Road.*

FIN DE SIECLE*: Hongkong Telegraph makes no mention of this; there is no looking forward to the 20th century, just general gloom due to the Boer War.

❖ *The Boer War, 1899–1902, between the Dutch settlers in South Africa (the Boers) and the British; essentially fought for the gold and diamonds of Transvaal.*

1900

Hongkong Telegraph
8 January 1900

The utter unsuitability of the Supreme Court for its present purpose was well shown this morning when it was explained to his Lordship that one of the leading barristers engaged in the case was late, owing to being obliged to change into warmer clothing. His Lordship accepted this explanation and said they had no means of warming the building.

---

* *Fin de siècle*: French, 'end of century'. The phrase at present also implies decadence, with especial reference to the end of the 19th century.

❖ *The Courthouse referred to here was roughly on the site of the present Queen's Theatre. The next Supreme Court, now housing the Legislative Council, would not be completed until 1912.*

His Excellency Li Hung-chang, who has been described as the Grand Old Man of China, arrived in Hongkong yesterday morning. ... This afternoon ... His Excellency landed at Murray Pier. ... The roadway between Murray Pier and Government House was lined with soldiers with fixed bayonets.

Hongkong Telegraph
15 January 1900

❖ *See also Minister Li Hung-Chang, p.135.*

Viceroy Li Hung-chang (1823–1901) Visiting Hong Kong, 1900
The Viceroy is seated with Sir Henry Blake, Governor of Hong Kong, probably in the grounds of the Government House. Standing behind and between them is Stewart Lockhart, the Colonial Secretary. The Viceroy's entourage is standing on his right. One of the greatest Chinese statesmen of the time, Li Hung-chang was, at various times, advisor and chief secretary to the Empress Dowager Tz'u Hsi, head of the Imperial Chancery, and finally the Viceroy, in 1900–1901, of the provinces of Chihli and Kwangtung. His interest in Hong Kong was reflected in his patronage of the Hong Kong College of Medicine — the forerunner of the University of Hong Kong.

Hongkong Telegraph
22 January 1900

We notice that Hongkong has at length become the proud possessor of a motor car. The machine in question is 'built for three' and was much in evidence on the Shau-ki-wan Road yesterday afternoon. It runs a good pace and splutters somewhat in doing so. This, however, is not a drawback, as it warns pedestrians ... to give it a wide berth.

Hongkong Telegraph
9 March 1900

It is reported ... that the Empress Dowager has decided to close the Peking University on the grounds that no progress has been made after a trial of one year. A decree is also said to have been issued closing all schools and colleges of Western learning ... on the grounds that there is no money in the Imperial Exchequer ... and further that these schools only turn out men hostile to the Conservative policy of the Government.

Hongkong Telegraph
10 March 1900

We do not wish to alarm our readers, but a tiger was seen in Queen's Road this morning. However, he was only a foot in length and so we do not suppose that homes will be desolated just at present. He was being carried round for sale by an enterprising Chinese who was asking the sum of a hundred dollars for him.

❖   _Probably either a tiger pup or a leopard cat; the latter resembles a tiger._

Hongkong Telegraph
29 March 1900

Boxers Create Trouble: It is stated that the Boxers Secret Society is creating great trouble in the neighbourhood of Jinchow, a town situated sixty miles to the southwest of Tientsin. A collision has already taken place between the Boxers and the Chinese troops and many of the latter have been slaughtered.

❖   _Essentially anti-foreign, the Boxer Rebellion gained in strength and eventually besieged foreign legations in Peking. Foreign troops were sent to relieve the siege, and the rebellion was put down in 1902._

Hongkong Telegraph
3 April 1900

Could Mr. Chater but see the road in Kowloon which bears his name he would weep. It more resembles a mud bath than anything else at the present and residents in the vicinity are thinking of applying for permission to raise a crop of paddy on it.

❖   *Readers who know Chater Road in the Central District of Hong Kong Island may be confused. For some strange reason, the early planners of Kowloon had duplicated a number of streets, among them Robinson, Macdonnell, and Chater Roads. In 1908 they were changed to their present names. Chater Road became Peking Road.*

To-day being the fifth day of the fifth moon is being observed with the customary ceremonies, and the Dragon Boat was seen this morning about 10 a.m. running through the Harbour … accompanied by the usual musical howls emanating from the Chinese instruments and throats. It seemed heathenish, yet we cannot help saying that there was a vividly rhythmical effect produced by the consonance of the musical instruments and the timely rowing of the modern *triremes.**

❖   *One might have expected a more enlightened or intelligent comment on the Dragon Boat Festival popular all over Southeast Asia. (Compare with* Hongkong Daily Press, *18 June 1915, p.331.)*

Hongkong Telegraph
1 June 1900

Dragon Boat Race, Hong Kong Harbour, c.1909
The long 'dragon' boat with men ready with their paddles is preparing for the race. These popular races are held annually during the Dragon Boat Festival, on the fifth day of the fifth moon, generally late May or early June. In this colourful and happy festival, dragon boat teams row vigorously to the beating of the drum to win the race.

The long and narrow boats are well-built and may be as long as 100 feet with 40–50 paddlers. So popular have the races become in recent times that many overseas teams, Asian and European, come to compete in this event. There are several popular versions of the origin of the festival, but the real origin is obscure and probably dates back to remote antiquity.

---

* Trireme: ancient Greek warship using three banks of oars as well as sails.

**Hongkong Telegraph
3 July 1900**

In Hong Kong there appears to be a great deal too much faith put in what one might call good luck. Take, for instance, the landslip which occurred at West Point ... yesterday morning. Here was a row of houses directly under a cliff some eighty feet in height, without any retaining wall ... to prevent ... a landslip occurring and carrying the crowd of Chinese living in the houses to Eternity.

❖   *Landslides, as they are now called, have continued to affect Hong Kong to the present time. There have been some horrendous ones killing many people and rendering many more homeless.*

**Hongkong Telegraph
19 July 1900**

The following is an extract from a letter in the *Pall Mall*:- 'Touching the popularity of Russia in China over all other "foreign devils", the simple reasons would appear to be that she bribes better than anybody else, and that she has no missionaries. To the missionary-cum-gunboat system pursued by this country in the land of Confucius we may, if we please, attribute much of the disfavour we experience there.'

**Hongkong Telegraph
11 September 1900**

Mr. E.R. Belilios, C.M.G., the well-known Hongkong admirer of Lord Beaconsfield ... is over in London on a visit. ... Mr. Belilios is one of the most wealthy men in the Far East, where he is a leading figure in the Jewish community.

❖   *A noted philanthropist, Belilios's wealth was made through the opium trade. When Lord Beaconsfield had modestly declined a statue erected in his honour, Belilios built the Beaconsfield Arcade (p.179), later replaced by Beaconsfield House, no longer extant.*

**Hongkong Telegraph
2 October 1900**

The Director of Public Works appears to be labouring under the delusion that the public exists for the convenience of the water supply and not the water supply for the convenience of the public. What is wanted in Kowloon is water and the sooner Mr. Orsmby can patch up his pumps and allow the Kowloonites to take their daily bath in peace, the sooner will those bugbears of the Official, the Unofficial Members and the Press, cease from troubling him.

❖   *Like most Hong Kong personalities, major and minor, of the past times, a street, in Tai Hang, was named after Mr Ormsby.*

Beaconsfield Arcade, Queen's Road Central, Hong Kong Island, c.1880
This handsome arcade was built in 1878 by an eccentric Jewish merchant and philanthropist, Emanuel Rafael Belilios. It stood next to the City Hall (Dent Fountain, donated by the Dent & Co. to adorn the City Hall, is seen in the foreground), and opposite the Hongkong & Shanghai Bank. Belilios's profound admiration for the British Prime Minister Disraeli (Lord Beaconsfield) was expressed in the naming the arcade the Beaconsfield Arcade. It should not be confused with the old Government Building on the hill above (red-brick building, still standing; see p.340) which Belilios leased from the Government in 1880, and named also simply 'Beaconsfield'. Belilios died in 1905 but the name he bestowed on the arcade persisted for many years. Beaconsfield Arcade was replaced, after the Second World War, by the architecturally inferior Beaconsfield House; the latter was finally demolished in the 1990s.

Ping-Pong. The euphonious name 'Ping-Pong' is not, as one might imagine at the first sound, a new form of Chinese tea; on the contrary, it is thoroughly English game, invented by a small body of well-known cricketers. ... The implements ... are of the simplest kind. In addition to your own dining table, all you need are a couple of small racquets and half a dozen small white xylonite balls.

Hongkong Telegraph
6 November 1900

❖   *True; it was invented in the 1880s as a diversion for wet weekends.*

1901

**Hongkong Telegraph
5 January 1901**

The latest thing in delusions comes from the United States lunatic asylum. One of the inmates fancies that he is a poached egg, and he has been looking for some years for a piece of toast large enough to sit upon. Mats and khaki coloured carpets have been offered by sympathisers, but he is not taking any.

**Hongkong Telegraph
23 January 1901**

Death of Her Most Gracious Majesty
Queen Victoria
Queen of Great Britain and Ireland
Empress of India

Shortly after nine o'clock this morning the Royal Standard was half-masted at Government House, Headquarter House and on H.M. Ships *Barfleur* and *Tamar*, announcing the sad news that Her Majesty the Queen is dead.

**Hongkong Telegraph
29 January 1901**

KING EDWARD VII. The proclamation announcing the accession to the throne of England of King Edward the Seventh was made by H.E. the Governor [Sir Henry Blake, G.C.M.G.] to-day at 4 p.m. on the Cricket Ground.

**Hongkong Telegraph
20 February 1901**

We learn that tramways are at last to be an accomplished fact in Hongkong; all arangements have been concluded with the Government and that, within a year, a tramway will be running from Kennedy Town to Shaukiwan … the tramway is to be on the American overhead system and is to be an electric one.

❖   *In fact the tramway only started in 1904, when the reclamation of the Central Praya had been completed.*

Government House, c.1880

It must be put to the credit of Hong Kong's early civil administration that the construction of the governor's official residence was not their top priority.

Various buildings were built before the Government House. Indeed, the plans of the building were only prepared, by Charles St. G. Cleverly, in 1851. Its construction, on Upper Albert Road, was completed in 1855, by which time Hong Kong had its fourth governor, Sir John Bowring, the poet and writer of hymns. The original Government House, shown in this photograph, was simple in style, yet imposing and elegant in appearance.

It has undergone several major alterations during its existence, the two most radical being in 1900–1902, and during the Japanese occupation. In the latter a tower was added and parts of the building given Oriental features, so that today the Government House bears little or no resemblance to its original form.

Typhoon Shelters: At the meeting of the Hongkong and Kowloon Wharf and Godown Co., Ltd. held yesterday, the Chairman, the Hon. J.J. Keswick touched upon ... the necessity for the provision of typhoon shelters for craft during typhoons. Mr. Keswick said: 'The Causeway Bay shelter ... is barely sufficient to receive small craft alone, and quite inadequate for the hundreds, if not thousands, of cargo boats and other craft that need protection in the typhoon season.'

Hongkong Telegraph
15 March 1901

❖   *See Typhoon Shelter, p.182.*

Typhoon Shelter at Causeway Bay, Hong Kong Island, c.1920
The shelter is seen packed with craft of various sizes, from the smallest sampans to large fishing junks, all anchored in neatly arranged rows. The narrow, streamlined sampans with covers have been sometimes called 'slipper sampans' because of their superficial resemblance to a Chinese slipper. The shelter boom was constructed in 1883 to protect the local water craft in times of typhoons and severe tropical storms.

Hongkong Telegraph
2 April 1901

There seems to be a mania in the Colony ... for adding another storey to buildings. ... We should like to know if the P.W.D. [Public Works Department] officials inspect each building before permission to make the addition is granted, for several that we have seen look as though they were too flimsily constructed to carry the extra weight. It will be instructive to note how many of these heightened buildings collapse.

❖ *A week later, the newspaper reported the collapse of a house in Wan Chai. The mania still persists and buildings still collapse.*

Hongkong Telegraph
8 May 1901

Mr. A.J. Raymond yesterday afternoon laid the foundation stone of the new Synagogue in Robinson Road ... greatly indebted to the generosity of Mr. Jacob Sassoon ... and his brothers. The Synagogue when completed would be dedicated to the Jewish community in Hongkong, in memory of his beloved mother, Leah.

❖ *Only 90 years after the completion, the Ohel Leah Synagogue, this exceptionally fine Sephardic-style building, was the centre of a bitter and acrimonious dispute over its demolition and redevelopment. Happily, on this occasion the conservationists had won and the synagogue still stands defiantly, surrounded on all sides by gigantic buildings.*

They are telling the story in Japan of a member of one of the American legations who recently ordered a jinricksha under the impression that it was something to drink.

Hongkong Telegraph
10 July 1901

❖ *A hundred years later, perhaps it should be explained that it is the original name for the rickshaw.*

Sun Yat Sen: ... it will be remembered he reappeared in Canton last September as the organiser of the rebellion. It did not succeed, for his followers ran short of supplies, but not before they had 'in twenty days won six battles and taken possession of five towns.' [When last seen] Sun Yat Sen was once more absorbed in his studies — this time in Yokohama.

Hongkong Telegraph
19 July 1901

Dr Sun Yat-sen and Co-Revolutionaries, Hong Kong, c.1888
Seated from left to right: Yang Heiling, Sun Yat-sen, Chen Shaobai, and You Lie. They were nicknamed the 'Four Outlaws' or the 'Four Bandits' because, inspired by Sun Yat-sen, they were plotting to overthrow the outdated and corrupt Manchu Dynasty. The man standing behind the four is Guan Jingliang, Sun's fellow-medical student at the Hongkong College of Medicine, where Sun Yat-sen graduated as medical doctor in 1892. As the result of their efforts, the popular uprising toppled the Manchu Dynasty in 1911, Sun Yat-sen becoming the first President of the newly-established Republic.

**Hongkong Telegraph
15 August 1901**

THE COCHRANE STREET COLLAPSE: ... These collapses are becoming of much too frequent occurrence in Hongkong and when one takes a stroll through certain districts of the city one's only wonder is that they do not occur with every shower of rain.

❖ *Poor materials and workmanship, adding extra storeys, and the faults in construction aggravated by heavy rain, were responsible; in this case, with many fatal casualties.*

Chinese Etiquette
The composite postcard depicts four scenes of common forms of Chinese etiquette: on meeting on the street and in the house, and the 'kowtow' — kneeling or prostrating. The Chinese traditionally have an elaborate system of etiquette which is diligently practised at all levels of society. There are numerous rules of behaviour and politeness, which date back to 500 BC, the time of the great Chinese sage Confucius.

**Hongkong Telegraph
3 September 1901**

Kowtow: ... [in] the last few days a great amount of argument has arisen as to the true significance of the term *kowtow* ... The easiest way ... to describe *kowtowing* is to tell what takes place. A man of lower grade calling on a Chinese gentleman *chin chins* him by shaking hands with himself and bowing, but if that same man goes to beg a favour he goes as a suppliant and *kowtows* to his would-be patron by falling on his knees and bowing his head to the earth. To *kowtow* to the Emperor of China is quite another matter. Then the man … goes down on his knees … and touches the floor with his forehead nine times, still remaining on his knees with his eyes downcast. Two equals meeting, as a rule do not *kowtow* … but if one elects to kowtow, the other does the same.

❖　　*This snippet on 'kowtow' was prompted by the discussion in the Chinese press on whether Prince Chun should kowtow to the Kaiser (the German Emperor) during the Prince's visit to Berlin. One paper argued that kowtowing to the Kaiser would be equivalent to acknowledging oneself to be subject to the Kaiser. The Prince was due to visit Berlin to apologise for the murder of Baron von Ketteler, German ambassador in Peking, during the Boxer Rebellion.*

IGNORANCE IS BLISS — Examination of the statistics relating to the population of Hongkong reveals the extraordinarily high infant mortality amongst the Chinese community, says the *Hospital*. It seems hardly possible to believe that out of every 1,000 Chinese born in the Colony, only 72 survive the first year of existence. This is what, however, the reports on statistics show. *Definite sanitary regulations* are gradually improving the condition of Hongkong, but apparently it needs other steps also if the Chinese population is to be preserved.

Hongkong Telegraph
26 October 1901

❖　　*This does seem unbelievable! But even if the figures are exaggerated, it paints an appalling picture. Behind Hong Kong's apparent success and prosperity of the period, hides the ugly truth of poverty, malnutrition, and high infant mortality rate among the Chinese population.*

Kowloon Walled City: We do not know whose duty it is to look after Kowloon Walled City, but we presume that the official buildings within it, at least, belong now to the Government. If this is the case we fancy that a little attention had better be paid to them before it is too late. … Why could not the place be put in a fair state of preservation and reserved as a public recreation ground?

Hongkong Telegraph
11 November 1901

❖　　*It was not known at the time that its status would become ambiguous and that neither China nor Hong Kong would bother about it. Some 90 years later,* Hongkong Telegraph's *appeal has been answered and the place restored as a public recreation ground. See Kowloon Walled City, p.186.*

Kowloon Walled City, Kowloon, c.1910
The city was essentially a walled enclave located at the bottom of a hill; an extension wall can be seen going up the hill from the city's north-west corner. It is reputed to have been built in the 17th century AD as a military stronghold, though the walls were apparently added in 1847, possibly as a precautionary measure against the British who had recently taken possession of Hong Kong Island (in 1841). Kowloon Walled City proved to be an anomaly in the Sino-British agreement over the New Territories lease of 1898: it was excluded from the lease and the jurisdiction within the city remained ambiguous for many years. After gradually falling into decay, its walls gone, and its interior reduced to slums, the city, by joint agreement with China, was cleared in 1990–95, and converted into a public park, with many of its historic features restored.

Hongkong Telegraph
20 December 1901

The quantity of opium which arrived at Canton from Hongkong during the third quarter of the present year is returned at 2,108.66 piculs. The duty paid was upwards of 63,259 H.K.Tls [Taels].

❖ *This was legal and with a handsome revenue for the Chinese Government. One is bound to ask why was it necessary to fight two 'opium wars', kill hundreds if not thousands of people, cast a big shadow over the relations between the two nations for many years, and then legalize the infamous opium trade?*

RICKSHAW RATES

Hongkong Telegraph
24 December 1901

In Victoria with a single driver:

Quarter hour	5 cents
Half hour	10 cents
One hour	15 cents
Subsequent hour	10 cents

The City of Victoria extends from Mount Davis to Causeway Bay and up to the level of Robinson Road.

❖ *In 1903, six boundary stones were placed defining the limits of the City of Victoria. Now merely items of historical interest, the stones are still in position.*

City of Victoria Boundary Stone, 1970s

In the 19th and early 20th centuries when the original settlement on Hong Kong Island was still known as Victoria, and before the city had spread throughout the island, the limits of the City of Victoria were defined by law and marked by six identical stones placed along its boundary.

All six still exist, five in the original position and one moved slightly in 1978 for better display.

The stones are cut from granite, pointed on top, and stand between 1 m and 1.2 m high above the ground.

They carry the incised brief inscription, as depicted in the photograph. Sometime in the course of the city's expansion, the boundary stones have lost legal significance and are now preserved as relics of historical interest.

Perhaps some readers may be interested in locating these stones, guided by the following clues to their position:

- Playground on the waterfront, north of Victoria Road.
- West pavement of Wong Nai Chung Road (shown here).
- East end of Bowen Road.
- Old Peak Road, near its junction with Tregunter Path.
- Hatton Road.
- East pavement of Pok Fu Lam Road.

1902

**Hongkong Telegraph
3 January 1902**

Yesterday's function at Government House … will, we hope, mark a certain turning point in the history of the Colony. … The presentation of the address and the speech by Dr. Ho Kai show very plainly that the Chinese Community have at last come to appreciate the fact that it is not the intention or object of the Government to oppress the Chinese at all, but that it wished to work hand in hand with them for the benefit of the Chinese, the Europeans and the general prosperity of the Colony.

**Hongkong Telegraph
21 January 1902**

The Island of Lantao, from all accounts, is about the only spot round Hongkong where large game can be met with. Mr. Hughes, of Messrs. Hughes and Hough, latest achievement was shooting a deer there last Sunday. We believe it was a wild deer, and there is no truth in the rumour that a Chinese is bringing action for damages on account of one of his sheep being shot.

❖ *Sheep were never raised or kept in Hong Kong (or Lantao); but shooting a wild deer, a beautiful and gentle animal, was despicable enough, though the* Hongkong Telegraph *did not appear to think so. Fortunately, we have since progressed sufficiently to prohibit all hunting in Hong Kong.*

**Hongkong Telegraph
30 January 1902**

The Empress Dowager: Amongst the celebrated personages of history there is no doubt that the Empress Dowager will be accorded a prominent position. Few women in the history of the world have done more to stir nations than she. … At the present time, with the fate of China trembling … she occasions the attention of the whole civilized world and can, by throwing her influence into one scale or the other, become, from the European point of view, an immense power for good or evil.

**Hongkong Telegraph
18 March 1902**

The vehicles licensed in the Colony during 1901 were: Rickshas, 1175 for Hongkong, 25 for Quarry Bay and 140 for Kowloon; Chairs, 556 for Hongkong and 24 for the Hill district [the Peak]; Gharies,* 7. The licenses issued to drivers and bearers numbered 11,085.

---

* Ghary: (Hindi origin) is a four-wheeled carriage, usually horse-drawn.

Ci-Xi, or T'zu-Hsi, (1834–1908), Empress Dowager of China, c.1898
A formidable force in Chinese history, the Empress Dowager began her career as a concubine of the Emperor Xianfeng, and on his death became regent. Opposed to reforms and modernization, she seized power from her nephew, Emperor Guangxu, in 1898. An inveterate intriguer, she acquired the nickname of 'Old Buddha'.

Hongkong Telegraph
21 March 1902

PRAYING FOR RAIN: [In Canton] The officials still offer sacrificial prayers to the gods for rain. This has been going on for some weeks. The butchers have been forbidden to kill pigs but the subordinate officials have been kept quiet by gifts, and so the daily consumption of pork has not been reduced. The country round Canton is very dry and only the immediate coming of heavy rains can avert a rice famine.

The 'Rain Prayer' Stone, Sheung Shui, New Territories, 1978

The Rain Prayer Stone is located on Top Hill, in Sheung Shui Wah Shan, the New Territories. It is a flat, dressed granite slab measuring 60 cm high and 32 cm wide, with Chinese inscriptions carved on both faces, both sides and top. They state that the stone was erected in 1839 during the reign of Emperor Tao Kuang, and dedicated to the god of 'rain and cloud'. It is reputed to have been placed by the Liu clan during a particularly dry season which threatened the crops. Since then, special ceremonies have from time to time been conducted near the stone, with prayers for rain.

POPULATION OF CHINA: According to a Japanese journal the latest census returns compiled by the Chinese Government show that the population of China is now estimated at 417,947,325 exclusive of Manchuria.

Hongkong Telegraph
29 April 1902

SANITARY BOARD NOTICE: In view of the PREVALENCE OF CHOLERA in Hongkong the public are hereby warned against the consumption of OVER RIPE FRUIT, UNCOOKED VEGETABLES and UNBOILED MILK or WATER.

Hongkong Telegraph
17 May 1902

FIRE BRIGADE: A circular was sent round a few days ago requesting the members of the Fire Brigade, who were in favour of one dollar for every fire they attended, to sign it, but it came back without any signatures.

Hongkong Telegraph
8 July 1902

Members of the Fire Brigade, Hong Kong, c.1880
Four young volunteer members of the fire brigade pose for the photograph. The first Hong Kong Fire Brigade, consisting entirely of volunteers — European and Chinese — was formed in 1856; it was ill-equipped and inexperienced. It took several disastrous fires to awaken the Government to the necessity of employing a fully-trained professional fire brigade, which was finally established, in 1895, at first under the wing of the Police Department.

Hongkong Telegraph
1 August 1902

MR. RUDYARD KIPLING was offered a Coronation Honour but refused it.

❖ *This is surprising, for Kipling was known as the champion of the British Empire and everything that went with it.*

Hongkong Telegraph
4 August 1902

IN THE TRACK OF THE TYPHOON:- The rain is blinding and the wind deafening … [as] you are watching the roaring water spurring up from the choked traps. … The lake outside Watson's is extending along Queen's Road. … close to the premises of Messrs. Lane, Crawford & Co. is lying a heap of dripping bamboo fallen from a building in the course of erection. … The Race Course is flooded to about four feet. … Land slips occurred in many parts. … altogether, Hongkong will have cause to remember the typhoon of August 2, 1902.

❖ *A good description, but bad though it was, this was not one of the worst typhoons to hit Hong Kong in its recorded history. The three worst ones were in 1874, 1906, and 1937, separated curiously enough, by 31 and 32 years' intervals.*

Hongkong Telegraph
13 August 1902

GLOBE-TROTTING M.P.'s: One of the misfortunes of the Far East is that when globe-trotting M.P.'s who have touched at Chinese … ports for a few hours return home they either write books on 'the Orient' or become perfect bores in the House [of Commons] whenever they can get a chance of dropping a word edgeways to show their travelled knowledge.

These 'globe-trotting' M.P.'s were frequent visitors in Hong Kong before its return to China.

Hongkong Telegraph
15 September 1902

Zoroastrian New Year: Hongkong is certainly a very cosmopolitan city, enjoying the benefit of being the home of useful men with different customs and religions. … Each is of service to the other, all exchanging knowledge. … Though … most of us are not holding any celebration to-day, the Parsees have their new year's day to keep up, and we hope they will enjoy many returns of it. … This is the 1,272 year of Yezdizerd.

❖ *From the very start and to this day, the Parsee community has been active in business and other spheres of Hong Kong life.*

The Opium Trade: A meeting of the Society for the suppression of the Opium trade has been held at Lambeth Palace, the Archbishop of Canterbury presiding. The meeting stigmatized the opium trade as a blot on the English name, and an injustice to China.

Hongkong Telegraph
11 October 1902

Leprosy in Hongkong: Leprosy is said to have been imported into the Colony, and two cases are reported to have been notified in the vicinity of Possession Street.

Hongkong Telegraph
5 November 1902

❖ *It is likely that the disease was present in Hong Kong before but was not detected. It continued to increase until an isolation and treatment centre had been set up on Hei Ling Chau (island). The centre functioned until 1970s when it was finally closed, leprosy being no longer a problem.*

The Currency Question: On the motion of Mr. Ho Fook, seconded by Mr. Kum Fook, it was resolved that the Government be requested to take steps to inquire into the advisability or, otherwise, of adopting a gold standard for this Colony.

Hongkong Telegraph
13 December 1902

❖ *Because of its trade with China, Hong Kong currency used silver as its standard. The above inquiry was prompted by a catastrophic and totally unexpected fall of silver earlier that year. In the event, the silver standard of the Hong Kong currency was retained.*

At noon to-day the eagle flag of Germany floated out above the new German Club in Kennedy Road … built in three storeys … lighted throughout by gas … on each floor there is wide verandah from where an excellent view of the harbour can be obtained.

Hongkong Telegraph
31 December 1902

❖ *Traders from Germany were active in Hong Kong from the earliest time. In spite of two setbacks during the two world wars, when their trade in Hong Kong ceased completely, they are still active in Hong Kong today. See Club Germania, p.194.*

Club Germania, Kennedy Road, Mid-Levels, Hong Kong Island, c.1910
This imposing 5-storey German Club bears testimony to the significant growth of the German mercantile community in Hong Kong before the First World War (1914–18). Club Germania opened on Kennedy Road in December 1902, the club's two earlier premises were located on Queen's Road East and on Wyndham Street. With the decline of the German trading activity, as a result of two world wars, the club eventually closed, its building becoming part of St. Joseph's College.

1903

Hongkong Telegraph
19 January 1903

A clip from 'HONGKONG AS SEEN BY OTHERS':- In the long experience of England in governing colonies a form of government has been evolved ... known as Crown Colony Government. Its essential feature is the entire absence of any popular element in the administration and the direct control exercised by the Colonial Office in London over all acts of the local authorities; the theory on which this is based is this, that, whereas a representative government in Hongkong which rested on a general franchise would place the British residents under the heel of the Chinese, a franchise which extended only to white British subjects would put the mass of the population and the great majority of the taxpayers at the mercy of a handful of merchants, and that under such circumstances the best way to secure honest and efficient administration is to place the control of affairs in the hands of a distant body of trained officials.

A few days ago the new guns at Belcher's Fort were fired for the first time, with the result that a large number of windows were shattered in Kennedy Town.

Hongkong Telegraph
22 January 1903

❖   *Hong Kong had two Belcher's Batteries, Upper and Lower. The note probably refers to the Upper Battery which had a huge 10-inch gun — almost certain to shatter, when fired, the windows in Kennedy Town directly below. The barrel of this big gun was discovered when Belcher Gardens were built after the war and was displayed there. After Belcher Gardens had been redeveloped in the late 1990s, the gun was moved to the new Museum of Coastal Defence at Lei Yue Mun.*

ARRESTS IN HONGKONG: In consequence of information received, European and Chinese detectives proceeded to No. 20 D'Aguilar Street … and there effected certain arrests. … we hear that some two hundred recruits were raised in Hongkong, that several thousand suits of uniform have been manufactured … and that a quantity of arms, ammunitions, canned provisions and general food supplies have been exported from Hongkong to the neighbourhood of Canton. … It is said that the plan of action was arranged to take place tonight when the inhabitants of Canton would be proceeding, according to custom, to the pagodas and other places of worship.

Hongkong Telegraph
28 January 1903

❖   *It must be stressed that the Hong Kong authorities were not sympathetic to the budding revolutionary movement in China.*

**Hongkong Telegraph
21 February 1903**

From the Editorial:
NEW TERRITORY. It will be a matter of some satisfaction to the rate-payers that the New Territory, until now considered as a white elephant for Hongkong since its acquisition from China five years ago, has at last come in for a genuine share of attention from investors in landed property. … Hitherto it has proved a burdensome luxury to Hongkong, but there are those who are confident that our New Territory is bound to develop to such an extent as not only to be able to pay its own way, but be a decided commercial advantage.

The Island House, Tai Po, c.1910

When the New Territories were leased to Britain in 1898, the first accommodation provided for the new administration was in the form of temporary matsheds hastily erected in April 1899 on a hill above Tai Po Village. Perhaps some uncertainty was still felt about the new lease, for permanent buildings were not constructed until several years later.

One of the first was the Island House at Tai Po, shown in this photograph, which stands alone on what used to be an islet, but is now connected to the mainland by a causeway.

The house was built in about 1905 to serve as residence for senior government officers administering the newly leased territory. The building took more than a year to complete, being interrupted by a strike of local workers employed on its construction.

It is an elegant two-storey house with colonial-style open verandahs, and is constructed in red brick covered for the most part in white plaster. At the corner of its main wing, a tower leads into a loft from which in the old days a beacon used to light the way for vessels using the Tolo Channel.

Set in its charming garden, the Island House had served for many decades as the residence of the Commissioner, later retitled the Secretary for the New Territories.

Sometime in the late 1980s, it seemed to have lost favour with the secretaries as a place of residence, and was allocated for the use of the World Wildlife Fund.

PLAGUE AT GOVERNMENT HOUSE: A case of plague was reported from Government House yesterday afternoon. Of course, it was a case occurring in the coolie quarter, and steps were immediately taken by the Sanitary Board authorities to thoroughly cleanse and disinfect the premises. The Government House party removed to their Peak residence to-day.

Hongkong Telegraph
25 March 1903

'It's a mistake to suppose that "joss" is a Chinese word,' says a retired ship's carpenter to a representative of a home paper. 'I've travelled a good bit in the Orient … and among the odds and ends of interesting information I picked up was a knockout of the genuineness of "joss" as a Chinese word. … A Chinese priest in Hankow told me there was no such word in Chinese. He explained that the word was a corruption of the Spanish word 'Dios' [God], and had come into use through the missionaries. Many early missionaries, he said were Spanish priests.'

❖   *This is correct. The term does not appear to have been used before the settlement of the Portuguese in Macao. The same applies to 'mandarin' which also owes its origin to the Portuguese.*

Hongkong Telegraph
29 April 1903

It will be of interest to know that the once familiar Vestal monument at Happy Valley … has been moved from its original position to a distance of about 30 feet … this has been necessitated by the utilization of the ground by the Hongkong Electric Tramway. We are also informed that the Kuhlan monument … will soon be removed to a site in the Happy Valley cemetery. … the Vestal monument, dedicated to those who lost their lives whilst in service on the China Station in H.M.S. Vestal, was erected in 1845.

❖   *See Kuhlan Monument, p.198.*

Hongkong Telegraph
5 May 1903

With regards to the electric tramways at Hongkong … the great disadvantage … as far as the public is concerned, is that its alignment is restricted to those roads in the vicinity of the harbour. … It is intended to have separate cars for Europeans and natives, which will run independent of each other.

❖   *The service finally opened, from Kennedy Town to Shau Kei Wan, in 1904, but the discriminatory arrangements were dropped.*

Hongkong Telegraph
28 May 1903

'Kuhlan' Monument, Morrison Hill Road, Happy Valley, Hong Kong Island, c.1900

The monument, seen on the right, was erected in the late 1850s to commemorate the men lost in anti-piracy operation, in 1855, by the combined forces of the American steam frigate *Powhatan* and the British sloop *Rattler*. The two ships engaged and destroyed a large stronghold of pirates off Kuhlan Island (now spelled Gaolan), about 110 miles south-west of Hong Kong. The fighting was fierce with large losses inflicted on the pirates. Four men from the *Rattler* and five from the *Powhatan* were killed in the engagement. In a rare tribute to the adversary, it was admitted that through their cause was evil, the pirates had fought with great courage. The monument to the men of HMS *Vestal*, lost in a similar operation ten years previously, was erected in 1845 not far from the Kuhlan monument. Both monuments were later moved to the Happy Valley Cemetery.

Hongkong Telegraph
6 June 1903

From the Editorial:

The Kowloon-Canton Railway has, for the past twenty years or more, been the subject of report and comment, yet ... the scheme which was to have given such a fillip to the development of our township on the mainland has not yet attained the embryonic stage.

❖   *Indeed! It would take another eight years before the trains would start.*

As an elite residential district, Conduit Road ... has come very much into favour since it was opened about three years ago. It was not long since that we announced the sale of a plot of land for a private garden. Another lot with an area of 3,576 square feet has been applied for and will be sold. ... The annual rental of the lot is $8, and it will be sold at an upset price of $180.

❖   *It was in fact sold for $200(!) to Sir Paul Chater, Hong Kong's financial giant and philanthropist. On it was built a palatial residence which he called the Marble Hall.*

Hongkong Telegraph
18 July 1903

Sir Paul Chater's Mansion, Conduit Road, c.1930
This palatial residence, called 'Marble Hall', standing directly above the central business district of Hong Kong, was built for Sir Catchick Paul Chater, the doyen of Hong Kong's merchant princes — a fitting abode for one who had given so liberally to all that was calculated to uphold the territory's success.

Born in Calcutta in 1846 of Armenian parents and said to be of noble descent, C. P. Chater came to Hong Kong in 1864 to take up a modest position as a bank clerk. He resigned shortly afterwards to start his own business as an exchange and bullion broker. Ambitious and extremely capable, he branched out into real estate; from then on his rise in the commercial world of Hong Kong was nothing short of brilliant.

Chater embarked upon a wide variety of projects and commercial undertakings — all invariably successful. In 1887 he originated the Praya Reclamation Scheme, probably the most important factor in Hong Kong's expansion as a business centre.

He was a prominent philanthropist and public benefactor, and a keen patron of the arts. Few men in Hong Kong's history have done so much for the commercial advancement of the colony as Sir Catchick Paul Chater. Many of Hong Kong's prosperous public companies owe their inception to his foresight and courage. He died in 1926, greatly honoured and respected.

Marble Hall was built around 1900 and stood on its site for half a century. It was demolished in the 1950s when the Mid-Levels succumbed to high-rise building development.

Hongkong Telegraph
5 August 1903

Hongkong's troubles are to be increased next month by the addition of a new daily newspaper with the voluminous title of *The Morning Post of South China*. A journalist from Japan is the editor. We sympathise deeply with Hongkong. It will soon be as bad as Shanghai in this respect.

❖ *A touch of jealousy perhaps on the part of the* Hongkong Telegraph*? In fact, the first issue of the* South China Morning Post*, as it would be called, appeared on November 6, 1903.*

Hongkong Telegraph
19 August 1903

Here is a study in natural history from the China Times:- Ten thousand ducks have been sent into the fields in the district of Chin-Kiang for ridding the country of locusts. It is reported that the experiment has been successful and the locusts are rapidly disappearing. So are the ducks.

Hongkong Telegraph
20 August 1903

The *Times* correspondent at Seoul describes the situation created by the rivalry between Russia and Japan as very serious, and the extension of Russian activity into Korea as most ominous.

❖ *Rumbles of a conflict to come. One year later the two nations would be at war.*

Hongkong Telegraph
28 August 1903

From the Editorial:
Before the following lines appear in print, the inaugural meeting of the Hongkong Society for the Prevention of Cruelty to Animals will have been held this afternoon.

❖ *An important milestone in the history of Hong Kong.*

Hongkong Telegraph
29 August 1903

An examination open to all qualified natural-born British subjects, for appointment in the Civil Service of India or for Eastern cadetship in the Colonial Services … will take place in London commencing on …

❖ *The key words are 'natural-born'. The essence of the colonial policy and mentality was the fact that in practice a distinction was made between a natural-born British subject and a mere possessor of a British passport. Although this distinction became less pronounced after the war, it came back with full force, in the 1980s, when more than two million holders of the Hong Kong British passport found themselves second-class citizens.*

Some American Impressions of Hongkong:- Hongkong can boast some magnificent buildings four or five storeys high. ... Queen's Road Central and Des Voeux Road in the heart of the business district are thoroughfares of which many European and American cities would be proud. ... However, while the buildings are massive, they are in many instances bizarre in their architecture. The style is glaringly modern. ... Instead of a noble simplicity, the Hongkong taste seems to run to frills and furbelows. ... The Hongkong Club, which is really the only club in the city of importance ... is extremely exclusive. It is harder for a camel to pass through the eye of a needle than for an average American to obtain admission.

Hongkong Telegraph
10 September 1903

Wong Yau, a farmer charged at the magistracy this morning with being in unlawful possession of 24 taels of raw opium, and offering a bribe of $2.60 to a constable, admitted the indictment and explained with regard to the second that as the policeman had worn his shoes out when chasing him he offered the money to buy a new pair.

Hongkong Telegraph
6 November 1903

A newspaper is born! On 6 November 1903, the first issue of the South China Morning Post *was published in Hong Kong. The* SCMP, *as it became widely known, would outlive its contemporaries, the* Hongkong Telegraph, *the* Hongkong Daily Press, *and the* China Mail, *to become one of the greatest newspapers in the Far East. It is still going strong ... Here is a paragraph from its first Editorial:-*

The modern newspaper has taken the place of the old-time ambassador. The cynic has said the ambassador is sent abroad to lie for the good of his country. The newspaper is sent abroad to tell the truth for the good of humanity. Whereas the ambassador, by means of weary months of negotiation, may make or prevent a war; a newspaper by means of a few trenchant articles, so be that they have truth behind them, will rouse a public to resent aggression, to reform abuses, to mould the policy of governments. Such is the power of the modern newspaper.

South China Morning Post
6 November 1903

**Hongkong Telegraph
12 November 1903**

THE SUPREME COURT: A granite block, bearing a suitable inscription in letters of gold, has been swung plumb and laid true into its appointed place. In a hollow in the great stone were placed, for the edification of archaeologists of some future generation, copies of the newspapers of Hongkong and specimens of each silver and bronze coin of the Colony, of the latest minting. The official ceremony [was] performed by … the Governor with the aid of the traditional silver trowel.

❖ *It would take another nine years before the Supreme Court would open. Historians and archivists should note the presence of the time capsule for if and when this great building is pulled down, the contents of the capsule should prove to be invaluable historic relics.*

Supreme Court Building, Statue Square, Central District, Hong Kong Island, c.1920

The Courts of Law began operating immediately when the Colony was established, remaining in temporary premises until the early 20th century. The foundation stone of the Supreme Court Building was laid in 1903, though the construction was not completed until 1912. The architect's plans were prepared by the London firm of Webb and Bell and its construction supervised by the local Public Works Department. The result was the splendidly imposing building seen today facing Statue Square. The style of the building is said to belong to the 'English School', but features the classical elements of tall granite Ionic columns and an armorial balustrade. It is surmounted by a graceful dome and four pinnacles at each corner. After housing the Law Courts for some seven decades, the building became, in 1985, the official home of Hong Kong's Legislative Council.

1904

KOWLOON HOTEL: This Hotel is situated in a quiet locality ... and surrounded by a delightful garden. It is an ideal place of residence. The building stands on an eminence, giving a magnificent view of the Harbour and the City of Victoria. It is within easy access of the Kowloon wharves, where the principal mail steamers disembark passengers and from where there is a regular ferry service to Hongkong.

South China Morning Post **6 January 1904**

Kowloon Hotel, Tsim Sha Tsui, Kowloon, c.1925
The 7-storey, modern-looking Kowloon Hotel was in the centre of the busiest and the most active area of Kowloon, and was deservedly popular. It was completed in 1923 and was still there after the Second World War (1945), but gave way to redevelopment in the 1960s.

Ah Ting thought that pigs and men would make good companions on his steamer. He was fined $25 or in default a month in gaol for carrying pigs on a passenger boat.

South China Morning Post **20 January 1904**

**South China
Morning Post
10 February 1904**

THE WAR, Official Declaration: The Japanese Consulate has kindly forwarded the following letter for publication:- 'To the Editor of the S.C.M.P.: Dear Sir, I beg to inform you that this morning I have received the telegram from our Government to the effect that war has been formally declared against Russia by His Imperial Japanese Majesty on the 10th February 1904.' Signed Masaichi Noma, Consul for Japan.

❖   *The war was a disaster for Russia, which lost its foothold in South Manchuria.*

**South China
Morning Post
20 February 1904**

Legislative Council: Letter from Rt. Hon. Alfred Lyttleton, Secretary of State for the Colonies:-

'I have recently had under my consideration the question of the amount of salary paid to the Governors of first class Crown Colonies, and I have come to the conclusion that the emoluments ... Are not sufficient to allow of their supporting the dignity of their position. ... [I] invite the Council to vote an increase in the Governor's salary ... from £5,000 to £6,000 a year. ...'

❖   *It must have been of some comfort to know that Hong Kong was regarded as a first class colony. Incidentally, it may be assumed that Lyttleton Road, in the Mid-Levels, was named after the Rt. Hon. Alfred Lyttleton.*

**South China
Morning Post
22 February 1904**

A certain solicitor defended a Chinese who was charged with assault. After the case was finished the solicitor, who had been successful in reducing the ... sentence to a mere trifle, entered the prisoner's room ... only to find that he had defended the wrong prisoner.

**South China
Morning Post
7 March 1904**

PHILHARMONIC CONCERT: It was a small but highly appreciative audience that assembled in the St. Andrew's Hall on Saturday evening to listen to the excellent programme ... of this recently resuscitated Society for its first concert of the season.

❖   *The Hongkong Philharmonic Society was first formed in 1895, and the society's orchestra gave its first concert the same year at the 'Theatre Royal' of the City Hall, under the baton of George P. Lammert of the well-known firm of auctioneers. This early society had absolutely no connection with the present Hong Kong Philharmonic Society and Orchestra, which began after the Second World War as a branch of the Sino-British Club.*

LEGISLATIVE COUNCIL, PEAK RESIDENTIAL AREA: The Attorney-General moved the first reading of the Bill entitled An Ordinance for the Reservation of a Residential Area in the Hill District. … This measure has as its object the reservation of that portion of the Island of Hongkong commonly known 'The Peak' as a place for the residence of persons other than Chinese. The reservation of this district is desirable in order that a healthy place of residence may be preserved for all those who are accustomed to a temperate climate.

South China Morning Post **29 March 1904**

❖ *Thinly disguised as a health measure, a more outrageous example of racial discrimination can hardly be imagined. See also* Hongkong Telegraph *31 July 1888.*

The Peak, Hong Kong Island, c.1890
The photograph shows a portion of the Peak still sparsely developed. Scattered below the slopes of Mount Kellett are several residential buildings, sometimes described as 'palatial'. On the left, a handsome building, is the Chalet. The long-terraced house in the centre is the Hillside; below it and to the right — the small tallish building is the Peak Church (also known as the Chapel.) At the top, the extreme left, is the Peak Police Station, on Mount Gough. The early settlement of the Peak, in the late 1860s, was slow but gained momentum after the opening, in 1888, of the Peak Tram. Restrictions imposed at the time on the Chinese residing on the Peak made it an exclusive European residential enclave.

South China Morming Post **4 April 1904**

PRAYA EXTENSION: As the works have now practically reached conclusion, it may be useful to give a brief account of their origin and progress. The Praya Reclamation ... was initiated by Sir C.P. Chater ... under the Ordinance No. 16 of 1889. ... The actual construction ... was commenced in February 1890, so that about fourteen years have been occupied in its execution. ... [it extended] the entire frontage of the business part of the City ... the whole surface of the old Praya wall had to be raised ... the total area dealt with was 65 acres, and the total weight of materials used in the works ... 3,500,000 tons. ... In addition to the sum expended upon the Reclamation itself ... about $1,000,000 has been spent in the erection of buildings upon it.

❖ *This was the second large reclamation of the Central District.*

Central Praya Reclamation, c.1902

An early visitor wrote about Hong Kong in 1853: 'An unproductive mountainous, lumpish isle ... As there was no level space elsewhere, the English have built their town of Victoria along the seafront ... the town struggles to the length of three miles; breadth or length it has none, being backed by rugged precipices and mountains.'

It was clear from the start that if the new town was to have any substance and prospects of development, more flat land would have to be reclaimed from the sea. With that in view, Governor Sir John Bowring proposed a modest-scale reclamation in 1855. The idea was shelved when a strong objection was voiced by the traders, most of whom owned seafront lots each with its own pier; reclamation would place their lots inland and entail building new piers. However, the reclamation went ahead in 1868 and was completed in 1873. This was the First Reclamation Scheme which pushed the new praya to the present Des Voeux Road.

It was not until 1890 that the much larger Second Reclamation Scheme was begun. The work lasted 14 years and when completed, in 1904, 65 acres had been reclaimed.

The waterfront had moved on the newly reclaimed land, granting the waterfront a new and imposing look.

The photograph shows the Second Reclamation Scheme during its concluding stages.

The estimated population of Hongkong for 1903 was 325,631. There were 1,034 births and 6,185 deaths, 1,252 of which were from plague.

South China Morning Post **18 April 1904**

ALEXANDRA BUILDING: Another handsome addition to Hongkong's buildings is now free from the hands of the contractor ... built by Hongkong Land Investment. ... The building is worthy of its fine position. It stands on the triangular portion of reclaimed land between the converging Chater and Des Voeux roads. ... The building is surrounded by open verandahs designed in a restrained style of Renaissance ... a welcome addition to the higher class of architectural building in the Colony.

South China Morning Post **4 May 1904**

Alexandra Building, Central, District, Hong Kong Island, c.1910
Alexandra Building was one of the several great imposing buildings completed between 1899 and 1905 on the newly reclaimed land after the major Praya Reclamation. Named after Queen Alexandra, wife of the reigning monarch Edward VII, it was completed in 1904 and stood in the triangular space formed by the converging Chater and Des Voeux Roads; it was five storeys high in the colonial style with arched verandahs. Less than 50 years later, in 1952, it was demolished to be replaced by a larger and more modern Alexandra House. The second fared no better and was demolished in 1975 to be replaced by an even higher and more modern Alexandra House. One is bound to wonder how long will the third one last?

South China Morning Post 2 July 1904

The Chinese invention of paper has received additional confirmation from Sven Hedin, who in his recent journey found Chinese paper that dates back to the second half of the third century after Christ. This lay buried in the sand of the Gobi desert. ... According to Chinese sources, the paper was manufactured as early as the second millennium before the Christian era. The characters of the newly-found manuscripts made it probable that paper making from vegetable fibres was already an old art in the third century A.D.

❖ *Sven Hedin was a famous Swedish explorer of Central Asia in the early 20ᵗʰ century.*

South China Morning Post 30 July 1904

THE ELECTRIC TRAMWAY — AN OFFICIAL OPENING: Shortly after 10 o'clock this morning an interesting little ceremony took place on the Praya ... when Mrs. P.H.H. Jones [wife of the Director of Public Works] drove the first public car over a length of electric railway line. ... Mrs. Jones took her seat at the front of the car and having been photographed ... she turned a lever somewhat too far ... with the result there was a flash and the car jumped forward — and the carriage slipped away towards Wanchai.

South China Morning Post 15 August 1904

A correspondent writes regarding the experience with the electric tram ... he waited eagerly nearly a quarter of an hour opposite the City Hall for a car to go out to Shaukiwan, but seeing no car rolling up he got tired of waiting and took a ricksha. On the way he met six cars coming west all in a string, but not one going east.

❖ *For those of us still using trams, this sounds all too familiar!*

South China Morning Post 16 September 1904

Considerable amusement was aroused among passengers near the Central Market this morning by a Lilliputian ricksha-coolie lustily shouting to a tram-car to get out of his way!

Tramcar, Hongkong Tramways Co., c.1905
The Tramways Company began operating in July 1904 using single-deck cars. The one pictured in this photograph was used for first-class passengers and had an enclosed centre portion with two benches running lengthways. Although originally it was intended to have three classes, by the time the trams were put into operation, two different designs were used for first and third classes. The familiar double-decker trams were introduced in 1912, at first with an open top, but eventually, in 1925, fully enclosed. The lower deck was for third-class passengers and the upper deck for first class, with different fares; this distinction was abolished in 1972. See also *Hongkong Telegraph*, 3 July 1912.

GOVERNMENT NOTIFICATION: It is hereby notified that on and after the 30th October 1904, the time of 120 EAST LONGITUDE will be adopted in the Colony. The effect of this will be that local time will be advanced by 23' 18".

❖ *By this Hong Kong, in effect, has adopted Zone Time. Each zone is an area of the earth bounded by two lines of longitude 15 degrees apart, within which time is the same and differs from that of the adjacent areas by one hour. It was already in use in China but not in Kwangtung. By this act, Hong Kong had adopted zone time independently.*

South China Morning Post
17 October 1904

Murray Parade Ground, 1881
Named after General Sir George Murray, Master-General of Ordnance, the parade ground occupied roughly the area on which the present Cheung Kong Center stands.

A parade ground in the middle of Central, Hong Kong, on which garrison troops were often seen parading, was undoubtedly a splendid sign of the British Imperial presence. The parading troops in this photograph, with an officer in charge on horseback, were most likely the 27th (Iniskilling) Regiment on Foot, which served in Hong Kong from 1879 to 1882. Major Alan Harfield, an eminent military historian, writes in his book *British and Indian Armies on the China Coast, 1785–1985*, that the regiment's history 'contains little of note for 1880 but during 1881 it records that the regiment was given its annual inspection by Major-General E. W. Donovan, who was the Commander of the Forces in China … .' It is more than likely that this inspection is the parade depicted in this photograph. The two buildings in the background are still there. On the left is St John's Cathedral, built in 1849. On the right is the four-storey red-brick building on top of Battery Path. At the time the photograph was taken, it belonged to a wealthy Jewish merchant, E. R. Belilios, who named it Beaconsfield, apparently as a sign of his admiration for Disraeli (Lord Beaconsfield). See also French Mission Building, p.340.

PROJECTED CASINO IN MACAO: For some time past it has been known that negotiations were proceeding with the Portuguese authorities for the establishing of a casino ... in the Colony of Macao. ... The friendly relations ... between the two Colonial Governments is our excuse for the suggestion that representations might be made by the British authorities to the Portuguese Government in order that the founding of the casino at Macao may never be eventuated.

South China Morning Post **22 October 1904**

❖ *Gambling seems to be considered a worse vice than opium!*

NEW MILITARY HOSPITAL ON BOWEN ROAD: Situated on one of the most prominent sites in Hongkong, amid a wealth of subtropical vegetation, and commanding a beautiful view of the harbour and surrounding district, the new Military Hospital in Bowen Road should form one of the chief features in Hongkong. For some twenty months work has been progressing.

South China Morning Post **17 December 1904**

Military Hospital, Bowen Road, Mid-Levels, Hong Kong Island, c.1925
Often referred to simply as the Bowen Road Hospital, this splendid group of buildings in red brick, commanding an excellent view of the harbour, was built in 1903–06 for the use of the garrison and was officially opened on 1 July 1907. It consisted of two blocks, each three storeys high, containing wards and the central, administrative block, all clearly seen in this photograph. The total number of beds was about 150. Even during the Japanese occupation, 1942–45, part of the hospital was used for the sick British prisoners-of-war requiring hospital care. The hospital continued after the war until 1967, when the new military hospital in Kowloon replaced it. The Bowen Road building was then handed over to the Government and converted into school premises.

1905

South China Morning Post 3 February 1905

Mr. Stanley Gibbons, the famous stamp collector, was among the passengers who arrived yesterday by the *Sachsen*.

❖ *He began his renowned stamp collection business in 1856, and today the Stanley Gibbons Stamp Catalogue remains the bible of stamp collectors all over the world.*

South China Morning Post 1 March 1905

The firm of F. Blackhead and Co. … will celebrate its fiftieth anniversary to-day … it calls for more than a passing remark … Were old Mr. Schwartzkopf, the founder of the house of Blackhead, to come back to earth he would be struck dumb with amazement at the vast strides which science has evolved. … Sailing up and down these rugged … shores in the early forties … he realised the difficulty of obtaining ships' supplies in a country … bitterly opposed to foreign intrusion … Whampoa was then a place of great importance … the seat of a large portion of the foreign trade … as foreign vessels were not allowed to go further up the Pearl River. It is from this start in Whampoa that the firm of F. Blackhead and Co. dates its jubilee.

❖ *The very enterprising German firm was mentioned earlier in* Hongkong Telegraph, *17 January 1889. See also Tsim Sha Tsui Bay, p.13, for 'Blackhead Point'.*

South China Morning Post 11 April 1905

China appears to possess advantages for the concealment of persons. … Sun Yat Sen, the professional organiser of revolution in the Celestial Empire, has a price of $50,000 set on his head by a grateful country, and finds his life in hourly danger in the United States, England, and Europe generally … The only country he is safe in is China. 'Once in a place like Canton, the rest is easy. The population is so large that one is lost among the millions', he says in an interview.

❖ *Indeed, Dr Sun Yat-sen was kidnapped in London and kept in the Chinese Embassy. He would have been sent to China to an almost certain execution, but for the intervention of his long-time friend Dr Cantlie.*

Not many weeks since we referred to the construction of roads in the New Territory, and we now understand that a new thoroughfare, now in the initial stage of survey, will connect Castle Peak with Shataukok, a large market city just over the border, near Starling Inlet in Mirs Bay. The road will be some twenty-one miles in length.

❖ *This is the old road that would pass through Yuen Long and Fanling; the road connecting Kowloon and Castle Peak had already been constructed.*

Hongkong Telegraph
12 May 1905

Government notification has been issued to the effect that the street along the west side of the new harbour office, lying between Wing Lok Street and Connaught Road Central, will in future be designated Rumsey Street.

❖ *Named after Commander Robert Rumsey, R.N. (Ret.), the Harbour Master. He arrived in Hong Kong in 1885 to serve as assistant harbour master; retired in 1903. One would have thought his 18 years of service had hardly merited a street named after his name.*

Hongkong Telegraph
13 May 1905

Letter from Governor Matthew Nathan to Major-General Gascoigne:- Sir, I have the honour to transmit the enclosed copy of Government Notification No. 156 and to inform you that the main thoroughfare recently opened across the Kowloon Peninsula has by my direction been named Gascoigne Road in commemoration of your connection with the dedication to the public of the King's Park which the road partly traverses.

❖ *Major-General Sir William Gascoigne was the General Officer Commanding Hongkong Forces 1899–1902.*

Hongkong Telegraph
3 June 1905

Intimations:
Reward of $5,000 offered by the Undersigned for the Arrest and Conviction of any Person or Persons who are in the habit of Smuggling large quantities of Opium into this Colony. Chin Joo Heng Co., Opium Farmers.

❖ *Chin Joo Heng Co. was concerned primarily, of course, about the loss of revenue; the opium farm monopoly at the time cost the firm in excess of half a million dollars.*

Hongkong Telegraph
20 June 1905

Farmers Thrashing Rice Kowloon City, Date Unknown

Rice is the staple food of one-third of the world's population, mainly of India and Southeast Asia. It needs abundant water and sunshine, and grows best where it can be irrigated.

The beginning of its cultivation goes back into the mists of pre-history. Archaeologists still debate how far back in time (10,000 years ago, some maintain) it was first grown. In China, it is grown in most of the provinces south of the Yellow River, and its importance in the life and welfare of the people may be glimpsed from the fact in the Chinese language 'to eat rice' is synonymous with taking a meal.

In Hong Kong of bygone days, before massive urbanization of the New Territories, rice was grown extensively in its small but fertile valleys assisted by the abundant monsoon rains. Rice

paddies were a familiar sight, with men and women busy transplanting seedlings into the muddy soil; soon the fields would blossom into masses of beautiful, living, delicate green. Two crops of rice per year are normally produced, but in Hong Kong, and perhaps elsewhere, three crops were sometimes managed. It was good quality rice, so superior, in fact, that a story was often heard of the rice from Sha Tin valley being exclusively reserved for the emperor's table.

Little, if any, machinery was used in harvesting the crops. Once ripened, the seeds were loosened from the stalks by thrashing (sometimes spelled 'threshing') the bunches into wooden vats, with cylindrical rattan tops, as seen in this photograph, or simply against the hard floor. The seeds are then fed into a winnowing machine, in which a wheel turned by hand creates a wind, thus separating heavier grain from lighter ones.

The disappearance of rice growing in Hong Kong is not surprising. Farming is hard work. Urbanization of the countryside brought easier and more profitable occupations than farming.

The peasants over in the New Territory are now gathering in their first rice harvest of the year. The grain is reported to be of an exceptionally good quality and is selling in the local markets at from $2.30, for medium, to $3 for first-class quality, per picul.

**Hongkong Telegraph
13 July 1905**

H.E. the Governor has proclaimed that the New Territories Land Ordinance 1905, shall come into operation on and from the 1st August next.

❖ *Designed 'to benefit the poor struggling peasants in the New Territories' and to deal 'satisfactorily, cheaply, easily and summarily' with disputes which may arise, the Ordinance proved in practice difficult to apply and was the source of much conflict.*

**Hongkong Telegraph
29 July 1905**

H.E. the Governor Sir Matthew Nathan, K.C.M.G., was 'At Home' at Government House yesterday, principally to his Chinese friends, of whom some 150 were welcomed and suitably entertained for a couple of hours.

**Hongkong Telegraph
26 August 1905**

From the Editorial:
Kowloon-Canton Railway: To-day, the members of the Legislative Council were asked … to vote an additional sum of $50,000 towards the expenses incurred in the survey and preliminary work in connection with the construction of the Kowloon-Canton railway. … It is exceedingly satisfactory to know that all needless delays and lengthy pauses are being brushed aside … and it bears out our previously conceived opinion that Sir Matthew Nathan is a man of action rather than words.

❖ *The actual work on the railway began in the spring of 1907.*

**Hongkong Telegraph
8 November 1905**

Nathan Road, 1906: Folly?

Sir Matthew Nathan, governor of Hong Kong from 1904–7, was unique in many ways among holders of that office. He was young (appointed at age 32,) an engineer, a bachelor and a Jew.

His competence and farsightedness were also unique. He pushed ahead the Kowloon-Canton Railway. He actively promoted education, particularly in technical fields. He is probably best remembered by his namesake road in Kowloon, which he planned and which became known as 'Nathan's Folly'. Time showed the epithet unwarranted and proved the wisdom of his effort as it became a vital factor in Kowloon's development.

It should be explained that the southern part of the thoroughfare we know today, up to Austin Road, had already been constructed, probably begun as early as 1865,

and was called Robinson Road.

Nathan had it extended north to become the main artery of the city, though its linkage with Taipo Road occurred much later. In 1908, after Sir Matthew had left Hong Kong, the old Robinson Road section and the new extension were named Nathan Road.

Even if it was not entirely Nathan's creation, the road is one of the finest streets in the territory and a lasting reminder of a great governor. See also p.284.

Nathan's health, never robust, was further aggravated by a fall from a horse. But he did not retire after leaving Hong Kong in 1907. Further appointments culminated in the governorship of Queensland.

On his departure, the *South China Morning Post* wrote:

'The general regret at the departure of Sir Matthew Nathan from Hong Kong is a tribute to his fine personal qualities, as well as to his splendid administration ... we sincerely trust that the genial gracious spirit of his administration will not vanish with his departure.'

1906

Intimations:
D. Mona, Tattooer, 60 Queen's Road Central.
The PUBLIC are informed that my Parlours are open from 9 A.M. all day. My 32 years experience in Tattooing is a guarantee of good work and prompt execution. ... H.R.H. The Duke of York, and H.I.H. the Emperor of Russia, both honoured me with their patronage.

Hongkong Telegraph
1 February 1906

PORTUGAL WILLING TO SELL MACAO. FRANCE ANXIOUS TO ACQUIRE:
The Chinese Minister to France has telegraphed ... stating that Portugal has expressed her willingness to sell to either Great Britain or France the Portuguese Colony of Macao. France ... has expressed her anxiety to acquire Macao from Portugal.

Hongkong Telegraph
9 February 1906

❖ *This was, of course, vigorously denied by both France and Portugal, and the Chinese Minister in question was credited with an attempt to show, perhaps mistakenly, the underhand intrigues of European nations.*

From the Editorial:
Hongkong and Singapore: Rivalry between colonies is an excellent institution ... stimulating ... the opponents to increased effort and thereby widening the horizon of both parties. Singapore has always been credited with a sneaking jealousy of the prosperity of Hongkong, the magnitude of its great industrial works, and its influence as the naval base of the Far East.

Hongkong Telegraph
12 April 1906

Prince Tsai Tsze of the Chinese Travelling Commission made a speech at the Mansion House [London] ... in the course of which he said the present journey of the Commission was a testimony of China's desire to form more friendly relations with Western nations. He hoped that this tendency would continue to develop until a Lord Mayor of London, in the near future, would propose the health of Chinese guests in Confucius's language and the guests would reply in the language of Shakespeare.

Hongkong Telegraph
17 April 1906

❖ *Noble aspirations! Incidentally, Prince Tsai was so overcome by the smoky atmosphere of the British capital, that he was unable to take part in various cultural visits arranged for the commission.*

**Hongkong Telegraph
2 May 1906**

Lane Crawford & Co.
Gentlemen's Summer Outfitters
<u>New Summer Goods Just</u>
<u>Received</u>
Straw Hats, Panama Hats
Elwood's Celebrated Sun Hats
Regulation Wolseley Helmets
Indian Pith Helmets
In all the Newest Shapes

❖   *This was the age of the popular myth that for a European to appear in the tropical sun of Hong Kong without a straw hat or a pith helmet, was to invite almost certain sunstroke.*

**Hongkong Telegraph
5 May 1906**

THE COLONIAL CEMETERY: It is officially notified that, as it has become necessary to extend the Colonial Cemetery at Happy Valley, and as the work will interfere with some existing graves, it is proposed, reverently and decently to take up the remains in certain graves, to re-inter them in adjoining ground. … Survivors, friends and relations who may desire to make any objection to this removal are requested to address the Colonial Secretary within three months.

❖   *There follow particulars of the graves …*

**Hongkong Telegraph
21 May 1906**

From the Editorial:
The jetsam which floats up with every mail from Europe reveals … the wonderful ignorance which prevails even amongst those who are otherwise deemed to be educated, regarding the position of Great Britain's Far Eastern possessions. No doubt many correspondents with the home country have received letters addressed to 'Hongkong, India' while it is on record that during the war Hongkong was frequently believed to be an integral portion of Japan.

❖   *India perhaps no longer, but I received a letter once, in the 1960s I think, addressed to me in 'Hong Kong, Japan'.*
'The war' probably refers to Russo-Japanese war of 1904–05.

Colonial Cemetery, Happy Valley, Hong Kong Island, c.1890
The cemetery, more recently known as Hong Kong Cemetery, is a large Protestant burial ground on the western slopes of Happy Valley overlooking the Race Course. It was opened in 1845, after the earlier burial ground at Wan Chai had become full. The photograph bears out a contemporary description of the cemetery as 'a carefully tended expanse of turf, with a pretty little chapel'. Magnificent tropical trees scattered among the graves and monuments complete the picture. Morrison Hill is seen in the far background, and a portion of the Race Course on the right.

Plague does not appear to be on the wane. Ten Chinese cases (all fatal) are returned for to-day.

Hongkong Telegraph
17 & 18 May 1906

And
Of the eleven Chinese cases of plague reported to-day eight terminated fatally. The total for the year is now 478.

Small mirrors on the back of church pews, to enable worshippers, while bending to pray, to see if their hats are on straight, are the latest up-to-date church improvement. A New York firm puts in the soul-satisfying equipment for three hundred dollars.

Hongkong Telegraph
5 June 1906

❖ *What will they think of next?*

**Hongkong Telegraph
29 June 1906**

From the Editorial:
From the debate which has taken place in Britain's House of Commons it is quite clear that a large section of the Liberal Party is in favour of abolishing the Indian opium trade with China. … The Secretary of State for India reminded the House of Commons that the opium trade … brought in a revenue of some £3,000,000 to the Indian exchequer every year and he asked how they were to replace it.

**Hongkong Telegraph
26 July 1906**

Steam has by no means made sailing vessels obsolete. The total number of them in the world is still 65,934 against 30,561 steamers.

❖   *Amazing statistics! Still more amazing how they were acquired.*

**Hongkong Telegraph
7 August 1906**

… for the information of the Sanitary Board … the new Western Market has been completed and has been established by His Excellency the Governor-in-Council as a New Market.

❖   *This was, in fact, the north block of the Western Market; the south block (unconnected with the north block) was built in 1858 and demolished in 1980. The north block was later declared a historic building and had been successfully converted into a shopping mall.*

**Hongkong Telegraph
3 September 1906**

A dispatch from Peking to the local mandarins states that the Conference of Ministers … held in the presence of Their Majesties, has decided that China shall be granted a constitution in February 1910. The Chinese will also be allowed parliamentary representation on the same date.

❖   *Too little, too late. The drive towards the revolution had already started and could not be stopped.*

**Hongkong Telegraph
12 September 1906**

Although no typhoon signals were hoisted this afternoon … the sampan men and women did not, apparently, like the appearance of the weather, and for fully an hour there was a continuous procession of sampans and boats of all sorts, proceeding from the West to Causeway Bay, to seek shelter.

❖   *How right they were! On 18 September, Hong Kong was hit by one of the worst typhoons in the territory's history.*

Typhoon in Hong Kong, 18 September, 1906

Among the natural disasters, typhoons — a local name for tropical cyclones — have proved to be the biggest natural threat in Hong Kong history. They affect the coastal regions of South China with remarkable regularity, mainly during the months of July to October. Many may pass, bringing much rain but doing little damage. A few, which strike full-on, may cause great devastation and loss of life.

Little accurate information about typhoons in Hong Kong prior to the setting up of the Royal Observatory in 1883 is available; several were known to have caused severe damage, in particular three — in 1841, 1874 and 1881.

The typhoon shown in this picture, struck Hong Kong on the morning of 18 September, 1906. Although it lasted a mere two hours, it caused enormous damage to property and heavy loss of life. Its effects were especially devastating, as it came swiftly and unexpectedly, without any inkling of its proximity. The Observatory's weather forecast for Hong Kong the day before read: 'Variable winds, moderate, probably some thunder showers.'

The photograph shows the ferocity of the typhoon as it caused havoc in the harbour, while the *Hong Kong Telegraph*, later that day, gave a realistic account of the disaster as follows: 'In the short space of barely two hours this morning, a typhoon of phenomenal velocity swept over Hong Kong, laid a great part of the city in ruins, annihilated the fleet of shipping which has been the Colony's pride and worked unexampled destruction to hundreds … Never in the history of the Colony has such a calamity overtaken her prosperity, and it never did damage and destruction even approaching that wrought by the typhoon this morning sending half the Colony into the direst distress … It came with a swiftness that could scarcely be imagined and it raged with a ferocity which carried everything before it.'

**Hongkong Telegraph
18 September 1906**

TERRIFIC TYPHOON, HOLOCAUST IN HONGKONG, SCORES OF STEAMERS SUNK, JUNKS AND SAMPANS OVERWHELMED, TWENTY FRENCH SAILORS KILLED, HUNDREDS OF NATIVES DROWNED.

❖ *These headlines speak for themselves. It was a disaster of immense magnitude and massive loss of life. Five petty officers (not 20) of the French gunboat* Fronde *were killed in a collision; a monument to them stands in the Happy Valley Cemetery. The typhoon remained the major news item for many days. The magnanimity of the Chinese community was especially notable.*

SS *Hankow* in Hong Kong Harbour, 14 October 1906
The ship is shown extensively damaged by fire. A crowd of curious onlookers has gathered to look at the stricken ship. In the foreground, an old-fashioned fire-engine is seen. The ship, belonging to the Hongkong, Canton & Macao Steamboat Co. (Butterfield & Swire), arrived in Hong Kong from Canton on 14 October 1906, laden with cargo and carrying about 2,000 passengers. The fire started in the aft of the vessel and within minutes the whole ship was ablaze. It was estimated that at least 130 people had perished in the fire. The disaster, coming so soon after the devastating typhoon of September 1906, was an added misfortune for Hong Kong.

THE BURNING OF S.S. 'HANKOW': At three o'clock in the morning the *Hankow* laden with valuable cargo and carrying about two thousand Chinese passengers arrived at Hongkong from Canton. ... The *Hankow*, belonging to Messrs. Butterfield & Swire, has always been a favourite with native residents. ... [it] will never be known exactly how many were on board for all traces of them have disappeared in the devastating flames or in the waters of the harbour ... [the fire] began ... in the bow and within five minutes the ship was a mass of flames.

**Hongkong Telegraph
14 October 1906**

❖ *It was subsequently ascertained that 130 people had perished in this disaster.*

The Peking Government has been informed by the Intelligence Department that Dr. Sun Yat-sen, the notorious head of the Chinese Red Republic Party, has recently been recognised on a foreign steamer coming to China, and instructions have therefore been sent to all Viceroys and Governors of the Empire to be (on the lookout) and if possible arrest him. We believe that a reward of over $20,000 is offered for the capture of the man, 'dead or alive'.

**Hongkong Telegraph
26 October 1906**

❖ *See also* South China Morning Post*, 11 April 1905.*

Truth will out, even in a misprint: 'The motor car has come to slay.' Thomas A. Edison* says he expects soon to place the automobile to the reach of all. It would be better if he would find a way to place all of us out of the reach of the automobiles.

**Hongkong Telegraph
6 December 1906**

KOWLOON-CANTON RAILWAY: It is difficult to conceive the progress of constructing the Kowloon section of the railway to Canton without paying a personal visit to the scene. ... The central scene is at the Lion's Head mountain which will be pierced by a tunnel. ... The first sign of the Kowloon railway operations is found at Lai-chi-kok, where a light railway ... meanders across the main road and passes along the wharf where piles of materials are waiting to be transported up country.

**Hongkong Telegraph
13 December 1906**

❖ *See Construction of Beacon Hill Tunnel, p.224.*

---

* Thomas A. Edison: famous American inventor.

Kowloon-Canton Railway, Construction of Beacon Hill Tunnel, Kowloon, 1907.
The photograph shows the South Face Camp of the tunnel construction. In the construction of the railway, the work on the Beacon Hill Tunnel was undertaken first in order to facilitate the supply of materials and equipment to the north section of the railway. Construction of camps on either side of Kowloon Range began in 1906, but the disastrous typhoon of September 1906 had delayed the work. Because of the lack of local village housing, huts for workers had to be constructed on the site, seen here on the left. The tunnel was completed in 1910.

Hongkong Telegraph
20 December 1906

At last … the project to tunnel the channel between England and France is assuming something of a practical form. For years the subject … has been discussed backwards and forwards, engineers have produced plans, and innumerable schemes … have been evolved, but to no avail. There was always that bogey of a French invasion by way of a tunnel. A humorous writer has remarked that the question of a channel tunnel has been a great bore in the past; it seems probable that it will be a still greater bore in the future.

Later comment:
Both Calais and Boulogne are hostile to the proposed Channel Tunnel scheme.

❖ *We trust the reader will spot the excellent pun! It is interesting to note that the question had been discussed as a practical possibility as early as that.*

1907

The Panama Canal: This great canal is for maritime uses exclusively, but when finished … our country will benefit by it only to a limited extent.

❖   *Its construction began in 1882 and completed in 1914.*

South China Morning Post 1 January 1907

Mr. James Berry, the gentleman who once held the post of public hangman, was conducting service at a … Baptist chapel the other evening. He is not to be regarded as a revivalist, however.

The Kowloon Pigeon Club advertises its annual show to be held on the 13th and 14th inst. An effort is being made to make the show as representative as possible and birds may come in from the outposts.

South China Morning Post 2 February 1907

Professor Mendeleeff, the world-renowned chemist is dead.

❖   *Most of us studied at school his famous 'Periodic Table of Elements'.*

South China Morning Post 5 February 1907

HONGKONG AND OPIUM: During the year 1906 the number of chests imported shows an increase of 3,638 on the previous year, or 47,566 while the exports from the Colony show an increase of 5,508 chests.

❖   *A very thriving trade by all accounts. The opium was taken by steam-launches and junks to various adjacent ports, no longer illegal but subject to duty.*

South China Morning Post 2 April 1907

For being drunk in Pottinger Street, Kakuchi, a Japanese barber, was fined $2.

❖   *One wonders, what would the fine be on Queen's Road?*

South China Morning Post 3 April 1907

Holland is considering a law prohibiting the descent of aeroplanes and flying-machines on its territory.

South China Morning Post 16 April 1907

South China Morning Post 10 May 1907

From the Editorial:
The dumping of dead bodies on the street is an evil which does not cease with the decrease of plague ... and the lamentable fact that nearly 400 bodies were deposited in the public streets during the first three months of the year makes the discussion in the Sanitary Board meeting most interesting.

❖ *This was still the case in the 1930s though to a lesser degree. In the present affluent Hong Kong, it is difficult to imagine the appalling poverty, disease and malnutrition which affected the less fortunate in those early years.*

South China Morning Post 8 June 1907

SUN YAT SEN'S VIEWS: From the pamphlet written ... by Sun Yat Sen, the Chinese Reformer, who is reputed to be the instigator of the present uprising:- The whole nation is ripe for revolution ... the newspapers and the recent publications in China are ... full of democratic ideas. ... It is evident ... that the downfall of the Manchu Government is but a question of time.

South China Morning Post 28 June 1907

From the Editorial:
The announcement that the Emperor William has accepted King Edward's invitation to visit England in the autumn will cause genuine pleasure, and it may be the prelude to happier relationship between the peoples of Great Britain and Germany.

❖ *Seven years later the two nations were at war (the First World War); incidentally, Edward and William, or Wilhelm II as he was known in Germany, were cousins.*

South China Morning Post 9 July 1907

ORIGIN OF SPECTACLES: Known by the Chinese but discovered in Europe. The Chinese who are usually supposed to have invented everything first, certainly imported their knowledge of spectacles, most probably from the Jews settled at K'ai-feng-fu. The first certain mention of spectacles occurs in a work published about AD 1460.

❖ *Readers may be interested to know that Leonardo Da Vinci, the incredibly versatile genius of the Renaissance, described the principle of contact lenses in 1508!*

Tin Hau Temple, Tai Miu Wan, Sai Kung, c.1920

The temple, overlooking what is popularly known as Joss House Bay, is the oldest in the territory. Although extensively renovated many times, the original building was constructed in AD 1270, only a few years before the Sung dynasty fell under the onslaught of the Mongols.

The photograph shows the temple standing on a barren coast with a few fishing sampans sheltering nearby. Today, it has a large, well-constructed pier and is frequently visited by worshippers.

The temple's principal deity is Tin Hau — the queen of heaven and the patron goddess of seafaring people, fisherfolk and sailors. The temple is richly decorated within and without with murals, handsome carvings, and brightly embroidered cloths. One of the halls is furnished as Tin Hau's bedchamber, another contains a statue of Buddha. Tin Hau is essentially a Taoist deity, and the presence of Buddha in the temple testifies to a strong Buddhist tradition in the area.

Although there are more than 40 temples dedicated to Tin Hau in Hong Kong, the goddess' birthday is celebrated at this temple annually, on the 23rd day of the third moon. Hundreds of fishing junks and sampans, gaily decorated with banners, sail on that day into the bay to celebrate the occasion. Tin Hau is extremely popular in Hong Kong, perhaps because she is by tradition a native of South China, and her birthday is always a happy and colourful holiday.

The temple can now be reached by a road behind it. Visitors should not miss the opportunity to also view an ancient inscription carved on a boulder, a short distance behind the temple, dated AD 1274. See also p. 288.

**South China
Morning Post
12 July 1907**

From the Editorial:
Dealing with the financial aspects of 1906, the report shows that there was a surplus of $202,401.10 on the actual working of the year.

**South China
Morning Post
13 July 1907**

An advertisement:
Now is the time to buy Chamberlain's Colic, Cholera and Diarrhoea Remedy. It is certain to be needed sooner or later and when that time comes you will need it badly — you will need it quickly. Buy it now. It may save life. For sale by all Chemists and Storekeepers.

**South China
Morning Post
2 August 1907**

SEVERE CATASTROPHE: At 5.20 last evening a portion of the Hongkong Hotel building fronting Queen's Road collapsed without warning.

❖   *Two people died, three were injured with broken limbs, and two were still missing at the time of the report. Twenty years later, the ill-fated hotel would be ablaze with a huge fire, though fortunately with only one fatality.*

Hongkong Hotel, Praya Central, Hong Kong Island, c.1900
The finest hotel in Hong Kong at the time, the six-storey Hongkong Hotel stood prominently on the waterfront (the Praya), on the corner of Pedder Street. The offices of Jardine, Matheson & Co. can be seen on the opposite corner. The hotel had a modest beginning, in 1868, as a three-storey building on the site previously owned by Dent & Co. In 1890–92 it was totally renovated and had three storeys added . It boasted of numerous bedrooms 'lofty and well-ventilated and open on to spacious verandah', (from the *Hongkong Guide,* 1893). But already the Praya is being extended, as the photograph shows, and the hotel would soon lose its prime position overlooking the harbour.

Although the Chinese Government continues to exude edicts and proclamations without stint, the personage in whose name these documents appear continues to remain a lay figure whose actions are controlled by the Empress Dowager. Secluded from the world and excluded from a voice in the deliberations of his advisers, the Emperor is little better than a puppet ... of those who in reality govern the Empire. ... No more pathetic figure commands the compassion of the outside world than Kuang Hsu for he has less freedom of actions and liberty of expression than the meanest of his subjects.

Hongkong Telegraph
2 October 1907

Viceroy of Canton Visiting Hong Kong, September 1907

The elderly, bearded gentleman of imposing appearance in the centre is the viceroy of Canton, Chang Jen-chun. He was to play an important role in the future of the University of Hong Kong and the resulting firm and friendly relations between Canton and Hong Kong.

Born of a literati family, in the province of Chihli, Chang entered the Chinese civil service early in life. After a number of important jobs in which he had proved himself a capable administrator, he was appointed governor of Honan in 1902, that of Kwangtung province in 1903, and finally, viceroy of Canton, in 1907.

It is noteworthy that while in Hong Kong Governor Sir Frederick Lugard was laying plans for the establishment of the University of Hong Kong, Viceroy Chang had expressed similar interest in the university, foreseeing its importance for the burgeoning academic ambitions of the young people of Canton. The photograph depicts the viceroy's arrival in Hong Kong, when he attended the investiture of the Director of Public Works William Chatham as Companion of the Order of St Michael and St George.

He also paid a visit to Governor Lugard, when the future of the university must have been discussed. A warm personal relationship had been established between the two men which contributed greatly to the peace and stability of the region.

Viceroy Chang visited Hong Kong again in 1909. His final act was to raise $200,000 — a very considerable sum in those days — for the endowment fund of the university. Sadly, he missed the laying of the foundation stone of the university in 1910, for he left Canton the previous year to take up a post in Nanking.

Hongkong Telegraph
4 October 1907

Seldom have we heard of children committing suicide in Hongkong, but this is what happened in the Central District late last night. ... A young servant girl, about fourteen years of age ... was found early this morning hanging.

❖ *Sadly, today we hear of it all too often; though now they are usually schoolchildren jumping to their deaths from high-rise buildings.*

Hongkong Telegraph
4 November 1907

[In Canton] the Police Authorities have given orders to prohibit the gambling dens ... from hanging out lanterns at their doors in the night. This step is taken to diminish the danger of fire.

Hongkong Telegraph
7 November 1907

From the Editorial:
The dastardly outrage which was committed at the Peak yesterday, in which a European lady was brutally assaulted, calls for more than mere passing note. It is a dangerous sign when Europeans cannot walk there in broad daylight without being subject to the attention of that class of community which lives by preying upon its neighbours.

❖ *Note the emphasis on 'European'. It was commonplace at the time for the English-language media to express a far greater indignation at any offence committed against Europeans than against the Chinese.*

Hongkong Telegraph
16 November 1907

The National Game: It is not generally known that down to the year 1748 cricket was an illegal game in England. Any person allowing it to be played on his land was liable to a fine of £20, and three years' imprisonment, while the 'implements' were to be burned. This was under a statute of Edward IV, enacted because the popularity of the pastime was interfering with archery.

1908

Sir Robert Hart's Retirement: He has served the Chinese Government for just on half a century. ... It would be quite impossible ... to note some only of the many services that Sir Robert has rendered the Chinese Government on innumerable occasions. ... No other European in modern times has been trusted in like degree by the Chinese.

❖ *First Inspector-General of the Chinese Imperial Maritime Customs, he had served in the post since 1863. He was an exceptionally capable organizer who by his high integrity won the respect and confidence of the Chinese.*

Hongkong Telegraph
3 March 1908

Kowloon and Victoria British Schools: the following new rules are printed in the Gazette: 'Admission to the Schools is limited to children of European parentage; the Inspector of Schools may, if he thinks it desirable, refuse any application for admission subject to appeal to the Governor whose decision shall be final'.

Hongkong Telegraph
7 March 1908

From a speech by Sir Thomas Jackson (Chief Manager of Hongkong & Shanghai Bank, 1868-1902):
'... [The Bank] occupies so conspicuous a place in the economic conditions of the whole of the Far East that special interest will be felt in the report of the proceedings at the first annual dinner held in London on the 18th ult. ... The start of the Hongkong bank was very peculiar. It arose out of a tremendous speculative boom that existed in Bombay in 1864. ... people of Bombay cast their eyes toward China and said we were going to start a Bank of China with its head office in Hongkong. ... The Hongkong and Shanghai Banking Corporation [was launched] with a capital of five million dollars, commencing business in March 1865. The first manager in Hongkong was Mr. Victor Kresser, and the first in Shanghai was Mr. David McLean.

❖ *A bit of interesting history.*

Hongkong Telegraph
20 March 1908

**Hongkong Telegraph
25 March 1908**

Hongkong University ... We are glad to learn that the idea of a Hongkong University, whose real value will be measured by the degree by which it becomes an educational resort for Chinese students, has the support of the Governor of Hongkong [Sir Frederick Lugard]. But the scheme ... has been brought well within the horizon of realization by the munificence of a much respected Parsi resident of Hongkong, Mr. Mody, who has given a donation of a hundred and fifty thousand dollars towards the founding of a University of Hongkong.

Mody, H. N., Prominent Parsee Merchant and Philanthropist, c.1908 Hormusjee Naorjee (later Sir Hormusjee) Mody arrived in Hong Kong in 1858 to a modest position of a clerk in a small local firm. He soon started trading on his own, and making, in the 1860s, major profit from the trade in opium. However, he later switched to share and bullion brokerage, in which he became eminently successful. Mody was personally involved in many of the more important public projects, such as the Praya Reclamation of 1890–1904 in the Central District. He had special faith in the development of Kowloon at a time when it was almost an empty area, and invested heavily in real estate there; Mody Road in Kowloon carries his name. But among his contributions to Hong Kong, the greatest was the Main Building of its university, built entirely at his expense. For this and for many other benefactions to Hong Kong he was knighted in 1910, the year the foundation stone of the University Main Building was laid. He died in 1911, greatly admired and respected.

OPIUM SUPPRESSION. AN IMPERIAL DECREE. The bane of opium consumption has increased to such an extent in this Empire that the poison has penetrated our vitals. … men have been known to squander their properties and shorten their lives. … philanthropists … from … abroad have started associations and societies for the purpose of exhorting people to abstain from selling and buying opium. … If people of other countries show this feeling, how much more should it be our duty … to eradicate the habit from our midst. … We hereby command the Ministries of the Interior and of Finance to lose no time in agreeing upon the manner of making investigations as to carrying out our instructions … within the limit of time set by Imperial Edict. Let there be no evasion of duties else the culprits will receive condign punishment at our hands.

Hongkong Telegraph
30 March 1908

❖ *The sentiment of the edict is admirable, but the contradictions are glaring when it is remembered that China not only exacted legal duty on imported opium, but also grew and processed its own.*

An American named A.G. Garr, residing at 8, Ladder Street, was prosecuted at the Police Court, this morning … for failing to report a case of small-pox which had broken out in his house. … The patient- Miss Marie Gardner, a nurse in the employ of the defendant — has since died. The accused pleaded ignorance. … The magistrate imposed a fine of $15.

Hongkong Telegraph
31 March 1908

❖ *It is almost impossible to imagine the health hazards of those past years. The anti-bacterial drugs and antibiotics had not yet been discovered. Regular occurrence of epidemics of plague, smallpox and cholera ravaged Hong Kong; tuberculosis, with no effective treatment, was very common, while malaria, dysentery, meningitis, typhoid were endemic in the place.*

A NAVY FOR CHINA: There was a meeting of the Grand Council [in China] the other day to consider the establishment of a Navy for China. A certain member of the Council expressed the opinion that there was no hurry for China to organize a Navy. Whereupon Duke Tsai held that, in the absence of a Navy, China was rated among the third-class Powers by the Hague Conference.

Hongkong Telegraph
8 April 1908

Hongkong Telegraph
14 April 1908

MR. A. H. RENNIE DROWNED. The sad and distressing intelligence was received in Hongkong late this afternoon that Mr. A. H. Rennie, one of the most prominent of Hongkong's commercial community, had been drowned in the harbour.

Rennie's Mill at Junk Bay, c.1907

Many Hong Kong 'belongers' know of Rennie's Mill as an area of the western slopes of Junk Bay housing a cluster of poor houses — a settlement with known Taiwan (Kuomingtang) connections. But not many know the sad tale of the mill.

Alfred Herbert Rennie, born in 1857, was a Canadian who came to Hong Kong in 1890. He obtained a post of a clerk with the Government Public Works Department but resigned in 1895. It was then that he conceived a plan to start a flour mill. It was a bold and innovative idea, as Hong Kong, apart from shipbuilding, had few local industries at the time. After obtaining financial backing from two prominent businessmen, C. P. Chater and H. N. Mody, the Hong Kong Milling company at Junk Bay was launched, probably around 1903–04. The land was bought at Junk Bay and the mill was built between 1905 and 1906. Rennie threw himself heart and soul into the new enterprise. He was the promoter, manager, director and chief organizer of the mill. All went well at first and the mill began to produce flour in 1907. But difficulties appeared very early. Previously, Hong Kong obtained flour supplies directly from the United States, and bakers were reluctant to switch their suppliers. Moreover, problems of disposal of waste products of the mill proved a serious obstacle. At any rate, Rennie's Mill failed a mere year after starting. Poor Rennie, disillusioned and defeated, committed suicide in April 1908, drowning himself in Junk Bay in full view of his failed dream project. The photograph shows Rennie's Mill, probably around 1907.

THE STATUS OF MACAO: The Macao correspondent writes that the English and Chinese newspapers have published the report that the Government at Peking is dispatching to South China an Imperial Commissioner charged with the duty of conferring with the Government of Macao on the question of delimitation of the boundaries of that colony. ... the correspondent considers it his duty to state that the Lisbon Protocol signed by H.E. Henrique de Barros Gomes, Minister for Foreign Affairs, on behalf of Portugal, and Mr. Duncan Campbell, Commissioner of the Chinese Imperial Maritime Customs, on behalf of China, was the first international document in which China recognised the sovereignty of Portugal over Macao. Art. 2 of the said Protocol states that 'China confirms perpetual occupation and government of Macao and its dependencies by Portugal', as any other Portuguese possession.

❖ *A most interesting document to be sure, if the information is correct. But the remarkable part is the signing by the Englishman (or Scotsman?) on behalf of China.*

**Hongkong Telegraph
1 May 1908**

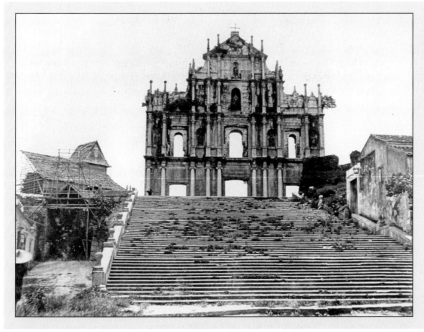

Ruins of St. Paul's, Macao, c.1874
The photograph may have been taken after the severe typhoon of September 1874, which was one of the worst in the history of the region. Ruins of St. Paul's (Sao Paulo), of which only the great facade remains standing (after the great fire of 1835), does not appear to have suffered any more damage by the typhoon. The buildings on the right and left, however, were severely damaged; they were later demolished leaving the magnificent steps of St. Paul's free.

**Hongkong Telegraph
4 May 1908**

A quarrel over a small debt … resulted in … a swollen hand and … a charge of assault. Li Wai, a coolie, it appears, owed Lo Pin Fong, a hawker, ten cents — a debt which the former would not pay … for many moons.

❖   *It does make one reflect on the relative value of money at different periods of time.*

**Hongkong Telegraph
24 June 1908**

Miss Stella Brumfield, of 49 Hollywood Road, paid $5 compensation this morning to the chair coolie, whom she was charged with assaulting yesterday. Accused, it was alleged, refused to pay the coolie his fare, and when he demanded it … threw two glasses of water over him.

❖   *Shame, shame, a European lady behaving like this! Without throwing any suspicions, it must be borne in mind, however, that with brothels being legal at the time, there were many ladies of various nationalities, and of doubtful virtue, making their living in Hong Kong.*

**Hongkong Telegraph
20 August 1908**

The blood of the rhinoceros is very highly esteemed by Burmese and Chinese as a medicine for all kinds of ailments.

❖   *Today, the poor rhino is facing extinction because its horn is still eagerly sought after as a potent medicine.*

**Hongkong Telegraph
24 August 1908**

From Peking:
THE DALAI LAMA. In a memorial the Governor of Shansi reports that, since the arrival of the Dalai Lama it has cost the Province a great deal of money to entertain him and his retinue. The report adds that the Lama's followers have been creating mischief everywhere.

**Hongkong Telegraph
16 September 1908**

The marriage of Mr. Winston Churchill, President of the Board of Trade, and Miss Clementine Hozier, daughter of the late Sir Henry Hozier, K.C.B., and Lady Blanche Hozier, was fixed to take place to-day.

**Hongkong Daily Press
5 October 1908**

The World Chess Championship, played partly at Dusselforf and partly in Berlin, has been won by Lasker by eight games against Tarrasch's three.

❖   *Emanuel Lasker, the German-Jewish chess master, had been the world chess champion for an incredible 26 years, from 1894 to 1920, losing the title in 1921 to Capablanca, a Cuban.*

Shau Kei Wan Village: c.1910

Cultivated fields in the foreground, a cluster of village houses, and a deep bay with sampans sheltering in it. It is difficult to imagine that this little village is today's crowded, bustling Shau Kei Wan. The transformation is mainly post-war; in 1910, the village must have appeared much the same as 1841, when Hong Kong was ceded to Britain.

Shau Kei Wan was not the only village on Hong Kong Island at the time of the takeover. Britain's Foreign Secretary Palmerston's oft-quoted remark that Hong Kong was 'a barren island with hardly a house upon it', was never meant to be taken literally. He would have been well apprised of the situation by Captain Elliot who was intimately familiar with the island and the harbour.

The remark was an expression of annoyance at Elliot's pre-emptive, and unauthorized, acquisition of Hong Kong, which neither Palmerston nor his government wanted; they had their eyes on Chusan Island (Zhousan).

What was Hong Kong Island like in 1841? It was barren of vegetation but not of habitation.

A rough census taken at the time estimated the Chinese population as about 7,500, of whom 2,000 were living on boats and the rest in some 20 villages and hamlets. The largest villages were 'Chek-chu', the present Stanley Village, with a population of 2,000, and 'Soo-ke-wan', now called Shau Kei Wan, with about 1,200.

Hongkong Daily Press
17 October 1908

Telegram:
Bosnia and Herzegovina have been annexed by Austria.

❖ *Seemed at the time like a quick and effective solution to this troubled land.*

From the Editorial:
Dr. Sven Hedin, who is now on his way to Europe after spending many months in Tibet, is reported to make no secret of his belief that the domination of Tibet by the Chinese will effectually destroy British influence in that country.

❖ *The famous Swedish explorer was dead right in his prediction.*

Hongkong Daily Press
22 October 1908

At an extraordinary general meeting of the Lusitano Football Club it was unanimously decided to change its name to Lusitano Recreation Club. The following were elected to serve on the Committee for the season 1908–9:- President, Mr. A.G. da Rocha; hon. secretary, Mr. C.M.C.V. Ribeiro; hon. treasurer, Mr. A.V. Barros; captain, Mr. A.J.C.V. Ribeiro; vice-captain, Mr. P. da Roza; committee, Messrs. J.C. Barretto, J.M. Britto, C.F. Franco, J.O. Remedios, and P.M. Remedios.

❖ *The interest of this announcement lies in the names. Transplanted from Macao to the early Hong Kong, they formed the nucleus of the Portuguese community; their descendants are still prominent in today's Hong Kong. See also p.52, photograph of the club.*

Hongkong Daily Press
27 October 1908

HOW IT FEELS TO FLY: Mr. Franz Reichel, who was with Mr. Wilbur Wright last month when the aeroplane made a 55 minute flight, describing ... his flight, says:- 'I have known that day a magnificent intoxication. I have learned how it feels to be a bird. I have flown. Yes, I have flown! I am still astonished at it, still deeply moved.'

❖ *I, too, am moved. Only one hundred years later and we take flying for granted, but we have space travel to look forward to for excitement.*

Antiquities & Monuments Office

The Time Ball, c.1900–1910

It now seems almost inconceivable that the radio is a 20th century invention. To be precise, Marconi suceeded in transmitting a wireless signal across a considerable distance on 12 December, 1901.

Accurate measurement of time is an essential element of our life, and today we are used to having it transmitted by radio, for example the famous 'beep' on RTHK. But before the invention of radio, other means had to be found.

One of these methods, which was used in Hong Kong during the early part of the 20th century, is depicted in these two photographs. The top one shows a small round tower on a hill in Kowloon (Tsim Sha Tsui) facing the harbour. The tower is located in front of the Marine Police Headquarters, both built in 1884. Suspended on top of the tower was a large hollow copper ball, seen in this photograph. A time signal was given daily at precisely 1pm by the dropping of the ball from the top of the pole to the bottom. The chronometers of ships at anchor in the harbour were then checked against the time ball manoeuvre.

In 1907, the ball, no longer clearly visible from the harbour, was moved to a higher position on top of the Signal Tower, on Blackhead Point, built that year for the purpose (bottom photograph). There it continued to give time signals until 1933 when the time ball manoeuvre was replaced by radio signals.

Both towers are still standing and are protected as historical structures. The first one, now known as the Round House, contains a small maritime museum. Both towers are well worth a visit, though unfortunately neither the time ball nor its mechanism are available for display.

Woman Playing the *Pipa*

The date is unimportant; the *pipa* is the musical instrument the Chinese love above all other instruments.

Music in China is a very ancient tradition; its beginning is shrouded in legend and myth. But there is no doubt that it was already well developed during the Chou dynasty, around 1100 BC.

The use of an orchestra also came early, it being used for official ceremonies or royal entertainment. A variety of instruments were used but none more loved, respected and admired than the pipa, a delicate pear-shaped, lute-like instrument, held tenderly in this photograph by a young musician.

The pipa is one of the oldest Chinese musical instruments, becoming the dominant instrument during the Tang dynasty (AD 618–907), but today still holds a supreme position among the rest of the instruments.

It has four strings and is played by plucking them with all five fingers of one hand. The resulting tone is resonant, yet delicate and clear.

It has a range of pitch and allows a variety of techniques, which has made it popular with all forms of Chinese music.

A true classical instrument, in the hands of a master, it is capable of conveying equally well the soft serene beauty of a Chinese melody and the loud battle scene with its clash of armour and cries of the wounded.

**Hongkong Daily Press
16 November 1908**

Telegram:

His Majesty The Emperor Kuang Hsu dies at 5 p.m. on Saturday (14th November).

❖ *The Emperor was only 37 years of age. The Empress Dowager, for several years the effective ruler, died shortly afterwards.*

**Hongkong Daily Press
27 November 1908**

THE SITUATION AT PEKING: Owing to the very strict censorship which is being exercised no news is obtainable from Peking. It is reported that a native newspaper [Ta Tung Yat Po] which published some reference to the affairs at the Palace was fined $300.

Telegram from London:
The Government promises to introduce a democratic Reform bill admitting female enfranchisement.

Hongkong Daily Press
8 December 1908

On Christmas: It was not before 1862 that the first Christmas Card was issued by a London firm. The first cards bore pictures of robins, holly & c., and were very modest productions.

Hongkong Daily Press
24 December 1908

1909

Having spoken for nearly nine days, Mr. Rufus Isaacs, K.C. ... concluded in the Court of Appeal on Dec.1 the longest speech ever made by counsel in that court.

China Mail
6 January 1909

❖   *Rufus Daniel Isaacs (1860-1935), first Marquess of Reading, British statesman, advocate and Lord Chief Justice. Was made Viceroy of India in 1920, and given the title of marquess in 1926, the only Jew to be so honoured.*

From the Editorial:
The finding of twenty Chinese stowaways on the E. and A. Company's steamer *Eastern* on her arrival in Sydney has caused no little commotion in the Australian press. The very mention of a yellow man entering their country seems to throw [Australian politicians] into a state of frenzy. It is a pitiful spectacle in the opening decade of the twentieth century.

China Mail
7 January 1909

❖   *The White Australia Policy was formally abolished in 1972.*

The following Bulletin was issued at Government House this morning:- Lady Lugard has not had a good night, but her condition is otherwise satisfactory.

China Mail
12 January 1909

❖   *Wife of Sir Frederick Lugard, the Governor, Lady Lugard was in fact seriously ill, later diagnosed as having appendicitis.*

Reception at the Government House, Hong Kong Island, 1907
The guests are posing for a photograph, very informally, on the steps of the back entrance of the house leading into the garden. The guest of honour is the Chinese General, seated in the middle of the front row. Several of his retinue are standing at the back. On the General's right are Lady Lugard and Major-General Broadwood. Governor Lugard and Mrs Broadwood are on his left. Among others present are Commander Basil Taylor of the Royal Navy, Mr Henry May (the Colonial Secretary, and later Governor), the Chinese Consul in Hong Kong, Mr Cheung Pat Sze, Dr Ho Kai and Mr Boshan Wei Yuk (of Po Shan Road).

Sir Frederick Lugard (1858–1945) served as governor of Hong Kong from 1907 to 1912. A capable man in both civil and military fields, he proved equally capable in Hong Kong. His chief interest was education and his greatest achievement was the founding of the University of Hong Kong, of which he became the First Chancellor. Lugard's noble idea was to create a citadel of higher education which could serve as the foremost bearer of Western culture in the Orient. Whether or not this lofty idea had entirely succeeded, the university has grown from strength to strength to attain the highest reputation in the region. After leaving Hong Kong, Lugard was elevated to peerage in 1928, and continued a brilliant career in Africa.

From the Editorial:
Mendelssohn's Centenary: On Feb. 3 1809 — just one hundred years ago — Felix Mendelssohn-Bartholdy saw the light in the house of a wealthy Jewish citizen of Hamburg. [His] career ... was one prolonged blaze of triumph from start to finish. ... From his successes as a child prodigy to the production of 'Elijah' he scarcely knew what the word failure meant. ... His personal charm won him friends in all ranks of society; his brilliant feats of virtuosity enchanted the public; he basked in the sunshine of total favour. ... In many ways he was the resuscitator of Bach and the present day earnest study of this great maestro's work is largely due to him. Mendelssohn, who was married in 1837, was one of the shortest lived of the wonderful band of men who were born in 1809, a band which included such giants as Gladstone, Lincoln, Chopin, Darwin, Poe, etc., for he succumbed on November 4, 1847, not having completed his thirty-eighth year.

China Mail
3 February 1909

From Peking:
The Imperial Sepulchre requires an expenditure of $6,000,000.

China Mail
13 February 1909

Pedder Street is practically in the hands of the contractors at present. The two new buildings for Jardine, Matheson and Co., and the Post Office, and the addition of the Hongkong Hotel, when completed, will rank amongst the finest out east.

China Mail
20 February 1909

❖ *None is extant today; the Post Office was the last to go, in 1976.*

From the Editorial:
Hongkong's Opium Divans. ... Speaking in the Legislative Council ... His Excellency the Governor Sir Frederick Lugard announced that the British Government cannot depart from the policy it had resolved upon in the matter of the opium divans of Hongkong. These will have to be closed, but instead of the drastic steps ... first intended ... half the divans [will] be closed in March 1909, the remainder in March 1910.

China Mail
12 March 1909

❖ *'Divan', a Turkish word, has several meanings, one of which is a low settee without a back. Here it is used for opium 'parlours' where customers could recline on divans while smoking opium. See Opium Smokers, p.244.*

Opium Smokers, Hong Kong, c.1900–10
The scene may well have been taken in one of the opium 'divans', or public smoking-rooms, which flourished in Hong Kong in the 19th and early 20th centuries. The production and sale of opium in Hong Kong, referred to as 'opium farm', was regulated as a monopoly, sold to the highest bidder. In 1909–10 the divans were closed, and by 1917, following an agreement with China, all trade in opium had ceased. So ended the shameful chapter of the China trade.

China Mail
10 April 1909

Hongkong street names all remind us
We may make our names sublime
And departing leave behind us
Street plates to last all the time.

China Mail
11 June 1909

Miss Florence Nightingale, who has just entered her ninetieth year, has received innumerable congratulatory messages and bouquets. She is very feeble, and is now confined at all times to her rooms.

❖ *For the few who may not know, Florence Nightingale was the founder of the modern nursing profession and became famous for her work during the Crimean War in 1854. She died in 1910.*

From Colonial Secretary: Intimation:
Hongkong Opium Farm: Notice is hereby given that Sealed Tenders will be received at the Colonial Secretary's Office, Hongkong, till noon on Tuesday, the 31st day of August, 1909, under 'The Prepared Opium Ordinance 1891–1909', that is to say, the sole privilege of preparing Opium and of Selling within the Colony.

❖   *It is scarcely believable that there was even an ordinance governing preparation and sale of opium.*

China Mail
6 July 1909

Telegram:
Louis Bleriot has successfully crossed the Channel from Calais to Dover in his aeroplane. He did the distance in 26 minutes.

❖   *Certainly a milestone of the 20th century.*

China Mail
26 July 1909

From the Editorial:
Just at present there is a veritable craze for Marathon races. In England, Scotland, the United States, Canada, Japan and some of the treaty ports of China these races have been run. … A few months ago we drew attention to a joint letter which three famous English doctors … addressed to every English public school, in which they said: 'We consider school and cross country races exceeding one mile in distance as wholly unsuitable for boys under the age of nineteen, as the continued strain involved is apt to cause permanent injury to the heart and other organs …'. Like other things, the Marathon craze will run its course and die away; let us hope it will not leave too many wrecks in its wake.

❖   *An interesting statement showing yet again how wrong predictions can be. Marathon races are more popular today than ever.*

China Mail
31 July 1909

Commander Peary has telegraphed to the New York Times that he reached the North Pole on April 6th.

China Mail
8 September 1909

**China Mail
6 November 1909**

The Condition of Queen's Road: The time is fast approaching when the force of public opinion will compel the Colonial Administration … to cleanse Queen's Road. We mean in a moral sense. It is … a disgrace that in a Colony of the British Crown, amply endowed with churches and missions … setting a model [to] the adjacent Empire of China … that no lady can go shopping after 5 o'clock without coming into contact with a very unpleasant side of life.

❖ *This refers, of course to prostitution. Public opinion or not, legal brothels in Hong Kong were abolished in the early 1930s.*

Chinese Gentlemen in the Botanical Gardens, c.1880

The interest of this photograph lies in what young, well-bred Chinese gentlemen wore during an outing in the early Hong Kong. The basic male attire is a loose pair of trousers and an equally loose-fitting jacket; the latter may be long, extending to the ankles. The trousers are tucked into long stockings which are neatly bound with black garters below the knees or just above the ankles. Shoes are made of cloth, often silk, and have thick soles, sometimes as much as one inch. Men wear satin skull-caps, but usually go bareheaded in summer.

This photograph was almost certainly taken in summer — hence the absence of outer garments, hats and the presence of fans. China is probably the only country in the world where men use fans. (In the West the use of fans is confined to women.) Fans are made or a variety of materials and are often very decorative. It is common for lines of poetry to be written on them.

The queue, introduced by the Manchu (Ching) dynasty is worn by all men and should normally hang down behind. The forehead is usually shaven.

The Botanical Gardens were founded in 1864 and are still in the same location today.

The Chinese people would be well advised if they leave the question of costume severely alone. They have evolved, in the course of their long history, a style of raiment entirely suitable to their habits and their country, and it would be a thousand pities if they abandoned their present mode of dress for the absurd fashions of the Occident.

China Mail
13 November 1909

DALAI LAMA AGAIN: Their Excellencies ... Senior and Junior [Chinese] Residents in Tibet, have notified the Throne that the Dalai Lama intends making a tour to Russia, and they suggest that an Imperial Edict should be issued to disallow the visit.

China Mail
19 November 1909

From the Editorial:
Exit 1909; ... what will make 1909 for long famous in many annals will be Lieut. Sir E.H. Shackleton's achievement in approaching to within one hundred miles of the South Pole.

❖ *Well, hardly! Two years later, Amundsen (Norwegian) and Scott (British) separately reached the South Pole, though the latter perished on the return journey.*

China Mail
31 December 1909

1910

From Clergyman's Experiences in China:
The Rev. E.J. Hardy, M.A., the author of a well-known book *How to be Happy Though Married* ... gives a short account of his life in the Far East ... 'The Chinese nation I regard as the greatest on Earth, for the Chinese can live on next to nothing, and he has no fear of death. Their intelligence is remarkable, and so is their power of adaptability. When first went out in Hongkong I found a large number of the soldiers in some outgoing districts ... armed with only bows and arrows. Three years later ... they were fully equipped with excellent rifles and were well drilled. The only peculiarity was that they knelt to present arms.'

Hongkong Telegraph
8 January 1910

**Hongkong Telegraph
3 March 1910**

In response to the Chinese Residents submission, the Throne has issued the following Edict:- 'The Dalai Lama of Thibet was well treated by the late Emperor and the Dalai Lama should have attended to his religious duties. ... However ... he has become proud, lascivious, loose in his conduct, and violent. This misconduct of the Dalai Lama has seriously developed till it has reached the utmost limit. Thus he began to disobey the Imperial orders and tyrannise over Thibetans. ... In the 30th year of Kwanghsu ... he fled from Thibet ... the said Dalai Lama is hereby deprived of his title in view of effecting punishment ...'

❖ *The Edict continues with recommendations to Thibetans to search among the youths of Thibet (Tibet) for a new Dalai Lama. See also* China Mail, *19 November 1909.*

Holyoak Family, c.1910
Photographic collections, dispersed among various institutions in Hong Kong, contain many photographs of European and Chinese families of Hong Kong, but unfortunately very few of the people in these photographs can be identified today. The one here is an exception; it shows the Holyoak family, obviously enjoying afternoon tea in the garden of their home—an English social tradition firmly transplanted to the colonies. The style of ladies' hats and dresses proclaims it to be about the early 20th century, probably shortly before the First World War. An elderly Chinese woman, a family retainer or possibly a housekeeper — an indispensable feature of the households — stands

modestly behind.

Percy Hobson Holyoak came to Hong Kong around 1903 to work for Reiss & Co, an old business house trading in Hong Kong since 1864. The firm did well during the early 20th century, but failed in the slump of 1921–22 and was liquidated in 1923.

It was immediately taken over and reorganized under new ownership as Holyoak, Massey and Co, with Holyoak as the senior partner.

Holyoak himself became a prominent member of the Hong Kong business community and was active in community service: Between 1915 and 1926, he served on the Legislative and Executive Councils and was at one time chairman of the Hong Kong Chamber of Commerce. He died in England in 1926.

Tobacco and Disease: Smokers will be delighted to learn that a military doctor has discovered … that smoking, instead of being bad, is good for health. Better still, smokers are almost immune from meningitis. … The discoverer of this new scientific fact is Dr. de Kermabon, of the French Army.

❖ *Smokers may or may not be delighted to learn that this was the biggest piece of nonsense that had ever emanated from any doctor.*

**Hongkong Telegraph
25 April 1910**

DEATH OF KING EDWARD: The following telegram [dated 6 May] has been received from the Secretary of State for the Colonies … 'Profoundly regret to inform you that His Majesty the King passed away at 11.45 to-day'.

❖ *See the next snippet.*

**Hongkong Telegraph
7 May 1910**

From the Editorial:
'It is not to be wondered at' said a learned Chinese pundit 'that this year your great Empire loses its master and is troubled with rebellion, for the tailed star is in the sky and that is always the sign of grief and disaster to great empires'. … Our present Visitor, now visible from about three in the morning till a little before daylight, is called Halley's Comet.

**Hongkong Telegraph
11 May 1910**

A new brand of coffee 'freed from caffeine' is now on the market. Something like a spiritless whiskey, or white blacking or non-adhesive glue, we suppose.

❖ *So that is when decaffeinated coffee really started!*

**Hongkong Telegraph
4 June 1910**

When will the new Law Courts be finished? The heavy rains of the past two days have … caused havoc with law books. As for lack of accommodation in the Summary Court, it is enough to make a saint howl with indignation at the *laissez-faire* spirit of the Hongkong Government.

❖ *The building was finally completed in 1912 having taken nine years to construct (see* Hongkong Telegraph, *12 November 1903, and photograph on p.202).*

**Hongkong Telegraph
2 July 1910**

Hongkong Telegraph
27 July 1910

From the Editorial:
Many Servicemen do not regard Hongkong as an ideal station to which to be drafted for a spell of years. Especially this is true concerning the women and children of the Garrison, for they have every reason to dread the heat and ills of a Hongkong summer. ... We are glad to learn that an arrangement has been made for the supply of electric current to the Victoria and Wellington barracks.

❖   *Which means doing away with the old unhealthy oil lamp.*

Hongkong Telegraph
25 August 1910

At about 5 o'clock yesterday afternoon, a Chinese, who turned out to be the master of a junk trading between Hongkong and the mainland ... reported that his boat had been boarded by seven men, some of whom were armed with choppers, about two or three days previously. Once on board the desperadoes seized the junk master and members of his crew and battened them down in the hatchway. ... the pirates cleared eighty five piculs of salt from the captured vessel and with their spoils cleared out of the island, abandoning the junk.

❖   *Piracy continued to be a menace in Hong Kong waters well into the 1930s.*

Hongkong Telegraph
31 August 1910

From the Editorial:
THE HARBOUR TUNNEL SCHEME: For many years past the subject of tunnelling the Harbour so as to give a permanent solid connection between Hongkong and Kowloon has been brought under public discussion. ... To some people the mere idea of a tunnel reaching from Hongkong to Kowloon appears to be the figment of a fanciful imagination.

❖   *Apparently during an acute shortage of water, in 1902, the matter received more than usual attention.*

Hongkong Telegraph
2 September 1910

Our Colony's Defences: As regards the volunteer movement and its organization, Hongkong at present moment affords very unfavourable comparison ... with Shanghai, Penang or Rangoon. Why this should be so is somewhat difficult to divine. In plain words, volunteering is not popular in this Colony. For the apathetic attitude by our young men towards a valuable asset in the Colony's defence one hears many causes cited including cliqueism, favouritism and failure to reward long service and proficiency in the ranks.

❖ *This is not borne out by contemporary witnesses. In fact, in the first decade of the 20th century, the enthusiasm of the Volunteers was high, and 'men of suitable age were "expected" to belong to the Volunteers' (Phillip Bruce,* Second to None, *p.108). In any case, 30 years later, the Volunteers showed exemplary courage fighting the Japanese in the Battle of Hong Kong.*

Hong Kong Volunteer Defence Corps, Hong Kong, c.1914
The photograph shows the Volunteers on exercise somewhere in the New Territories, probably during a training camp. The artillery unit is practising firing two 15-pounder BL Field Guns (breech-loading guns firing 15-pound shells). The Hong Kong Volunteers were formed in 1854 to replace the much depleted Hong Kong garrison during the Crimean War. The Volunteers fought with distinction defending Hong Kong against the Japanese during the Second World War. The Corps was renamed the Hong Kong Regiment in 1969, and soon afterwards was granted the title 'Royal'. It was disbanded in 1995, prior to Hong Kong being returned to Chinese sovereignty.

Most of us are aware of the suppressive measures taken by the Hongkong authorities in the matter of gambling. In the earlier days of the Colony's history gambling was a licensed pastime just the same as it is in Macau or Canton at the present moment. ... Legislation spelling total suppression has been tried and has not met with success.

❖ *This item gives an entirely wrong impression of Hong Kong's attitude to gambling. Unlike Macao or Canton, the Hong Kong Government has*

Hongkong Telegraph
3 September 1910

always been opposed to legalized gambling. The licensed gambling mentioned in the article was a short experimental period. Under Governor Macdonnell's strong advocacy, a limited number of gambling houses was licensed in 1867. Macdonnell believed that this would reduce corruption among the police who often exacted protection money from gambling houses. The experiment was a failure, as other abuses appeared, and the licenses were cancelled in 1872, never to be resumed. Horseracing and the present-day Mark Six, both controlled by the Hong Kong Jockey Club, may be discounted as non-profit gambling, as the net profits are channeled into cultural and educational projects.

Gambling, Hong Kong or Macao, c.1905
A number of gamblers are engaged in playing 'fantan' and other games. Fantan, reputed to be an ancient game, is based on guessing the number of porcelain buttons placed under a cup. Gambling flourished in Macao where it has been legally allowed. In Hong Kong, however, except for a brief trial period, gambling is prohibited by law, but illegal gambling dens are nevertheless present.

Hongkong Telegraph 10 September 1910

Tradition asserts that four thousand years ago there lived a mandarin … who constructed an aeroplane to carry himself. He tried to ascend in the presence of the Emperor with the aid of forty seven rockets, but the rockets exploded prematurely, and the Mandarin was so badly burned that the Emperor ordered him beheaded.

❖   *One may assume that the beheading was an act of mercy.*

From the Editorial:
Too much importance can scarcely be attached to the great part which our New Territory is destined to play in the future of Hongkong's history. On every side of the fruitful land, evidences are ... apparent that it is going to be the great feeder of the Colony, not only providing an outlet for the Island's congested population, but also making a home for new industries. ... Of course, the main factor in this movement is the starting of the Kowloon-Canton railway which is expected to be in full working order by next July.

❖ *A very accurate prediction of the development of the New Territories.*

Hongkong Telegraph
17 September 1910

OFFICIAL OPENING OF THE KOWLOON RAILWAY. The official opening this afternoon of the British section of the Kowloon-Canton Railway represents an epoch-making event in the Colony's history. In it we see at last the realisation of years of unfulfilled expectancy, and the successful consummation of a scheme beset from the beginning with difficulties and carried out despite almost insuperable obstacles. True, we cannot describe the Kowloon-Canton Railway as complete until the Chinese have brought their section down to the boundary and the two have been connected up. But we on our side have accomplished our part of this great undertaking, and before very many months have elapsed we should be in direct railway communication with the Capital City of Canton.

❖ *Although the Chinese side took only a year more to complete, the full Kowloon-Canton service was not operative until 1913. See Kowloon-Canton Railway, p.254.*

Hongkong Telegraph
1 October 1910

The agitation [in Canton] against the queue is spreading daily. ... Yesterday while taking a short walk on the new bund I counted no less than 23 queueless men. This may not appear a great number but when one considers that not long ago it was death to remove the appendage it shows how much the times are changing.

❖ *Indeed, they were. Repeated references to the abandoning the queue at the time seem to confirm falsity of the notion that the queue was only discarded* after *the fall of the Ching Dynasty.*

Hongkong Telegraph
29 October 1910

Kowloon-Canton Railway, Opening of the British Section of the Railway, 1 October 1910
The ceremony marking the completion of this important project, and opening the railway to traffic, was held on 1 October 1910 at Tsim Sha Tsui in temporary matsheds seen in this photograph (the Terminus Building was not yet ready). Sir Henry May, Officer Administering the Government (in the absence of Governor Lugard), accompanied by Lady May, formally opened the new railway; they are seen in the centre walking to the dais to begin the proceedings.

**Hongkong Telegraph
5 November 1910**

In 2900 BC the Chinese recorded events by knots in lengths of cord. As these did not prove enduring marks, recourse was taken to notches in bamboo sticks and tablets. Here again it was found that the cuts did not last and it occurred to an ancient Chinese savant who had spent much time observing the claw marks of birds in the mud and wet sand, to take such signs and the representations of animals, birds and fishes to convey words and ideas. Such was the origin of pictorial writing.

**Hongkong Telegraph
24 November 1910**

Doctor Sun Yat Sen has been severely censured by the Government authorities for his revolutionary speech at the Chinese Club in Penang. It is said he was gravely warned that serious consequences would follow a repetition of such conduct in public.

❖   *One cannot imagine that this would worry Doctor Sun, for he must have known that the days of the Ching Dynasty were numbered.*

From the Editorial:
The 'dangerous characters called Jesuits' who have been expelled by the Revolutionary Government in Portugal from all territories belonging to that unhappy country, proved on inspection to be really very harmless: modest and retiring men ... fine scholars too, and interested only in learned questions. ... this is sheer religious persecution, and we as free men, as lovers of liberty, abhor it and are disgusted by it.

❖   *Earlier this month, the Portuguese monarchy was overthrown by the revolution; hence expulsion of Jesuits. In Hong Kong Jesuits have set up fine schools and have promoted many cultural activities.*

Hongkong Telegraph
26 November 1910

Yesterday, the new tariff of charges in the third class of the tramways came into force. Six cents is now charged for what was formerly a five-cent ride, if paid in copper. Silver is still accepted by its face value. The Tramway Co. have been compelled to take this step because of the depreciation of the baser coin.

Hongkong Telegraph
5 December 1910

From the Editorial:
In the majority of instances a mere term of imprisonment is far from producing the desired effect, a direct incentive to indulge in further mischief, whereas a taste of 'cat' in nine cases out of ten, instils a wholesome discipline on the criminal which at once justifies the use of such form of punishment. ... The use of the 'cat' with greater frequency and freedom in Hongkong will confer untold benefits on the community.

❖   *'Cat' derives from 'cat-o-nine-tails' — a whip consisting of handle and nine tails, each with knots on it (reference to a cat which was believed to have nine lives). Flogging with a 'cat' is a terrible punishment. In Hong Kong, it was generally caning inflicted with a rattan cane, which was much less severe, but Governor Macdonnell (1866–1872), a man of stern character, is said to have replaced caning with 'cat' flogging. 'Cat' is used here probably figuratively, for 'caning'.*

Hongkong Telegraph
29 December 1910

1911

**Hongkong Telegraph
13 January 1911**

'Please don't spit on the pavement or any public places. The Society for the Suppression of Promiscuous Spitting in Public Places'. Such was the notice being distributed in the public streets today.

❖   *If this is not a joke, what happened to this society? We could still do with one today.*

**Hongkong Telegraph
2 February 1911**

The sad death occurred this morning of Mr. H.R. Cochrane, accountant of Mercantile Bank of India. He fell from the verandah of the bank mess into Queen's Road, opposite the Grand Hotel, at an early hour this morning. It is surmised that he must have fallen while walking in his sleep.

❖   *Cochrane Street, connecting Lyndhurst Terrace with Queen's Road Central, was not named after this unfortunate man, but after Rear-Admiral Sir Thomas Cochrane, Naval Commander in the 1840s.*

**Hongkong Telegraph
6 February 1911**

TIGERS IN THE NEW TERRITORY: A great deal of ridicule was recently cast upon the story of a tiger having been killed in the New Territory. ... [It] was seen at Fanling ... on Saturday evening by three European railway officials who happened to be travelling on the train. When sighted it was only some fifteen yards off the line, and was so keenly engaged in making a meal off a goat that it never even lifted its head or shifted off the place when the train passed.

❖   *True story or not (European railway officials were quite likely to have had a few drinks), there is no doubt whatsoever that tigers appeared not infrequently in the New Territories at the time.*

**Hongkong Telegraph
7 February 1911**

The first case under the new regulations in which no opium smoking is allowed in eating houses was heard this morning. ... His Worship said the case would be met by binding [the offenders] over to come up for judgement in the sum of $50 each.

❖   *At last a step in the right direction.*

Aberdeen, c.1920

Located on the southern side of Hong Kong Island, Aberdeen was not named after the city in Scotland, but the Earl of Aberdeen, who succeeded Lord Palmerston, in September 1841, as the British foreign secretary; and who incidentally was opposed to the retention of Hong Kong as a British possession. The Chinese, however, called the harbour of Aberdeen, Shek Pai Wan and the village inland Heung Kong Tsai (Little Hongkong).

At the time of cession of Hong Kong to Britain, Aberdeen had a small farming village on shore, but a much larger boat population sheltering in its well-protected harbour. This photograph shows a mass of sails, and although taken much later, depicted a scene that had not changed for centuries. In the early times, the place had an unsavoury reputation. Reverend Eitel, writing in his book *Europe in China*, in 1895, described it as 'the haunt of pirates … dreaded by peaceful traders'.

There is little doubt that the boat people of the local waters descend from the early sea-faring aborigines who had left ample archaeological evidence on the local seashores of their activities from as far back as 6,000 years.

A junk is a unique vessel. With its patched sails, high stern and a distinctive hull, it may seem almost bizarre to foreign eyes, but it is highly functional. The boat people were the first to build watertight compartments in their boats, thus safeguarding against rapid sinking, and perforated rudders, which are highly effective while offering less resistance to water.

Today, the sails are gone, replaced by motors; modern-day trawlers are moored alongside junks, while on shore the farming village is now a mini-metropolis.

Intimation:

Short-hand Typist Required. No other than Males need apply, must be competent. Apply to … stating salary required.

❖   *Surprised? Equal pay for men and women was not achieved in Hong Kong (Government and University) until 1970s!*

**Hongkong Telegraph
25 February 1911**

**Hongkong Telegraph
7 March 1911**

It is usually the fate of festival days marking changes in the climate to present conditions the exact reverse of what was expected. To-day was no exception. It is the Festival of Excited Insects, excited because they were to awake to-day from their winter sleep. The gods have been unkind to them, however, and rain and lowering clouds damped their ardour.

❖   *A very interesting festival, also known as the Budding Moon, seldom observed today except in farming communities.*

**Hongkong Telegraph
18 March 1911**

LOCAL AVIATION: A large number of spectators gathered to-day at Shatin Village in the expectation of seeing Mr. Van den Born give the first aviation exhibition in Hongkong. Unfortunately the wind proved too high to allow of the aviator flying. It is hoped that the weather conditions tomorrow will be suitable.

Trial Flight at Sha Tin, 18 March 1911

This was a momentous day for Hong Kong. Only eight years after the Wright brothers had succeeded in lifting their aeroplane into the air and flying several hundred yards, a similar feat was to be attempted in Hong Kong on 18 March 1911. A makeshift 'airfield' was hastily prepared on a stretch of beach at Sha Tin and a large number of eager spectators, including Governor Sir Frederick Lugard and his party, had gathered at Sha Tin Village in expectation of seeing the brave Belgian gentleman by the name of Van den Born give the first aviation exhibition in

Hong Kong.

Alas, they were disappointed; the wind proved to be too high to allow the aviator to take off. The disappointed crowd had dispersed, while the governor and his party took the next train back to Kowloon.

A flight did take place successfully the following week, but according to Dr Edward Pryor's informative and carefully researched lecture, reported in the City News in March 1955, the 18 March flight went ahead after the wind had suddenly dropped, though by that time many of the visitors had already departed.

PORPOISES IN THE HARBOUR: An unusual spectacle was witnessed in Hongkong Harbour this morning … a shoal of porpoises passed right through the narrows. There were some thirty or more porpoises in the shoal, and the average length of the fish appeared to be about ten feet. A number of launches followed the wake of the unaccustomed visitors.

❖ *If they averaged 10 feet, they were probably dolphins (porpoises, which are similar, are generally smaller). Their appearance in Hong Kong waters is common though usually not in the busy harbour. Both, porpoises and dolphins, are, of course, not fish but mammals; the editor should have known better.*

Hongkong Telegraph
23 March 1911

Photographic Advert: Your own baby, if you have one, can be enlarged, tinted and framed for $2.

Editorial comment: But so many people prefer to let nature do this enlarging, tinting and so on.

Hongkong Telegraph
11 April 1911

For the second time within a few months, a shipload of smuggled Chinese coolies have been thrown overboard in the Pacific Ocean and drowned. The men were all being taken from Lower California, Mexico and on the approach of the revenue cutters were heartlessly dumped into the sea, there to perish … the cutter 'Orient' witnessed the first murder, and attempted to save the helpless coolies but was too late.

❖ *One is left speechless at this horrible act of barbarism.*

Hongkong Telegraph
15 April 1911

MOTORS IN THE COLONY: The number of accidents due to motor cars … during the last few weeks … together with the reckless manner in which they are now driven, has led to new police regulations being framed to control traffic. There will be … a prohibited area within which motor cars will not be allowed to encroach. This area extends from the 'Parade Ground' [Murray Parade Ground] to Pokfoolum Road, and from Queen's Road to Bonham Road.

❖ *Motor cars were permitted, however, to reach Caine Road via D'Aguilar, Wellington and Arbuthnot Roads. A wise decision; if only it could be enforced again! See also Motor Car, p.260.*

Hongkong Telegraph
24 April 1911

Motor Car, Hong Kong, c.1920
Although the first petrol-driven internal combustion engine appeared in the 1880s, the first model with the essential elements of a modern motor car, or automobile as it is sometimes called, dates from about 1900–01. The motor car in the photograph is, of course, a much later model, of the 1920s. It is difficult to fix precisely the date when motor car first made its appearance in Hong Kong; probably around 1903–05. It was not received kindly by the public and attracted a good deal of unfavourable comment in the press. But by 1910–12, it became clear that the motor car 'had come to stay' (one newspaper had mistakenly printed 'had come to slay'), so much so that in 1913, the Clock Tower on Pedder Street, a much loved landmark, was pulled down in the interest of safe traffic.

Hongkong Telegraph
8 May 1911

6778 people visited the Museum at the City Hall last week.

Hongkong Telegraph
16 May 1911

The death has occurred at Peking in his sixty ninth year of the notorious Li Lien-ying, the Chief Eunuch of the late Empress Dowager Tzu-Hsi. … The power wielded by Li Lien-ying was colossal. … His successor, Chang Yuan-fu, is already a bye-word in the capital. … When his downfall comes it is devoutly to be hoped that he and the deceased Li Lien-ying will be the last of their obnoxious breed.

❖ *Obnoxious breed it was indeed. Believed to have been introduced into the court during the Han dynasty, eunuchs used their power to foment discord, and were largely the cause of intrigue, malice, wickedness, confusion, and revolt.*

Chinese Civilization ... from the very earliest times [in China] the taste for learning was cultivated and has continued to be a distinguishing characteristic of our people ... through all its history to the present day. Centuries before Homer there existed in the country a literature which attests to the very highest state of intellectual attainment.

Hongkong Telegraph
17 May 1911

The new Post Office is gradually shedding the unsightly but necessary structures of the builders, and beginning to assume its proper aspect. From the harbour it has a most imposing appearance and is certainly an outstanding architectural feature of the Colony.

Hongkong Telegraph
18 May 1911

❖   *Demolished in 1976, and replaced by a hideous, box-like but utilitarian structure on the waterfront.*

The General Post Office, Central District, Hong Kong Island, c.1920
This splendid building, in red brick with arched verandahs, which could make any city proud, was built between 1903 and 1911, replacing a much smaller one on Queen's Road Central. The picture shows its magnificent corner turret at the junction of Connaught Road and Pedder Street. Barely noticeable in the foreground, is the statue of the Duke of Connaught facing Blake Pier, moved here from the Statue Square in 1907. The General Post Office Building was demolished in 1976 to be replaced by the new one on the waterfront next to Blake Pier (now the Outlying Islands Pier).

**Hongkong Telegraph
2 June 1911**

HEALTH IN THE TROPICS: Dr. James Cantlie, formerly of Hongkong, is reported to have expressed the following views ... the younger the age at which a man proceeds to the tropics the greater the risk of contracting disease. ... I never have any hesitation in recommending a healthy man of between 30 and 50 to proceed to the tropics to take up work there; but I do my best to dissuade anyone under 21 doing so. ... It usually takes about 2 years after taking up residence in a warm country that effects of climate are manifested, and it depends upon soundness of wind and limb, and the strength of character of the individual, what the future is to be.

❖   *The same Dr Cantlie who was one of the founders, in 1887, of the Hongkong Medical College, and who after retirement in Scotland was instrumental in rescuing Dr Sun Yat-sen from the Chinese Embassy in London where the latter was held after being kidnapped. Like most medical men at the time, Dr Cantlie regarded Europeans largely unsuitable for life in tropics. We know better now. It was not the climate or the heat, but indulgence in alcohol and the prevalence of infectious diseases, mostly without specific cure, that made life in the tropics difficult.*

**Hongkong Telegraph
3 June 1911**

Official Notice: Unless with the express permission of the Department of Public Works, no wheeled vehicles will be allowed on Kennedy Road other than the following:- a ricksha, bicycle, tricycle or other similar machine not propelled by a motor, and a perambulator [pram for short] or other similar machine. Any such wheeled vehicle must proceed round the bends of Kennedy Road at a moderate speed.

**Hongkong Telegraph
21 June 1911**

The first public appearance of the top hat in its shiny modern form was in London on January 10th 1797 and proved to be nothing if not sensational. The wearer was John Heatherington, a Strand haberdasher, and the unwonted sight of his new and shiny head gear caused such a turmoil in the street that he was charged with breach of the peace and 'inciting to riot' and was bound over to keep peace in the sum of £500.

**Hongkong Telegraph
4 August 1911**

Kowloon-Canton Railway: It is reported that H.E. the Viceroy [of Kwangtung] appointed officials to draft up a series of regulations in connection with the running of the ... Railway. ... One series deals with the management of the employees of the railway. ... Fog signals and the firing of bombs will be introduced in cases of bad weather. ... The employees of the Railway when on duty will not be permitted to entertain passengers. Special apartments will be set apart for the convenience of female passengers, prisoners and lunatics.

❖ *The last regulation must be particularly reassuring for female passengers!*

Wealthy Chinese, who have come down to Hongkong in the last few months, having bought up all the suitable houses. ... on the Island as residence, are now ... turning their attention to Kowloon. ... we should see a very important development of the territory within a very short time. There appears to be no confidence among the Chinese that the revolution movement in Canton ... will die out. So long as this feeling prevails we shall see the men who have something to lose in a great revolutionary explosion ... eager to establish homes where life and property are more safe and secure — and their first in this connection will certainly be centered on Hongkong.

Hongkong Telegraph
17 August 1911

❖ *Note the similarity to the flow of wealth and entrepreneurial ability in the 1950s.*

To-day a Chinese festival is held, which has a parallel in Europe 'All Souls Day' ... Celebrations on a huge scale are carried on in the Civil and Military Temple [Man Mo Temple on Hollywood Road], while many of the Chinese firms ... make special arrangements for the day. ... Paper offerings will be burnt, the donors hoping that these articles will reach those in the spirit world who are homeless and hungry ...

Hongkong Telegraph
6 September 1911

❖ *This probably refers to the festival known as the 'Festival for the Hungry Ghosts', celebrated on the 15th day of the 7th Moon; the comparison with 'All Souls Day' is not really apt. See photograph of Man Mo Temple, p.99.*

Hongkong is faced by a somewhat serious situation with regard to the rice supply. The Chinese in Hongkong rely almost entirely upon rice from Siam [Thailand]. The old crop in that country is now practically exhausted and the new crop is not yet quite ripe. As a result less supplies

Hongkong Telegraph
7 September 1911

are coming forward and during the last two months the price has advanced from $6 per picul to $10. Unless additional supplies shortly come forward from Siam, there is imminent danger that there will be a rice famine in Hongkong.

❖ *It was, indeed, serious. The situation was brought partially under control by stopping all exports of rice from Hong Kong, by strict measures against hoarding and speculation of rice, and urgent appeals to Siam for more supplies.*

Walled Village, Tuen Mun, New Territories, c.1930s
The village is Nai Wai (泥圍), one of several established by the To (陶) Clan, which straddle Castle Peak Road at Tuen Mun. A fine walled village ('wai' usually refers to a walled village) dating from the 14 century AD, it is square in plan with four corner towers. Many of the original houses inside have been gradually replaced with modern houses (one can be seen in the photograph). In the past, the villagers farmed the adjoining fields, growing mainly rice and vegetables.

***Hongkong Telegraph*
14 September 1911**

FOUND … a brown donkey, straying at West Point. Apply to the Inspector on duty, Central Police Station.

***Hongkong Telegraph*
19 September 1911**

From the Editorial:
The tragic incident … of a motor-car 'running amok' and crushing out of existence six men once more calls attention to the high price that mankind has to pay for his triumph over time and distance. The motor-car is with us at Hongkong and … 'has come to stay'. … We recognise that the motor-car is an agent of utility and convenience. … But, unhappily, while the owner of a car may not necessarily be a criminal, its ownership does not always supply faculties and attributes which Nature has denied.

❖   *Today we can recognize this as the beginning of a lethal record, as the motorcar in increasing numbers and with increasing speed collects an ever-increasing number of victims.*

KOWLOON-CANTON RAILWAY: CEREMONY: Despite the [rumours] ... of possible trouble at the opening of the railway, the ceremony passed off without a hitch yesterday ... After passing the British frontier the train that conveyed the visitors from Hongkong passed a line guarded by soldiers with bayonets fixed and a plentiful supply of ammunition. ... Unfortunately Their Excellencies the Governor of Hongkong and the Viceroy of Canton were unable to be present.

Hongkong Telegraph
5 October 1911

❖   *This was the first 'through train' after the Chinese section of the railway had been completed. Their Excellencies' absence is explained by the fact that the ceremony was postponed at the last moment from the 2ⁿᵈ to the 4ᵗʰ of October due to the former date being a day of religious observances in China.*

Kowloon-Canton Railway, Opening of the Chinese Section of the Railway, August 1911
The Chinese Section of the Railway was completed almost a year after the British Section. The occasions was marked by official functions and receptions some of which were attended by the Governor of Hong Kong, Sir Frederick Lugard. In the photograph, which was probably taken at Lo Wu, prominent Chinese and British guests are seen attending the opening ceremony.

**Hongkong Telegraph
14 October 1911**

Bella Penida, a chauffeur in the employ of the Exile Garage, was again brought up before Mr. J.R.Wood at the Magistracy this morning on a charge of exceeding the speed limit by driving his car at the rate of sixteen miles an hour instead of ten, as provided in the Ordinance at Praya East ...

**Hongkong Telegraph
20 October 1911**

HONGKONG AND THE REVOLUTION: Among the Chinese in Hongkong there are many different schools of opinion on the rebellion and the probabilities of success. Many of those born and bred in Hongkong ... are by no means as enthusiastic over it as the Cantonese. ... The former say that to them the result matters little for they are British subjects and their home is here. ... The Cantonese refugee follows the struggle keenly because when it is over he will be able to go home to his paddy fields ... but at the same time he has a devout hope that the revolution will succeed.

❖   *The newspapers were full of news of the revolution; not surprising, for this was one of the greatest milestones in China's history, terminating the last Imperial dynasty.*

**Hongkong Telegraph
24 October 1911**

THE REBELLION; EUROPEAN PRESS OPINION: The Daily Telegraph says that at present there is no need for foreign intervention. The Manchus have deprived China of all opportunities for educational development and self-culture. Such an effete government should be removed.

**Hongkong Telegraph
27 October 1911**

The overthrow of the Manchus is considered in revolutionary quarters to be imminent.

❖   *Canton declared its independence from Peking on 29 October.*

**Hongkong Telegraph
31 October 1911**

Telegram:
An Imperial Edict has been issued in which the Throne apologises for its Governmental mistakes, grants the National Assembly full power to form a constitution, provides for the reorganization of the cabinet and the exclusion of the Imperial Family therefrom.

❖   *Too little, too late!*

WINGED AEROPLANES: The Wright brothers, who have been experimenting quietly for months ... have begun preparations to test a new aeroplane which ... will, if successful, revolutionise the present types. The new machines will be ... without propellers. The brothers have been engaged in perfecting a device to apply power to movable wings in imitation of the flight of birds, dispensing with the motor-driven screw entirely and they believe that they have succeeded.

Hongkong Telegraph
3 November 1911

❖   *Their belief was premature; the new contraption was a dismal failure. The birds still reign supreme. Can one imagine a jumbo jet with flapping wings?*

The Nobel prize for chemistry has been won by Madame Curie. She and her late husband Pierre Curie were responsible for the discovery of radium. This is the second of the Nobel honours that the Curies have received.

Hongkong Telegraph
9 November 1911

❖   *She was recently reburied in a place of honour in France (actually she was Polish by birth by the name of Sklodowska). At the time of her award of the Nobel prize, Madame Curie, as a woman, was not entitled to vote!*

A life-size model of Dr. Sun Yat-sen, the Chinese revolutionary leader, has been added to Madame Tussaud's Exhibition.

Hongkong Telegraph
29 November 1911

❖   *The ultimate seal of renown?*

WOMEN IN CHINA: The leaders of the revolutionary movement which is now taking place in China announced that ... they will aim at encouraging friendly relations with foreigners, and this change would have a great and far reaching effect on the lives of women. ... Three thousand years ago, when our ancestors were roaming primeval forests, the position of the Chinese women was the same as it is today. She has remained stationary. ... Western lands are holding out helping hands to their sisters, who form part of the oldest civilization in the world. Modern literature and journalists are also largely responsible for the awakening of Chinese women. The two books published, within the last few years, on the Germs of Feminism and the Right of the Chinese Woman in the choice of a Husband, voice the modern ideas which are taking root in the country.

Hongkong Telegraph
1 December 1911

Chinese Ladies, Hong Kong, c.1900
The four young women are sitting on a bench, probably in the Botanical Gardens. The two attractive young women in the centre are well coiffured and dressed in pretty embroidered clothes. Their feet are bound as was the custom with women of the privileged class. On either side, the two women, wearing black clothes, are probably their maids, their feet are not bound. Foot binding was less popular in South China than in the north, and was generally less common in lower classes. Women farmers avoided the custom as it would seriously interfere with performing heavy work in the field.

Hongkong Telegraph
5 December 1911

THE ENGLISH PIGTAIL: In all that has been said of the shedding of the queue by the Chinese, we have seen no mention of the fact that our own sailors, as far back as the days of Elizabeth [I], wore pigtails. The sailors of Nelson's day took an immense pride in them.

PHILHARMONIC CONCERT: The Hongkong Philharmonic Society is a shining example of what can be done by a number of people who are sufficiently serious to work together regularly and constantly to attain a given objective. ... That this has been done was abundantly proved by the programme presented at the Annual Concert last time at the City Hall.

Hongkong Telegraph
9 December 1911

❖   *The post-war Hong Kong Philharmonic Orchestra, bearing no direct descent from the pre-war Society, began in 1947 as an amateur orchestra and delighted numerous audiences with its regular concerts. It turned professional in 1975 and has since grown into a full-sized fine symphony orchestra.*

Cheung Chau (長洲), c.1920
Cheung Chau, meaning 'long island', is shaped like a dumb-bell (the geographical term for it is 'tombolo'), and is located in the south-west area of the territory. The photograph shows the island's main village occupying the narrow sandbar between two rocky landmasses. The island has had a mixed population of farmers, shopkeepers, and fisherfolk for many centuries. A number of archaeological sites and an ancient rock engraving also point to prehistoric human activity on the island. Its sheltered western bay has always afforded safe and calm anchorage to numerous fishing boats, as the photograph reveals.

Hongkong Telegraph
15 December 1911

A telegram from New York states that an interesting experiment has just been carried out … to ascertain the time it takes for a telegram to encircle the globe. The telegram of nine words was dispatched from the editorial office via Honolulu, Manila, Hongkong, Singapore … and back to the starting point. The message was exactly 16.5 minutes on its journey.

Hongkong Telegraph
19 December 1911

COLONY'S BADGE: Among the matters which came before the Legislative Council … is an important resolution … 'that the existing badge of the Colony is not only inartistic but it is unsuitable for reproduction especially on flags'.

❖ *The badge represented a pastoral scene in which, among other things, a top-hatted and frock-coated Englishman was shaking hands with a Chinese man.*

1912

Hongkong Telegraph
3 January 1912

EMU'S MENU: Among the indigenous birds of Queensland [Australia] the emu is one of the most interesting. … In the stomach of a specimen which was recently killed were found four pennies and five halfpennies. Other things found inside the emu were:- nine 2 inch nails, five marbles … one umbrella ferrule, one key, one medal … two studs, three buttons, one safety pin, two staples, three washers and 24 pieces of broken china, while a large pin was found embedded in the liver. The emu was only young, and was a fine specimen.

Hongkong Telegraph
8 January 1912

The streets of Hongkong were once again decked with flags, the occasion being the official day of rejoicing upon the establishment of a Republic in China.

With fitting ceremony the Courts of Justice began today what will, it is hoped, prove to be a long career of usefulness. There are differences of opinion in regard to the architectural beauty and structural fitness of the Courts but it may be fairly claimed that they are an improvement upon the old premises in Queen's Road. An interesting fact about the Law Courts is that over 12,000 tons of granite have been used in its structure.

Hongkong Telegraph
15 January 1912

❖ *Ninety years later, opinions are unanimous that it is a fine example of the neo-classical architecture. Its usefulness has been of long duration, the building now serving as the Legco Building. See Supreme Court Building, p.202.*

Hongkong has reason to be proud of the part it has played in the sphere of tropical medicine. It was here that the plague bacillus was discovered and it was also in this Colony that initial steps were taken towards the extermination of the malarial mosquito. Hongkong itself has been transformed from a place with an evil reputation into one of the healthiest localities in the East.

Hongkong Telegraph
22 January 1912

❖ *During the first plague epidemic in Hong Kong, in 1894, Kitasato of Japan and Yersin of France discovered the plague bacillus in Hong Kong. However, the claim that Hong Kong had become one of the healthiest places in the East is a dubious one. Right up until the Second World War, typhoid, meningitis, cholera, smallpox, malaria, and especially tuberculosis were prevalent in Hong Kong in sporadic and epidemic forms.*

HONGKONG'S THEATRE: Dusty and draughty, unlovely and uncomfortable, unbearably cold in winter, intolerably hot in summer, inconvenient and in all respects woefully lacking and out of date ... [the theatre] excites no feeling of pride in the breasts of the residents of the Colony ... a theatre which would be a disgrace to a small provincial town in England.

Hongkong Telegraph
5 February 1912

❖ *The Hong Kong's only theatre, thus strongly castigated, was located in the City Hall.*

Hongkong Telegraph
13 February 1912

From Shanghai, February 12th, 'THE THREE EDICTS' :-
By the first the Throne accepts the Republic. In the second the Throne accepts the conditions agreed upon by Yuan Shi-kai and the Republicans. The third informs the Viceroys and Governors that the Throne retires from political power to meet the wishes of the people.

❖   *From Autocracy to Democracy — a truly gigantic step for China.*

Hongkong Telegraph
2 March 1912

The daring of the West River pirates seems to know no limits for on Thursday night they attacked the British Steamer *Tai On* on her voyage to Hongkong from Kongmoon escorted by a Chinese torpedo boat ... Fortunately no one was hurt by the bullets of the pirates, though some passed very close.

Hongkong Telegraph
4 March 1912

It was gratifying in a measure to those who have a pride in our unrivalled harbour and its limitless facilities for shipping to learn ... that the question of the projected commercial wireless for this Colony has not been neglected.

Hongkong Telegraph
5 March 1912

UNIVERSITY OF HONGKONG
OPENING CEREMONY
THE UNIVERSITY BUILDINGS
will be opened on
Monday March 11th 1912 at 2.30 p.m. by
His Excellency Sir Frederick J. D. Lugard GCMG, CB, DSO
Governor of Hongkong and Chancellor of the University
To be followed by a
UNIVERSITY BAZAAR

South China
Morning Post
12 March 1912

The modern thimble dates from 1684 when the goldsmith Nicholas Benschoten of Amsterdam sent one as a present to a lady friend.

❖   *A small item of useless but interesting information.*

South China
Morning Post
26 March 1912

The Board of the Interior [in China] has issued a new regulation forbidding the practice of footbinding throughout China.

University of Hong Kong at the Inauguration

Two years, almost to the day, after the foundation stone of the main building of the new university had been laid, the building was ready for the inauguration of the university, on 11 March 1912. The opening ceremony, in the presence of a large and distinguished gathering, was performed by Sir Frederick Lugard, the Governor of Hong Kong and chancellor of the university; it was followed by a highly successful and popular university bazaar.

The Main Building, a gift to the people of Hong Kong by a local Parsee businessman, Sir Hormusjee Mody, is a magnificent structure in the traditional red-brick university style. A local firm of architects, Leigh and Orange, designed and supervised the construction of the building of brick and granite. Described also as 'Renaissance' in style, it presents external and internal colonnades on two floors supported by rows of large granite pillars, and is surmounted by a tall clock tower and four turrets. Within there are open courtyards, two with tall palm trees planted in its first year of existence.

The Main Building is the centre of one of the oldest of the Far Eastern universities, which is acknowledged as the foremost bearer of Western culture, science and learning to the youth of the Orient.

One of the finest buildings of the British period in Hong Kong, it is a gazetted historic building.

South China Morning Post 28 March 1912

The official flag of the new Chinese Republic, hoisted at the Legation in London, has five bars of colour — red, yellow, blue, white and black.

❖ *The day before, on the 27th, Dr Sun Yat-sen — who was appointed provisional president — formally resigned presidency, making way for Yuan Shih-kai.*

South China Morning Post 30 March 1912

The notification appointing the Government Hospital at Kennedy Town to be a Leper Asylum for the segregation and treatment of lepers has been rescinded.

Few today will remember that leprosy was common in Hong Kong in the early times. The island of Hei Ling Chau was long used to segregate lepers, and was only discontinued to be so used in the 1970s.

Hongkong Telegraph 6 April 1912

Yesterday was Ching Ming, or day of pure brightness, when the Chinese delight to honour their dead. … In only one instance did the writer see a grave untended and as he passed it he thought of the neglected … weatherbeaten grey stones at Stanley that mark the resting place of the pioneers of the British Colony.

❖ *The 'neglected' stones are, in fact, the early garrison graves. Later, they were looked after by the Government and the Commonwealth War Graves Commission, and well maintained up to the present.*

South China Morning Post 9 April 1912

Now that the Revolution has ended, the indications are that a great future lies ahead of China … Manchu power has been completely overthrown and all its retarding influence swept aside. … The stupendous task of commercial and industrial reform is now about to begin.

South China Morning Post 10 April 1912

From the Editorial:
Two interesting items of news, which may well be coupled, are furnished in telegrams received within the last twenty-four hours. The first is that Mongolia has declined to join the Republic, the second is that a kind of holy war is said to be proceeding in Tibet.

❖ *No matter! Both would be swiftly brought to heel.*

For the first time in the history of … air flying a man leaped from an aeroplane at Jefferson Barracks [USA] this afternoon and descended to the earth in a parachute.

South China Morning Post 11 April 1912

London: Reuter's correspondent at New York states that the liner Titanic has sent a wireless message to the effect that she has collided with an iceberg, and asks for assistance. … The Titanic is reported to be sinking by the head. The women are being taken off the vessel in lifeboats.

South China Morning Post 16 April 1912

❖ *The news all over the world at the time was dominated by the incredible tragedy of the sinking of the* Titanic *which was widely believed to be unsinkable. Some 1,500 lives were lost because there were no sufficient lifeboats and rafts to carry all on board.*

Dr. Sun Yat-sen has decided to reside in Macao and the house he has chosen is already in a fair way to completion. His family has left for the Portuguese settlement and he will follow shortly.

Hongkong Telegraph 2 May 1912

❖ *Those who visit Macao are undoubtedly familiar with this house — an important historical building in the place.*

It is reported that Great Britain has declared it her intention formally to recognise the New Republic conditional upon the New Territory adjoining Kowloon being further extended.

Hongkong Telegraph 4 May 1912

❖ *The extension was not achieved.*

Eight overhead fans have been installed above the counters in the General Post Office. This consideration for the perspiring public is greatly appreciated these days.

Hongkong Daily Press 28 May 1912

From the Editorial:
If the inner history of the Chinese Revolution ever comes to be faithfully written it will … be found that the part played therein by the Chinese in Hongkong, particularly of the merchant class, was a much more active one that most people at present imagine to have been the case …

South China Morning Post 30 May 1912

Because of the right of asylum which they enjoyed at the very door of their native land, they were able to pave the way for the great uprising in a variety of ways; indeed, the view is held in some quarters that the rebellion was largely engineered from a block of buildings in Bonham Strand.

❖   *That the revolution, at least partly, was hatched at Bonham Strand may well be true, but as for 'asylum' — the meetings there were clandestine and Sun Yat-sen himself was declared in Hong Kong 'persona non grata'.*

Hongkong Waterfront, c.1920

There may be more than a few today who would find the waterfront shown here aesthetically more pleasing than the cramped jagged outline of the present one.

When this photograph was taken, the last massive reclamation in the central section of the town had been completed only 16 years before. It resulted in the shift of the mercantile offices to the east and the intrusion of the Chinese businesses into what was only a few years ago not merely the European business quarter, but also the residential part of town.

On the newly reclaimed land, massive, imposing-looking colonial-style buildings with corner turrets and arched verandahs were erected. Lining the new waterfront, renamed Connaught Road, they had totally transfigured the waterfront.

Let us now identify these edifices of the past: on the extreme left, just inside the photograph and projecting into the harbour, is the Victoria Recreation Club (now at Deep Water Bay). Moving right, next is the building of Butterfield & Swire, then a three-storey office of the *Telegraph*; then the large and imposing Hongkong Club, on its new site since 1897. There follows a gap which is Statue Square, in front of which stands a statue of Queen Victoria (seen here at an angle). Through the gap and beyond Statue Square, we can glimpse part of the Supreme Court (now the Legco Building), and still further behind on Queen's Road, the magnificent City Hall.

Next, two fine four-storey buildings, seen from the front side, are Queen's Building in front and Prince's just behind, separated by Chater Road. Further along the waterfront, next to Queen's, is St George's Building, then the King's Building and the narrow building without a name. Then comes Pedder Street and the last building seen on the right is the General Post Office.

HONGKONG'S FUTURE: ... notwithstanding some pessimistic forebodings, the confidence of the community and the Government in the future of the Colony has been strikingly shown in many ways ... Within the past ten years, for instance, the Colony has seen completed the extensive scheme of reclamation along the city water frontage, whereby 65 acres have been added to the city, 34 acres being building land, on which some of the finest business houses in Asia have been erected. [The writer] further refers to the erection of Government Offices costing over $1,000,000, and new Courts of Justice costing $865,000, not to mention the latest addition in the shape of the Hongkong University.

Hongkong Telegraph
7 June 1912

Queen's Building, Central District, Hong Kong Island, c.1905
The photograph shows the east and north aspects of this magnificent building, completed in 1899. Behind it, portion of the Prince's Building, completed in 1904, can be seen. The massive Praya Reclamation of 1890–1904 resulted in the new waterfront (see opposite page), later to be renamed Connaught Road, on which a number of large, imposing buildings was erected, like the Queen's. Together they had totally transformed the Central District into a stately and impressive area. None, however, survived the post-Second World War redevelopment fever.

**Hongkong Telegraph
14 June 1912**

The statement made by ... the Officer Administering the Government [in effect, the Acting Governor] on the subject of vehicle regulations ... 'Early in May' said His Excellency, 'I was concerned at the constant accidents caused by motor vehicles, and I obtained a report which showed that there are 21 motor cars in Hongkong, of which seven are privately owned, and 14 belong to four garages. No accidents had been caused by the former, while the latter had been responsible for 28 accidents during the 16 months ... which resulted in four persons being killed and four seriously injured, a very bad record.'

❖ *Most interesting statistics of Hong Kong's early motoring history. A bad record, indeed! Fourteen cars responsible for 28 accidents.*

**Hongkong Telegraph
17 June 1912**

Dr. Sun Yat-sen arrived in the Colony ... en route for Peking. He is at present staying at the Hongkong Hotel, and his movements abroad have been followed with great interest by the Chinese.

❖ *Although he had relinquished presidency, his advice was frequently sought by the new Chinese republic.*

**Hongkong Telegraph
3 July 1912**

HONGKONG'S DOUBLE DECKERS: The Tramway Company are proceeding apace, equipping cars ... with seating accommodation on top. Though it was at first doubted by many of the public, whether the 'double decker' would be a success in Hongkong, results have proved that the step was a good one ... The ride to Shaukiwan is a most enjoyable one.

❖ *The first 'double deckers' had open tops, but in 1925 became fully enclosed.*

**Hongkong Telegraph
9 July 1912**

CHINESE LADY DOCTOR: A Chinese woman, Dr. Yamei Kin, is at the Head of the Imperial Pei-Yang Woman's Medical School and Hospital, and is visiting physician to ... [several institutions] all of which are Government Institutions. She is the first woman to receive an appointment as head of her own work.

A telegram ... announces the death of the famous missionary, Dr. Griffith John. Shattered in health, and so weak that he could hardly stand on landing, Dr. John reached London early January this year, after more than half a century of work in China in the service of the London Missionary Society. ... Founded 'a remarkable mission which by 1905 had a Church membership of 6,500'.

Hongkong Telegraph
26 July 1912

His Holiness the Dali Lama and his acolytes are on their way back to Lhasa, singing their *Song of Degrees* ... and surrounded by the refinements of civilization, the whole crowned by the holy one's bath tub. Thus this contact with European luxury spoils native simplicity. A gracious rain was falling on the Tibetan inheritance as the August procession moved off, its members expressing their delight at escaping from the Indian climate. ... The anabasis of the Dali Lama is an episode to touch the heart.

Hongkong Telegraph
27 July 1912

❖ *Note the strange spelling 'Dali Lama'! In case readers have difficulty with 'anabasis', as I had, it may be translated as the 'military march into the interior', and was first used to describe the march of the Persian King Cyrus (the Younger) into Asia in 401 BC.*

Ex-Emperor Cuts Off His Queue: The Dowager Empress has induced the young Emperor to discard his queue, thereby setting to the members of the Imperial Household an example showing the reconciliation of the Manchus to the Republican Regime.

Hongkong Telegraph
29 July 1912

❖ *It is sometimes forgotten that while the Republic reigned officially outside, the Emperor continued to rule over his small isolated Forbidden City (the Imperial Palace) and his entourage well into the 1920s.*

SLEEPING POLICE: In view of the frequency of burglary ... of late we might be permitted once again to ask, 'Where are the Police?' To answer our query, they are, or some of them have been *asleep*. ... It may be a pretty and reposeful sight to see our supposed guardians of the peace wooing the Goddess of Sleep in the open air, but we need hardly point out that this is not quite what they are paid to do ...

Hongkong Telegraph
7 August 1912

Hongkong Telegraph **8 August 1912**	A boy at Wanchai was knocked down by a bullock cart yesterday and his leg was broken. ❖ *Bullock carts in Wan Chai in 1912!*

Hongkong Telegraph
9 August 1912

ANCIENT CHINESE WRITING: The British Museum has acquired a collection of ancient bones inscribed with archaic Chinese characters of a more primitive type than any yet found. ... the characters have been deciphered only in part. ... The bones having been inscribed with questions, were seared with hot irons, and the cracks which then appeared in the bones were interpreted according to certain rules of divination. ... The enquiries related to such things as the prospect of rainfall, harvest ... hunting expeditions, change of residence, and so forth. One eminent authority inclines to assign the date to the early part of the Chou dynasty, which lasted from B.C. 1122 to B.C. 249; but the moderate Chinese critics attribute them to the Shang dynasty, which lasted from B.C. 1766 to B.C. 1122. In any case they are the oldest forms of Chinese writing that have survived.

❖ *This must be one of the earliest references to what became known as the 'oracle bones'. Today some of these inscribed bones are attributed to pre-Shang period.*

Hongkong Telegraph
23 August 1912

Twelve months hard labour in each case was the sentence ... at the Police Court, today, on a man and a woman charged with kidnapping a child aged eleven years, from her mother. ... The police, it was stated, were unable to obtain the return of the child from the Country as they had not the amount required for the redemption of the child. The mother said she would have to pawn two other children to raise the amount required to get the stolen child back.

❖ *This seems to defy all reason — that a kidnapped child should have to be bought back.*

Hongkong Telegraph
24 August 1912

THE TIGER AGAIN: The police have received a report from the schoolmaster ... in ... Sai Kung, that on the 21st inst. he heard his pigs making a great noise and he looked out of the window to see what was disturbing them. To his surprise he saw a tiger making off with a pig that weighed 102 catties and was valued at $20.

❖ *See also* Hongkong Telegraph *7 February 1911, p.256.*

Sedan Chair, Hong Kong, c.1920s
Described as an enclosed chair for one passenger carried on poles by two bearers, sedan chair is not an exclusively Oriental mode of conveyance, but was used in Europe in the 17th and 18th centuries, and was even said to have been invented in France (the city of Sedan). On Hong Kong Island's hilly terrain, it proved indispensable and could carry passengers to heights where no rickshaw could possibly reach.

From the Editorial:
SLAVERY IN HONGKONG: … serious point is raised in the annual report … of the Registrar General of Hongkong that purchased children can be found in probably 90 per cent of the well-to-do Chinese families in the Colony. … [It is] the admitted fact that young children are rather freely disposed of for money … and it is safe to assume from this … that in many instances these children are deprived of all true freedom.

❖ *The problem of these 'mui tsai' children had troubled the official conscience of the Hong Kong Government since the 1860s but nothing was done (but see also Po Leung Kuk, p.143). The male children fared rather better for they were usually 'adopted' when there was no male heir; but the girls were mostly bought for domestic servitude. It is wrong, however, to call it slavery, since they had legal rights, especially in cases of proven maltreatment. Still, it was a reprehensible custom which did not stop until the end of Second World War.*

Hongkong Telegraph
30 August 1912

**Hongkong Telegraph
4 September 1912**

A Zeppelin airship has carried 57 passengers round Hamburg for two hours.

❖ *Although some attempts to launch an airship were made as early as 1870, the first practical airship was constructed in 1900 by Count Ferdinand von Zeppelin of Germany.*

According to a Chinese paper, General Li has decided to send 60 students abroad at a cost of taels 40,000 per annum. ... eight students to study Navy affairs in Great Britain ... six students to study military affairs in Germany ... twenty students to study mineralogy in Belgium ... ten students to study industrial affairs in America ... eight students to study law in France and mathematics in Italy respectively ... And eight students to study political economy in Japan. If the funds are not sufficient for so many students to complete their courses, rich people will be invited to contribute money for the purpose.

**Hongkong Telegraph
12 September 1912**

Thus it is that a force like the Hongkong Volunteer Corps should be regarded as providing the opportunity for useful service that any able man should be eager to embrace. ... The day may come when it will be realised volunteering is no mere hobby. It is a serious business, and an obligation on such as have strength and facilities for pursuing it.

❖ *That day did come — in December 1941 — when the Hongkong Volunteers fought hard and proved their worth defending the territory against the Japanese attack. See also Hong Kong Volunteer Defence Corps, p.251.*

**Hongkong Telegraph
23 September 1912**

A fine of five dollars or fourteen days was imposed at the Police Court this morning, for cruelty to a chicken by carrying it in a bag minus ventilation.

A chicken escaped from a roof and flew to the Telegraph and Telephone wires. Roosting there it short-circuited business and obstructed traffic by reason of the crowds that collected to watch the ludicrous attempts of three stalwart constables to dislodge it. In court today the bird will no doubt be reprimanded.

❖ *One can only hope that it was the same chicken, described in the previous snippet, avenging its incarceration without ventilation.*

What many scientists present pronounced a wonderful demonstration was given by Miss Helen Keller at Boston recently, when she sang the scale and spoke in three languages at the ontological congress at Harvard Medical School.

Hongkong Telegraph
24 September 1912

❖   *Helen Keller (1880-1968) became blind and deaf when 18 months old, yet achieved world renown when she graduated from a college and published several books.*

Somewhat of a sensation has been caused by the sudden disappearance of the compradore of the Hongkong and Shanghai Banking Corporation. He was missed on Sunday and it is said that defalcations which are laid to his account total about five hundred lakhs of dollars. The bank does not suffer much.

Hongkong Telegraph
30 September 1912

❖   *Two now seldom used words perhaps need an explanation: 'defalcation' which means misappropriation of money, and 'lakh', which comes from India and has been much used in the past in the Far East, means a hundred thousand.*

In China, as is well known, salt has been a great monopoly for three thousand years, and the salt-tax forms, with the ground tax ... and the maritime customs, the chief income of the state. Import of salt into China is forbidden ... and all the salt consumed by the population is derived from sea-water, salt marshes or salt springs.

South China
Morning Post
17 October 1912

❖   *The whole of China was divided into 14 salt-producing areas. Some popular uprisings have been recorded, such as during the Ming dynasty, when the local population objected to the government collecting their salt. Abandoned salt-fields can still be seen at Tai O, on Lantao Island.*

The chair and rickshaw coolies of Hongkong have gone on strike, owing, it is said, to their resentment of heavy fines recently imposed for loitering and obstruction in the streets. In Kowloon the rickshaws are plying as usual.

Hongkong Telegraph
29 October 1912

❖   *In those days, when apart from the tramways, rickshaws and sedan chairs were almost the only means of transportation, the inconvenience caused by the strike was very considerable. Fortunately, this one lasted only a few days.*

Nathan Road, Kowloon, c.1930

This unique photograph of Nathan Road about 70 years ago shows several interesting features: the modest, two-three storey-high colonial houses line both sides of the street; today all have been replaced by high-rise commercial buildings.

There are few people on the street and only three motor vehicles visible. One of them is the No. 7 bus, a small single-decker, on its way to the Star Ferry (the destination sign is clearly visible). At least this bus number and the route remain the same to this day.

A Sikh policeman is seen on the left, and in the middle of the road a traffic sign proclaims prominently the speed limit of 20 miles per hour. With hardly any motor traffic on the street and with less than 1,000 motor vehicles licensed at the time, this seems a wise precaution. If only this had been adhered to, there might have been fewer major accidents on the roads.

In the absence of definite landmarks, it is difficult to tell which part of Nathan Road is shown in this photograph, but it is probably not far from its junction with Gascoigne Road. The scene is one of slow and tranquil pace, so sadly missing from present-day Kowloon.

An aeroplane flight from England to India is now under consideration ... the distance along the proposed route is 4,800 miles and it is estimated that each day's stage would be 400 miles.

Hongkong Telegraph
30 October 1912

❖ *That is a total of 12 days, weather permitting! But considering that only nine years previously, Orville Wright flew his biplane, with his brother Wilbur running alongside, for just 36 metres (a tiny fraction of a mile) before diving to the ground, it had been a phenomenal achievement.*

POST OFFICE INSCRIPTION: The inscription on the wall of the Hongkong Post Office 'As cold water to a thirsty soul, so is good news from a far country', has been recently embellished by a heavy hard-wood framework of ornamental design.

Hongkong Telegraph
9 November 1912

❖ *The inscription, I believe, has been preserved.*

BOYCOTT OF THE TRAMS: On Sunday evening ... the neighbourhood of Sai Wan Ho was thrown into a state of excitement when some two thousand Chinese who take exception to the new regulation adopted by the tramway, excluding the tender of Chinese coin in payment of fares, held up the cars, threw stones at them, and in one instance assaulted the police, a Chinese detective being bitten on the thumb.

Hongkong Telegraph
25 November 1912

❖ *For a short while the Chinese tradesmen in Canton retaliated by refusing to accept Hong Kong money. The boycott of the trams lasted for one month. In an attempt to appease the protesters, the tramway company had offered free rides for Chinese passengers rather than accept Chinese coins, but the free rides had only lasted for two days.*

At the Police Court, this morning, Sergeant Thompson charged the master of a fishing junk with being in unlawful possession of 35 sticks of dynamite. He was asked if he intended using it for fishing and he replied that he used it for frightening sharks. ... Defendant was fined $250.

Hongkong Telegraph
17 December 1912

Hongkong Telegraph
18 December 1912

The Dairy Farm: So successfully do the Dairy Farm Ltd. advertise, that it is practically safe to assert that had they no shop premises, they would not suffer much. The fact that they have one of the cleanest and freshest looking stores in the City is a clear indication of the care devoted to the goods that they sell. Hams, in nice white cloths, may be seen, of a quality which is the hallmark of the firm's reputation, bacon of undisputed excellence, German sausages of all kinds, prepared under expert supervision. ... As for butter and cheese, the quality of these commodities is so well known that further mention of them would be superfluous.

❖   *The Dairy Farm Co., which is still flourishing today, should take notice of this highly complimentary account.*

Hongkong Telegraph
26 December 1912

Street noises represent one of by no means lesser evils from which ... the people who live in [Hongkong] suffer. But, as with mosquitoes, cockroaches, prickly heat and a host of other annoyances ... in time we get inured to them. We are nevertheless glad when we see that some attempt is made to mitigate the nuisance. It will be noticed that it now becomes an offence for a person to make or cause to be made any noise 'calculated to disturb or interfere with the public tranquillity' ... between sunset and the hour of six in the following morning. We would that the clause operated at all hours of the day and night.

Hongkong Telegraph
28 December 1912

The Time Ball at Blackhead Point is to drop on Sundays, and Government holidays, as well as on ordinary weekends, beginning on 1ˢᵗ January. ... For the benefit of captains of vessels about to leave, who have had no opportunity of correcting their chronometers while in Port, the Ball will, when necessary, be dropped at some other [daylight] hour on application to the Harbour Master.

❖   *See also p.239. Since the Time Ball Signal was available since 1884, it may be assumed that the present announcement refers to the additional signals on public holidays and weekends. The Time Ball was a large hollow copper ball painted black. Dropping the ball at precisely 1 pm served as a time signal and could be observed by the ships in harbour so that their chronometers could be checked. This continued until 1933, when the signal was replaced by radio signals.*

Main Depot of Dairy Farm Company, c.1908

The building is still there — at the junction of Wyndham Street and Lower Albert Road, on Hong Kong Island — though considerably altered. The Dairy Farm Company's origins go as far back as 1856, but the company was not properly established and incorporated until 1886. It has always maintained extensive grounds on the south side of the island and until 30 years ago even maintained its own herd of cows.

Company records show that the Main Central Depot, shown in this photograph, was first built on the site in 1892; extensive reconstructions have completely changed its appearance. It is likely that the two blocks which today comprise the building, bearing the dates 1913 and 1917, are the result of rebuilding.

The two blocks are of brick and stone foundation and stand on split levels following the steep slope of Wyndham Street. Their style is simple and colonial. The building has some historical significance as the Dairy Farm Company is a very old Hong Kong firm. After 1981 the building ceased to be used by the company and now houses the Foreign Correspondents' Club and the Fringe Club.

Sung Dynasty Inscription, Tai Miu Wan, Sai Kung, 1976
The inscription carved on a large boulder on the north shore of Tai Miu Wan
(Joss House Bay) records a visit of an officer named Yen I-chang, in charge of
the local salt production, in the year AD 1274 in the Southern Sung (Song)
Dynasty. We shall never know what caused Yen I-chang to resort to this unusual
method of chronicling what must have been a routine visit, but we shall be
forever grateful to his memory, for he left us a most remarkable and lasting
historical relic — an engraved inscription of some 108 characters, precisely
dated. The inscription is of particular interest, informing us of the Government's
control of the salt production and speculating on the fate of a couple of early
temples in the area. Skilfully engraved in a style consistent with the date, the
inscription is well preserved and easily read. However, its ancient literary style
makes interpretation difficult; a plaque offering a paraphrase in modern Chinese,
and a translation in English, have been installed near the inscription.

1913

Broadway was puzzled recently by dispatches from Pittsburgh that Mrs. Lily Langtry, who is under contract at $3000 a week to appear in a suffragette playlet written by herself, is not allowed to play there. ... It is denied that adverse criticisms in the newspapers had anything to do with cutting short the international star's engagement.

Hongkong Telegraph
11 January 1913

❖ *A bit of history: Lily Langtry, British actress was noted for her beauty, her acting, and for becoming the mistress of King Edward VII. At the time of this broken contract, she was 60 years old.*

VEGETARIANISM: The recent celebration ... of the Vegetarian Society serves to remind one of the quiet but very insistent campaign which has been and still is being carried on by those who spurn the eating of flesh. ... it is interesting to note that vegetarians are now backing up views by economic arguments. ... It is argued that meat of all kinds is becoming more costly, that as population increases it will become necessary to use land more economically. ... Will the economic argument eventually compel attention?

Hongkong Telegraph
17 January 1913

❖ *Evidently it did not. Today, one could be more forceful by bringing in the 'mad cow' disease and the more recent foot-and-mouth disease arguments.*

CHINA'S EX-EMPEROR : A LONELY CHILD: ... the immense precincts of the Winter Palace are absolutely deserted save for the Empress-Dowager, the Child Emperor, and a few eunuchs. ... The same hundreds of sheep, pigs and fowls stipulated by the Imperial household ordinances are still daily slaughtered, but being uneaten, are sold outside. The eunuchs, left uncontrolled, are rapidly stripping the Palace of all valuables. ... The Empress-Dowager weeps ceaselessly ... the Emperor is a dull, listless child, not knowing what has happened. He plays ceaselessly with toy soldiers in the halls ... that were trodden by the feet not only of his illustrious ancestors, but by Kublai Khan himself, and which once rang to the hurrahs of horsemen returning from the conquests of half Asia.

Hongkong Telegraph
22 January 1913

❖ *The* Telegraph *paints graphically a very sad picture. The Empress-Dowager died suddenly a month later.*

Chinese Family in Hongkong, c.1917

This handsome family is unfortunately anonymous, but it does convey the image of a reasonably well-to-do Chinese family in Hong Kong in the early part of the century. The head of the family, possibly a merchant, is seated in the middle. He is dressed in a traditional silk jacket and gown, wears a skull cap, and silk shoes. On his right, holding a child, is his wife, also suitably dressed for the occasion. In a similar position on the left is his secondary wife or concubine. Around them are their five children, ranging from a baby in arms to an adolescent boy also wearing a gown and skull cap.

Concubinage is an ancient custom in China, originating undoubtedly

in the desire of a family to have more sons.

Only one woman in a man's household holds the position of legal wife; all the others, and there could be several, are secondary wives or concubines. Although concubines are not on an equal basis with the first wife, their children are generally on an equal level to those of the first wife. In the present day, concubinage is prohibited in China, and is absent in the Western-oriented families, but is still found in traditional families, especially in cases where the first wife has failed to give birth to a son.

Notice that although it was 1917, the women's feet had not been bound. This custom was never popular in South China.

Hongkong Telegraph 1 February 1913

CRACKER-FIRING: It is notified in the Gazette that it is unlawful for any person … to discharge, kindle or let off any fireworks in the City of Victoria or within three hundred feet of the Praya Wall … except under permit issued by the Registrar General. The firing of crackers on any of the days observed as Holidays is governed by the above.

❖ *Never strongly enforced, this law was again promulgated in 1967, after the riots. However, the New Territories had never bothered to observe this order.*

THE SCOTT EXPEDITION: The Central News Agency announces that Captain Scott and his party perished in a blizzard after reaching the South Pole on January 18th 1912.

❖　*The news of this terrible tragedy took a year to reach the world, and would dominate the world press for some time. Britain was shattered by the news. What made the tragedy even worse was that on reaching the South Pole, Scott discovered that he was beaten by the Norwegian explorer Amundsen who had reached the Pole just a few days earlier.*

Hongkong Telegraph
11 February 1913

PLAGUE: We are informed that two cases of plague within the Colony have been reported during the last few days. This brings the number of cases for the present year to a total of three, which compares very favourably with last year's ... nine cases [in January] and twenty four [in February]. The rat return ... is equally encouraging.

Hongkong Telegraph
13 February 1913

The Ellis Kadoorie Schools, which have undergone considerable extensions and improvements, were opened this afternoon by His Excellency the Governor. There was a large assembly of both Europeans and Chinese who have an interest in the Schools. ... The site [of the school] is one of the best in Hongkong. It is on a lofty piece of ground overlooking Queen's Road. ... The college commands a fine view of the Harbour ... and the Chinese ideas on the subject of fungshui are satisfied. ... It is estimated that the new College Hall will be able to accommodate 1,500 pupils.

Hongkong Telegraph
24 February 1913

AMERICA'S NEW PRESIDENT: Our telegrams today tell of the inauguration of Mr. Woodrow Wilson as president of the United States of America, an event which will probably mark the beginning of a new epoch in the history of the great Republic.

❖　*More than that, he would initiate a new epoch in the history of the world, by becoming the chief proponent of the League of Nations, the predecessor of today's United Nations.*

Hongkong Telegraph
5 March 1913

Hongkong Telegraph
2 April 1913

THE CLOCK TOWER: So, the Clock Tower is to go at last; very few people will be really sorry, for neither its position nor appearance greatly recommended it for preservation. There are sentimentalists. … who will plead for its retention on the score that it is an ancient landmark. … There is nothing of antiquity about it, as the term is usually understood. It is still a comparative youngster as historic buildings go.

❖ *It is difficult to agree with this comment. Built by public subscription, in 1863, the tower was a handsome structure and at 50 years old, in a city which itself was only 70 years old, could be considered 'ancient'. Its role as a 'traffic hazard', with motorcars numbering less than a hundred, was a gross exaggeration; besides, standing at the top of Pedder Street, it did not encroach on Queen's Road. An admirable solution, which obviously did not occur to the town planners, was to make Pedder Street between Queen's Road and Des Voeux Road, a pedestrian mall. Contrary to the* Telegraph's *comment, the loss of the Clock Tower was genuinely regretted by many; it was the first victim on the list of historic structures which would grow rapidly in years to come, to be sacrificed in the name of progress.*

The Clock Tower, Central District, Hong Kong Island, c.1910
The Clock Tower, for many years a prominent feature of the Central District of Hong Kong, stood 80 feet high, at the junction of Pedder Street and Queen's Road Central. Funded by public subscriptions, which proved insufficient, the final result fell short of the original handsome design, so much so that when it was completed, in 1863, E. J. Eitel described it as 'an ugly tower obstructing the principal thoroughfare'. This was too harsh. Many a passer-by was grateful for its presence as he checked his watch against the tower's clock, and it earned a warm place in the hearts of Hong Kong people. In spite of its unfortunate location, the Clock Tower remained there until 1913, when due to the increasing traffic, now with motor cars added, it was deemed a traffic hazard and was demolished.

THE CHILDREN'S BILL: Yesterday the Ordinance amending the 'Offences against the Person Act of 1865' was passed by the Legislative Council; and, henceforth, any person over sixteen years of age, who has custody of a child, and ill-treats it in any way ... will be guilty of a heavily punishable misdemeanour ... but why has Hongkong allowed forty-eight years to pass before discovering officially that the life of its Chinese children was not altogether a bed of roses? That is one of the many puzzles connected with the Colony which we have given up trying to unravel.

Hongkong Telegraph
18 April 1913

Chinese Children, Hong Kong, c.1950s
These cheerful looking children are posing for a photograph sitting on a waterfront, probably at the western end of Connaught Road. They are probably children of the fisherfolk, or boat people, whose junks and smaller sampans can be seen alongside the quay.

The Sydney Chinese have recently celebrated the establishment of their Chamber of Commerce by a banquet. Their Consul-General presided, and many European and Australian merchants were amongst the guests. The toast of the Chinese Republic was drunk, and there was much talk of exporting wool and corn to China.

Hongkong Telegraph
8 May 1913

❖ *Chinese have been prominent in the Australian commercial and cultural life for many decades. A little research has revealed that the work of the Sydney Chinese Chamber of Commerce is presently carried on by the much-expanded Australia China Chamber of Commerce and Industry.*

**Hongkong Telegraph
11 May 1913**

Qualified Doctors: A copy of the Register of medical and surgical practitioners qualified to practise in the Colony appears in the Government Gazette. There are 30 names, of which three are those of ladies.

**South China
Morning Post
4 June 1913**

There is no doubt that since March 1912 China has been 'squeezed like a lemon' of her best art treasures, and that objects of a class hitherto unheard of and unseen outside of China have come under the hammer in the auction rooms of Europe and America.

❖ *A shameful situation, but true not only of China, but also of Egypt and Greece.*

**South China
Morning Post
9 June 1913**

What the Library of Congress [in USA] catalogues as the smallest book in the world is a volume, paper bound, measuring only two-fifth by two-fifth of an inch and which will easily rest on the thumbnail. It contains 48 pages of Japanese paper upon which are printed an introduction and the complete Rubaiyat of Omar Khayam.

❖ *Another interesting but useless snippet of information.*

Wyndham Street, Central District, Hong Kong Island, c. late 1920s
View north shows the bottom portion of the street where it joins Queen's Road Central. Note the two sedan chairs carrying passengers to some higher levels. Compare with Wyndham Street photograph on p.157, taken when it used to be filled with stalls selling flowers and wreaths, and thus nicknamed 'Flower Street'.

The evening muck-raking industry, as carried on in Wyndham Street, is as thriving as ever. … Dozens of lurchers and cadgers and sparrow-starvers can pick out all that they want from the heap without undue inconvenience.

South China Morning Post
11 June 1913

The first shipment of San Miguel Beer arrived in Hongkong by the *Ruby* today. This is the first time that San Miguel draft beer has been placed on the Hongkong market and it is confidently anticipated that it will speedily establish itself here. The beer is brewed from the best German malt and hops, contains absolutely no salic acid or other preservative, and is guaranteed a pure beer of excellent flavour. The percentage of alcohol is very slight — some 4 per cent — and the beer leaves no ill after-effects.

Hongkong Telegraph
13 June 1913

❖   *This item will no doubt be of interest to the 'San Mig' devotees. The confidence was fully justified, and the beer continues to be as popular in Hong Kong as ever.*

Opium to the value of $60,000 was burned on Thursday afternoon in nine great cauldrons. Addresses were delivered … music was provided by a band and the greatest enthusiasm prevailed.

❖   *It is difficult to reconcile this item with the available historical information: although opium divans in Hong Kong were closed between 1909 and 1910, and export of prepared opium was abolished, Hong Kong Government still maintained, in 1913, monopoly on 'opium farms' and consumption of opium continued.*

For some little time the Colony has enjoyed an immunity from the collapse of Chinese houses, which was unhappily too frequent in former years. Heavy rains often bring this about, but in many cases the ravages of white ants are perhaps responsible. At any rate it is fairly certain that the men who built Chinese houses in the Colony in the early years of its development have left a legacy of architecture which is a source of danger to human life and limb.

Hongkong Daily Press
16 June 1913

❖   *An interesting and timely observation, for three days later several buildings collapsed in Station Lane (Hung Hom) causing the death of 25 persons and injuring many others.*

Hongkong Daily Press **23 June 1913**	HONGKONG UNIVERSITY: The Dean of the faculty of Medicine [Dr. Francis Clark] has been officially informed that the General Medical Council of Great Britain has decided to recognise the degrees in Medicine and Surgery of this University, granted after examination, for registration in the Medical Register.

❖   *A very important milestone in the history of the medical education in Hong Kong which, incidentally, brought many students from Singapore and Malaya where such recognition was withheld.*

Hongkong Telegraph **1 July 1913**	LIFE IN HONGKONG, VIEWED THROUGH OUTSIDE EYES: Twenty servants is the usual complement of an ordinary household. The average Chinese of the servant class ... is wonderfully efficient, quiet in his movements, reliable, respectful, patient, long-suffering and even kind. ... Thus it is that, with nothing to do in the house ... European women get very lazy and bored with life in the East. The summer is trying ... in Hongkong, though the temperature in August and September is rarely above 84 ... it is moist and clammy heat. You cannot help feeling languid and fit for nothing.

Hongkong Telegraph **4 July 1913**	Undoubtedly the Revolution has produced among the women of China grave discontent with their present status, both political and social, and according to the testimony of missionaries some very exaggerated notions of the freedom enjoyed by women in the West are now prevalent.

❖   *The simple truth is that women in the West at the time had not attained full political or social freedom.*

South China Morning Post **7 July 1913**	This morning both the Chief Justice and the barristers ... dispensed with wigs on account of heat.

❖   *The reason was, in fact, that an enterprising thief had that morning purloined the electric fan used by the Chief Justice!*

South China Morning Post **8 July 1913**	The new tar macadam roads which have been laid in various parts of Kowloon appear to be a great success. They are easily kept clean, rain does not damage them, and so far they are standing the hot weather remarkably well.

❖   *Another milestone: a tar-surfaced road; 'macadam' was named after MacAdam, the Scottish engineer who invented the process.*

As the unit of population in China is not the individual but the family, it is apparent that the aggregation of families descended from a common ancestor and living on land inherited in common from the same source led ... to the formation of clans, the members of which bearing the same name recognised mutual interests. ... The most potent factor in its development is the belief in and practice of ancestor worship.

Hongkong Daily Press
9 July 1913

❖ *This is essentially correct. The clan aggregation and ancestor worship are still very much in evidence in the New Territories.*

Ancestral Hall of Tang Clan, Ha Tsuen, New Territories, c.1977

Since the dawn of their long history, Chinese people have worshipped their ancestors. It is the cornerstone of their religious beliefs. It is an expression of filial piety which applies equally in death as in life: respect for elders while living becomes, by natural extension, worship of them as ancestors when dead. Nothing is ever likely to change this. Nor is this purely an abstract, ethical doctrine: the living and the dead offer mutual help and intercede one for the other.

The ancestral hall is the heart and the centre of the clan's religious life: in it are the soul tablets of past generations arranged in rows on an altar. It serves as the clan's social centre, where festivals and other important occasions are celebrated.

In the New Territories where clan life is still very strong, ancestral halls abound. The one shown here, of the Tangs of Ha Tsuen, was built about 1790. It stands prominently on the main road to Lau Fau Shan. Like other traditional ceremonial buildings of this type, it is large and imposing, and consists of three halls separated by two courtyards open to the sky. Its roof has delicately carved supporting brackets of wood. In the main hall two large tablets bearing the characters *Hau* (孝) and *Tai* (弟) exhort Tang clansmen to follow the two principles of filial piety and fraternal love.

As the Tangs have lived in Ha Tsuen since the 16th century, this is probably not the first ancestral hall built by them.

Visitors may be puzzled by the sight of a large iron cannon on the porch of the hall. It was found in 1977 buried behind the village. It Is probably of Chinese origin, cast in the early 19th century. The local people have come to accept it as their lucky object, guarding the hall from some unseen danger.

**Hongkong Daily Press
11 July 1913**

A Chinese charged today with creating a disturbance by beating gongs at night, said he did not care for the law; the Chinese custom must be observed.

**Hongkong Daily Press
12 July 1913**

Sun Yat-sen has declared emphatically that he is out of politics for good; he has also declared that he is shortly leaving for England.

❖ *Sun Yat-sen, the great idealist and visionary, who had inspired the revolution and had selflessly stood aside for Yuan Shih-kai to become the President of the new republic, found himself outflanked and outplayed by the wily Yuan who attempted to proclaim himself emperor.*

**Hongkong Daily Press
13 July 1913**

A TALKING CINEMA: A new machine has been invented which not only takes and produces animated photographs, but records ... sounds and reproduces them in unison with the pictures.

❖ *Premature. It did not succeed until the late 1920s.*

Statue Square, Central District, Hong Kong Island, c.1920s
A fine view of the Statue Square, originally called the Royal Square, in the period when it was surrounded by statues. The magnificent Supreme Court completed in 1912, with its classical-style architecture and an impressive dome, forms one side of the square. In the centre is the statue of Queen Victoria seated in its ornate stone pavilion, installed in 1896 (facing the left bottom corner of the photograph). Two other Royal statues are in front, that of Prince of Wales (later King George V) on a pedestal on its right, and of Princess of Wales (later Queen Mary) on its left, both installed in November 1909. Portions of the Hongkong Club, on the left of this photograph, and the City Hall, on the right, are visible.

Complaints have reached us of the filthy condition of Statue Square, especially around the monuments. Weeds are much in evidence around the statue of King Edward [VII]. Will the authorities please note?

Hongkong Daily Press
14 July 1913

From the Editorial:
There has been great activity in regard to building operations to meet the urgent demands for house-room created by the immigration of some forty to fifty thousand Chinese who poured into Hongkong during 1911 [the revolution]. Pending the erection of sufficient dwellings for the accommodation of so large an increase, the existing dwellings became greatly overcrowded. ... The penalty to be paid for this overcrowding was a severe outbreak of plague, no less than 1,847 cases being recorded.

Hongkong Daily Press
15 July 1913

❖ *The problem is familiar to Hong Kong, though plague has, thankfully, been eliminated.*

There is a feeling in Vienna that a definite settlement of the differences between the Balkan States is imminent.

South China Morning Post
19 July 1913

❖ *Ha-ha-ha ...*

STANLEY: 'We found a village' says Rudyard Kipling 'which they call Stanley. Tenantless buildings of brown stone stared seaward from the low downs and there lay behind them a stretch of weather-beaten wall. No need to ask what these meant. They cried aloud 'It is a deserted cantonment and the population is in the cemetery.'

South China Morning Post
20 July 1913

❖ *This was written in 1889. The beautiful prose of Kipling cannot disguise the fact that he was wrong. By that time the sickness among the troops had abated significantly, and Stanley was not abandoned because of sickness, but because the garrison was more dispersed. The cemetery, in fact, contained graves of soldiers who had died between 1842 and 1860 when sickness was very prevalent, and not after.*

**South China
Morning Post
1 August 1913**

The Chinese were the first to issue banknotes. The Asiatic Movement [society] … recently acquired a banknote issued at Peking in 1800 BC in many ways similar to those now in use. It is of thick white paper, inscribed in blue ink, with the number, name of the bank, and date of issue, cashier's signature, and value in words as well as figures. Round the border is engraved the counsel:- 'However much you may possess, strive to be thrifty'.

❖ *This is surely not to be taken seriously! However, China was the first to use paper banknotes; my information is that it was first used in China between 7th and 9th century AD, to overcome shortages of coins.*

**China Mail
9 August 1913**

The New York journalist, Mr. Mears, has completed the fastest round-the-world journey in 32 days, 21 hours and 35 minutes.

Rock Engraving Shek Pik, Lantao, c.1960
Another ancient rock engraving at Big Wave Bay, Hong Kong Island, was described on p.116. This one at Shek Pik on Lantao island is different in pattern from other engravings in the Hong Kong area.

Here a strikingly geometric design — concentric squares and one spiral — is reminiscent of some of the geometric patterns stamped on Bronze Age pottery found in Hong Kong and South China. The connection, however, is far from clear.

Like other engravings, it is undoubtedly ancient

and probably had had a deep spiritual meaning for the people who carved it.

The engraving is located near the base of the Shek Pik Reservoir dam. To reach it, take a bus from Mui Wo to Shek Pik, get off the bus at the beginning of the dam; a road leads to the base of the dam and the engraving which is signposted. It can be a rewarding day's excursion.

Fifty ladies were summoned to appear at the Central Police Court, Sydney [Australia] ... to answer a charge of having contravened the city bye-laws by having passed along the city thoroughfares without having the points of their hatpins sufficiently protected.

China Mail
14 August 1913

HONGKONG'S HOUSING PROBLEM: Something must be attempted if the middle class section of Hongkong residents is to have its biggest problem solved. ... Surely if the Government can lay out money to help golfers, it can do something for residents who want comfortable homes at a moderate rental.

China Mail
21 August 1913

One British University in China is, as yet, and will be for very many years, quite sufficient to meet the demands of those who seek a Western education. That University exists in Hongkong, and in it can be found accommodation for hundreds of students from all parts of China.

❖　*This is a preposterous statement. The University of Hong Kong was a tiny institution by any standards; in the 1930s, its total student body was around 300. Even as the above statement was being printed, there were three universities founded in Shanghai alone.*

China Mail
23 August 1913

FORMOSAN PROGRESS: The camphor and salt monopolies, and the sugar and timber industries are the backbone of the island's prosperity ... The camphor monopoly was created in 1899 and strengthened by the Crude Camphor and Camphor-oil Monopoly Law in 1903. Formosa is the greatest camphor producer in the world.

❖　*The importance of this may be appreciated when it is realized that at the time camphor was the only known effective insect repellent. The camphor tree which produces the substance, is native to South China, Formosa (Taiwan) and Japan.*

South China Morning Post
26 August 1913

The silk industry of China is reputed to be 4000 years old. ... Today this product occupies the premier place among its exports, accounting for 25 per cent of the value of goods sent abroad ... but China has made no attempt to counteract by scientific remedies the effects of disease or to apply scientific methods to the industry. The result today is that the producing capacity of the Italian silk is four times that of Chinese.

China Mail
28 August 1913

Sam Tung Uk Village, Tsuen Wan, 1976

This photograph shows part of Tsuen Wan 25 years ago; at the bottom, the walled village Sam Tung Uk stands out clearly. Tsuen Wan, an old market town, was then a collection of small dilapidated villages, many in a sad state of decay. Rapid development during the past 20 years destroyed the old villages and in their stead there grew a modern New Town of Tsuen Wan seen today, with high-rise buildings, shopping plazas, and gardens. But Sam Tung Uk was saved. In 1980 it was repaired, restored, and preserved by the ever-watchful Antiquities & Monument Office and the Tsuen Wan Regional Council, as an example of a typical walled village. It is now a folk museum, a show-piece for visitors, with all its former residents resettled. It probably looks better than it has ever done in the past.

The original Sam Tung Uk was built some 200 years ago by the Chan family. Initially, as its name indicates, it contained three rows of houses, a fourth having later been added at its rear. The Ancestral Hall is in the centre, now splendidly restored. Even if somewhat over-restored, Sam Tung Uk is still an excellent example of a single-clan walled village and is well worth a visit. The MTR brings one almost to its doorstep.

China Mail
1 September 1913

This morning a gorilla escaped from Fillis' Circus and was eventually caught on the Praya. The animal, however, became so savage that its keeper chained it to a telegraph pole in Chater Road, where it remains at the time of writing.

❖ *Things were certainly more exciting in Central in those days!*

From the Editorial:
From time immemorial there have been two great scourges of humanity — Alcohol and Opium. To these must now be added that of Cocaine. … It is only within the last ten years or so that notice has been taken in the Press of an insidious and growing evil in the shape of Cocainism. … The horrors of morphinism, opium smoking, alcohol, Cannabis Indica, and all the intoxicants ever known in the history of the world, pale into insignificance beside the rapidly increasing holocaust of cocaine.

❖ *The editorial was prompted by the fact that only two days before, revenue officers had seized a large quantity of cocaine in a Kowloon godown.*

China Mail
6 September 1913

H.M.S. Tamar is not to disappear from the harbour at any very early date it seems. We are informed that at present there is no intention of immediately disposing of her, and that after paying off she will continue temporarily, as the quarters of the Commodore.

❖ *HMS* Tamar *became a depot, or receiving ship, in Hong Kong in 1897. From 1913 it was moored permanently alongside the west wall of the Naval Dockyard. When the Japanese invaded Hong Kong, in December 1941, she was scuttled and sunk rather than be allowed to fall into enemy hands. See also p.153.*

Hongkong Daily Press
24 September 1913

Today, being the anniversary of the birth of Confucius, was kept in fitting style by the majority of the Chinese merchants in Hongkong. All the big hongs were closed, as was also the cotton market, and the streets were made bright with flags. Doorways were festooned with flowers and balconies with strings of highly coloured lanterns.

❖ *The great sage has exercised the most profound influence on Chinese life and culture. Sadly, today, his birthday is not even a public holiday in Hong Kong.*

Hongkong Daily Press
27 September 1913

**China Mail
2 October 1913**

THE NEW WESTERN MARKET: The South Block of the new Western Market, the construction of which has just been completed by the Public Works Department, was opened to the public yesterday, the stall-holders ... celebrating its inauguration in Chinese fashion by much jossing and firing of crackers. The new building ... takes the place of an older market which was found to be too small to meet the requirements ... of the growing West Point District.

❖ *A mistake. The building described here is the North Block. The South Block (a separate building) was built in 1858 and demolished in 1980.*

Western Market, North Block, Hong Kong Island, 1977
The Western Market on Hong Kong Island consisted originally of the two separate blocks. They were constructed in the same style but at different times and on different streets. The South Block was built in 1858 and demolished in 1980. The remaining North Block, smaller and more compact than was the South, was completed in 1913. Located between Des Voeux Road Central and Connaught Road Central, its north facade faces the waterfront. It has walls of red brick on a granite base, and a large and handsome granite arch over its main entrance. It stands prominently among the surrounding high-rise modern structures as a small building of fine quality and style. Restored and protected as a historic building, it now houses a fashionable shopping plaza.

A PAVING EXPERIMENT: The oblong patch of paving at the bottom of Battery Path is a new departure as far as Hongkong is concerned. It is composed of compressed asphalt. ... If it [the experiment] proves successful ... it is hoped that its use will be extended to other roads in the city.

Hongkong Telegraph
6 October 1913

From the Editorial:
The dispute between China and Japan has, for the present at least, been settled ... but it would be foolish to underrate the gravity of the episode. ... In two ways it is of evil promise for the future. It reveals the powers of a bellicose faction in Japan, whose aggressive instincts and appetites are directed against China. ... For the first time for years the blunt occupation and seizure of Chinese territory has been urged as a mode of getting compensation for grievances real or fictitious.

❖   *The episode referred to was the murder of three Japanese in Nanking. A rumble of events to come; but for the time, Japan's ambitions would be diverted by the world-wide conflict of the Great War of 1914–18, in which she would side with the Allies with considerable benefit to herself.*

Hongkong Telegraph
1 November 1913

MUSIC BY WIRELESS: A curious instance of transmission of a melody by wireless telegraphy is reported from New York. According to this, the wireless operator on board ... as well as several of the ship's officers, had an opportunity of clearly hearing the British National Anthem played through the receiving apparatus on board station. It was later ascertained that this melody had been played on the yacht of Prince of Monaco at a distance of 800 miles. It is believed this is the first time a melody has been transmitted by wireless telegraphy over such great distance.

Hongkong Telegraph
6 November 1913

This morning ... a serious collision, involving as far as is known five deaths, took place in the harbour between the SS Soshu Maru and one of the Yaumati Ferry launches. ... Of the estimated number of fifty passengers on board the launch, over thirty have been accounted for and the latest reports put the number of dead at five, twelve being sent to hospital as well. The dead comprise a baby, a woman and three men.

❖   *The final count was 21 dead, mainly drowned, much higher than initially reported.*

Hongkong Telegraph
26 November 1913

Ascending the Peak on Double Ninth, c.1930
The 'Double Ninth' was originally the Day for Climbing the Hills, the festival when all good Chinese believed they must visit high places. Today, the pragmatic Cantonese combine it with the Ch'ung Yeung — the Autumn Festival, when ancestral graves are visited, swept clean, and offerings placed on the graves (similar to the Ch'ing Ming Festival in the spring). In North China, the two festivals are observed separately.

The origin of the 'Climbing the Hills' festival is obscure, but is reputed to have originated during the Han Dynasty (220 BC – 224 AD, when a virtuous scholar was advised to ascend the mountain with his family in order to escape an impending disaster.

Visiting and attending to the graves of the departed ones is an extension of the all-important tenet of ancestral worship, serving also as welcome family reunions.

The photograph shows a long procession of people ascending the Peak, on Hong Kong Island. The small building, in the centre of the photograph, is the gatehouse of the Governor's Peak residence — the Mountain Lodge. The gatehouse is still standing, but the Mountain Lodge was demolished after World War II, and a public pavilion built on its site.

Several sedan chairs can be seen in the centre, waiting for customers, and a few can be seen ascending with the crowd. Under a temporary cover, refreshments are being sold to the thirsty climbers.

THE MONA LISA: A telegram from Rome states that it is officially announced that the famous picture La Gioconda [the Mona Lisa], stolen from the Louvre in 1911 has been found in Florence and is now in the possession of the authorities. The alleged thief is Italian ... says that he stole the picture to avenge Napoleon's art thefts in Italy.

❖ *Leonardo Da Vinci's Mona Lisa is probably the most famous painting of all time; yet the identity of the lady in the painting remains a mystery.*

China Mail
13 December 1913

From the Editorial:
Further communications ... concerning the matter of high rentals ... induce us to further elaborate on the subject. Are the landlords as rapacious as they are represented? ... There are houses in Hongkong whose rents have been doubled within the past three years. We explained some time ago how property values were inflated in Hongkong. ... A block of twenty seven houses known as Belilios Terrace were originally let for $25 a month and the tenants had now been notified that a rental of $65 and taxes must in future be paid.

❖ *Multiply the figures by a factor of 1,000, and the story could be true today.*

Hongkong Daily Press
17 December 1913

A COMMON TONGUE: Chinese ... desire that a common tongue be established 'to unite the country, break down social barrier, increase national prosperity, engender patriotism, reduce unnecessary hardship, cause mutual understanding, remove local prejudices, produce social consciousness, help to develop nationality, facilitate the learning of written Chinese and thus to make the democratic Government more successful.' ... The *Peking Daily News* suggests that a uniform Mandarin should be taught in all schools.

❖ *In a nutshell, so that they can talk to each other.*

Hongkong Daily Press
18 December 1913

The band of the German flagship *Scharnhorst* played last night at the Hongkong Club, which was thrown open on the occasion to the wives and families of members and subscribers. Upwards of 250 ladies and gentlemen dined at the Club, and a dance followed.

❖ *Eight months later Germany and Britain would be at war.*

Hongkong Daily Press
31 December 1913

1914

**Hongkong Telegraph
2 January 1914**

FROST IN KOWLOON: The unusual phenomenon of frost was witnessed at Kowloon this morning. Big tracts of grass were covered with a thick hoar frost. ... The sight was an extremely pretty one, and it aroused much curiosity on the part of those who happened to be about before the sun's rays melted the frost. ... On enquiry at the Observatory the Director informed us that they had no report of frost. ... It was as long ago as 1891 that a temperature as low as freezing point ... was reported in Hongkong.

❖   *A typical Government response? Nothing is allowed to happen without a report!*

**Hongkong Telegraph
2 February 1914**

NOTICE: Will the gentleman who took by mistake a GREEN FELT HAT from the Peak Hotel on Friday evening, kindly return it to H.M.S. Alacrity? His own hat is at the Peak Hotel.

The Peak Hotel, The Peak, Hong Kong Island, c.1910
The large building dominating the scene is the Peak Hotel, built around 1890. Well situated (1,200 feet above sea level), and offering 'comfortable and cool accommodation' the hotel was popular for a while, but in the long term did not do well, and was demolished in 1937.

SIR KAI HO-KAI RETIRING AFTER 24 YEARS SERVICE [in Legco]: His Excellency the Governor announced at the meeting that ... 'owing to indifferent health the Senior Unofficial Member, whose fourth term of appointment as a member of the Council expires ... has been compelled to intimate ... that he would not be prepared ... to continue his service upon the Council.

Hongkong Telegraph
26 February 1914

❖ *So came to an end the career of public service of one of the most eminent Hong Kong personalities — a doctor, barrister and legislative leader. He died the same year. See also* Hong Kong Telegraph, *30 March 1882, and his photograph on p.62.*

The University of Hongkong has been presented with a valuable set of surgical instruments for teaching purposes by Messrs. A.S.Watson & Co. The Faculty of Medicine have reason to be grateful for the generous gift by a local firm, which will enable the important subject of operative surgery to be taught practically in the University's School of Anatomy.

Hongkong Telegraph
10 March 1914

❖ *Medical readers may be interested to know that this refers to teaching operative surgery procedures to undergraduates using cadavers. This unique course, not part of the curriculum in other medical schools, was introduced by Professor Kenelm H. Digby, but was discontinued after the war with Digby's retirement.*

The Colonial Secretary informs us that Hongkong has been declared infected on account of plague, by Bangkok, and that vessels from this port are required to remain in quarantine at Kokphra until ten days from the date of leaving Hongkong.

Hongkong Telegraph
17 March 1914

An interesting personality arrived ... from the North this morning, in Dr. G.E. Morrison, Political Advisor to the Chinese Government. ... Dr. Morrison, who is 52 years of age, has held his present appointment since July 1912, prior to which he was for many years Peking correspondent to *The Times*.

Hongkong Telegraph
27 March 1914

❖ *I am informed by Ms Elizabeth Heinz that George Ernest Morrison, Australian by birth, was one of the most famous correspondents of his day.*

Hongkong Telegraph
16 April 1914

THE TIGER: The chief ground for scepticism regarding the presence of a tiger on the island of Hongkong hitherto has been the fact that there have been no reports of the beast having attacked any living creature. Unbelievers have asked what the tiger feeds on. They are now answered by a report which has been made to the Police of a big bullock, having been killed and eaten by some wild animal … The day before yesterday the tiger was seen on the east side of Mount Gough.

❖ *The tiger was again seen very clearly close to Bisney Villa; it was of medium size, lying outstretched by the roadway sunning itself. As a further sequel, Ho Tung (later Sir Robert Ho Tung) had offered $100 for the capture of the tiger. The present-day residents of Hong Kong are certainly missing an exciting experience.*

Hongkong Telegraph
30 April 1914

Advantages of Living in Hongkong: Plague — heavy mortality; Rabies — quite prevalent; Piracy — rampant; Tigers — lurking around; Chinese Republic — financially rotten; China trade — at a standstill.

Hongkong Telegraph
9 May 1914

The licences issued by the Hongkong Police last year included the following:
    1,100 jinrickshas, 673 chairs (sedan), 5,880 drivers, 2,932 chair bearers, 13 private vehicles, 29 motor cars, 4 motor cycle drivers, 15 billiard tables, 222 licences to shoot and take game, 316 money changers, 91 pawnbrokers, and 7,929 hawkers.

Hongkong Telegraph
13 May 1914

A reader informs us that a whale 23 feet in length was seen in Tolo Harbour near Taipo, on Sunday, and that the police, from a launch fired three rounds at the mighty creature, which however disappeared.

❖ *The newspapers of the previous months were full of the sightings of a tiger, which had been seen at Magazine Gap, Lei Yue Mun, and Barker Road; a hunt was dispatched but failed to bag the tiger. And now a whale! One wonders whether Hong Kong had been gripped by a mass hysteria?*

Antiquites and Monuments Office

Bishop's Residence, c.1885

Shortly after the Nanking Treaty was ratified in 1843, formalizing the cession of Hong Kong to Britain, the first colonial chaplain, Reverend Vincent Stanton, was appointed 'to care for the needs of the European population'. It was not, however, until 1849 that the Anglican See and Diocese of Victoria was established. In the same year, St John's Church was opened, soon to be given the status of a cathedral. With the latter came the appointment of the first bishop — the Reverend George Smith.

Bishop's House, shown in this photograph, was built in 1851 on Lower Albert Road, conveniently close to the cathedral. As the bishop at the time usually assumed the duties also of the warden of St Paul's College, the house also accommodated the school.

It is gratifying to record that in spite of Hong Kong's gigantic appetite for redevelopment, Bishop's House is still standing, though very much altered and modernized in the interior. The design of the building is simple but dignified. It stands on granite foundations and its north-west corner is graced by a handsome octagonal tower — shown clearly in this old photograph.

**Hongkong Telegraph
14 May 1914**

A Government Gazette Extraordinary issued today states that … 'On and after the 20th May 1914, and until further notice every dog going … in the public thoroughfares or elsewhere shall be muzzled'.

❖　*It may be noted that regulations regarding muzzling dogs were much more strictly imposed at that time than now because of high incidence of rabies.*

**Hongkong Telegraph
12 June 1914**

From the Editorial:
A TIGER OR A CAT? First it was a tiger — a whopper at that too. Any number of people had seen it asleep and awake, walking unhurriedly across paths and scampering into brushwood, and so on. There could be no doubt that it was a tiger. Then it became a cheetah, or something like that. … Now it is a cat; a cat above the ordinary size but certainly not to be mistaken for a tiger … to say nothing of those seals that were said to have appeared near Dumbell Island. Hongkong has always been short of amusements, and an open-air menagerie would liven up matters a bit.

❖　*The* Telegraph *has fun with the tiger scare. It refers to a report of a large cat, probably a civet cat, still common in Hong Kong and protected. Even if exaggerated, some of the reports of tiger sightings must be true.*

**Hongkong Telegraph
26 June 1914**

Some Impressions of a Returned Hongkongite: 'It is good to be back again. I am convinced now that I did not mark Hongkong down at its true worth till I got away from it. I though it too … prim and respectable, but compared to England it is positively riotous. … I find a quite surprising number of alterations and improvements … at Kowloon … a new pier … Salisbury Road is now restored to the width originally intended … the roads in Kowloon … have greatly benefited by the improved method of tar-spraying. … I will not say what it was in my mind about the piracies that are still allowed to continue, about the smelly dustcarts, or even about the water drippings that fell on my hat and coat at Queen's Road this morning. … I will confine myself to thanking the Fates that I am once more in Hongkong.

❖　*These sentiments are shared by many ex-residents of Hong Kong. The lure of Hong Kong that binds us to it with strong bonds is sometimes difficult to understand.*

Chater Road, Central District, Hong Kong Island, c.1910–20
Named after Sir Paul Chater, Hong Kong's prominent businessman and philanthropist, Chater Road is viewed from the junction with Des Voeux Road Central in this photograph. The building on the right is Alexandra Building, completed in 1904, with A.S. Watson & Co., Chemists, a very old Hong Kong firm, occupying the ground floor. Opposite is the Union Building, completed in 1904–05. At the far end of Chater Road, Queen Victoria's Monument, in the Statue Square, can be seen.

THE ASSASSINATION IN BOSNIA: Martial law has been proclaimed here [Sarajevo]; the bodies of the Archduke Ferdinand and his wife … have been embalmed already. Both assassins are natives of Bosnia.

Hongkong Daily Press
1 July 1914

❖　*This was the spark which ignited the Great War of 1914–18.*

At the Magistracy yesterday, before Mr. J.R.Wood, an Indian named Shad Daud was charged with recklessly riding a pony, to the common danger of the public at Kowloon. P.C. Shannon told the Magistrate that he saw the pony along Chatham Road. … He was galloping and seemed to have no idea how to guide or control the pony … later saw him again in front of Humphreys Avenue … He could not guide it properly, so he beat it. He then came galloping along Chatham Road again, and narrowly missed knocking down a lady and a gentleman and two children. … Defendant was fined $5.

Hongkong Daily Press
13 July 1914

Hongkong Daily Press
27 July 1914

From the Editorial:
Once more Europe is face to face with a very grave crisis in the Balkans with some likelihood of war involving all the great Powers of Europe. Austria has declared war on Serbia. … The gravity of the situation lies in the attitude of Russia … towards an Austrian occupation of Serbia, and unless … Russia … can be persuaded to acquiesce in this, a war of unparalleled magnitude must result.

❖   *Russia did not acquiesce and the prediction was fulfilled when World War I was unleashed upon the world.*

Hongkong Daily Press
3 August 1914

Germany has declared war against Russia and mobilised her entire army. There is no news yet that the declaration extends to France, but France has called up all her reservists.

Hongkong Daily Press
4 August 1914

RUSSIA INVADES GERMANY. GERMANY INVADES FRANCE. GREAT BRITAIN TO INTERVENE. [In Hongkong] The Royal Naval Reserve, or such part of them as the Lord's Commissioner of the Admiralty may direct be called into active service.

Hongkong Daily Press
6 August 1914

Great Britain as well as France and Russia are now officially declared to be at war with Germany. The Colony of Hongkong, in common with all parts of the Empire is taking every measure for its own defence.

To the Editor of Hongkong Daily Press:
Dear Sir, Several of our friends have informed us that it is rumoured that Lane, Crawford & Co. have taken advantage of the war scare to raise their prices 30, 40 and even 50 per cent. Will you allow us … to most emphatically deny these statements, which are evidently circulated with a desire to injure our reputation for fair and honest dealing … yours etc. Lane, Crawford & Co.

Hongkong Daily Press
8 September 1914

Yesterday the Volunteer Corps Orders included the following under the heading of 'Discipline': Volunteers are reminded that each man is personally responsible for the upholding of the good name of the Corps. The noisy or unseemly behaviour in public places of men in uniform not only damages the Corps, but also reflects great discredit on the individuals themselves. ... In a 'Dress' notice attention was called to the order that all Volunteers must wear uniform at all times, any breach of this rule in future will be severely dealt with. ... Volunteers 'walking out' or attending public entertainments etc. must wear Khaki Jacket, trousers (or shorts and puttees) and belt and side-arms.

❖ *It must be remembered that most of the regular troops were withdrawn from Hong Kong for war in Europe, and the defence of Hong Kong rested almost entirely on the Volunteers. Fortunately, Hong Kong was not attacked, and the Volunteers had to wait for World War II to prove themselves in battle, which they did with credit.*

Hongkong Volunteer Corps at Fanling Station, New Territories, c.1914
The Volunteers seen in this photograph are preparing to embark on the train, probably at the conclusion of their training camp, which usually took place near Fanling. At the time the Hong Kong garrison was much depleted as the First World War was on and the regular troops were required in Europe; the Hongkong Volunteers filled the gap forming the main body of defence in Hong Kong.

Before Mr. J.R. Wood yesterday a man was charged with the larceny of a set of artificial teeth. From a story of the defendant, it appears that he and the complainant were at one time friends. The latter borrowed $10 from him, but failed to refund the amount, so he stole his alleged debtor's teeth! Complainant denied the defendant's statement ... and the Magistrate sent the thief to prison for six weeks.

Hongkong Daily Press
19 September 1914

❖ *Seems rather a stiff sentence for a stealing a set of dentures.*

Hongkong Telegraph
8 October 1914

THE TURKISH BATHS OPEN TOMORROW: We have been asked to announce that the baths in connection with the Hongkong Turkish Bath and Toilet Company Ltd., will be opened tomorrow afternoon, everything now being in readiness. From next week there will be special days for ladies — Tuesdays and Fridays.

❖   *Turkish bath, which probably has little to do with Turkey, has been described as one in which the bather, after a period of heavy perspiration in a room of hot steam, is washed, massaged, and cooled. It must have been great fun, and in the days when a bath at home was still a rare luxury, must have been very popular.*

Hongkong Telegraph
12 October 1914

IMPORTANT NOTICE: Any European desiring to leave the Colony should apply in writing for permission to do so to the Provost Marshal, Head Quarters Offices, at least 48 hours before the intended hour of departure, giving name, nationality, age, sex, height, complexion and occupation of the applicant. ... Applicants should apply in person.

❖   *The Provost Marshal is the head of the Military Police. One wonders what has complexion to do with a permission to depart.*

Hongkong Telegraph
16 November 1914

There is no truth in the report that the local volunteers have sent the sandwiches, supplied to them on a recent march, to the Museum as interesting antiques.

Hongkong Telegraph
4 December 1914

The fifth meeting under the auspices of the Hongkong Gymkhana Club takes place at Happy Valley tomorrow afternoon. ... A splendid programme has been arranged and an afternoon of excellent sport should result. Besides the customary events, there will be a mile race, as well as foot races for Indian troops. The band of the 25th Punjabis ... will be in attendance.

❖   *Gymkhana — competition in sports, especially horse-riding — has long been a favourite event in countryside England. No doubt, Hong Kong was attempting to recreate the atmosphere of the English countryside for the nostalgic expatriates.*

A Fox Hunt, New Territories, c.1920–30
The picture here is not of a gymkhana, but of a fox hunt. The hunting party, complete with the dogs, reputedly took place in Fanling, the New Territories. Although the South China red fox inhabits the New Territories, it was rumoured that European foxes were introduced for hunting. The terrain, however, favoured the fox (thankfully). The fox hunting was a failure and was abandoned while the club, formed for the purpose, was dissolved.

TOBACCO FOR THE TROOPS: … we have decided to join hands with the *South China Morning Post* in the scheme for opening a Tobacco and Cigarettes Fund for the Allied Army at the front. … Donations, from five cents upwards, will be thankfully received and acknowledged in our columns.

Hongkong Telegraph
9 December 1914

OBITUARY: We regret to record the death of Mr. James Johnstone Keswick, which took place in Scotland on December 26th. … The deceased gentleman was well known in Hongkong, being for some years prior to 1901, taipan of Messrs. Jardine, Matheson & Co., Ltd.

❖ *A great name in the hierarchy of the Princely Hong, J. J. Keswick had been a member of the Legislative Council, Chairman of the Hongkong Chamber of Commerce, and a founder, with Sir Paul Chater, of the Hongkong Land Co.*

Hongkong Telegraph
29 December 1914

Pak Tai Temple, Cheung Chau, c.1928

The temple dedicated to the Emperor of the North (Pak Tai) is surely one of the most interesting of the many temples in the territory, one not to be missed when visiting the land.

It was built in 1793, in the last few years of the reign of Emperor Ch'ien Lung, reputedly as a propitiating gesture to Pak Tai, seeking his protection against a calamity, though the exact nature of the calamity remains obscure.

Pak Tai himself was believed to have been a Taoist saint, though another version names him as a famous emperor of Northern Wei dynasty (AD 386–534). Indeed, almost every temple of Pak Tai has a different story of his origins.

The temple is a fine, lavishly decorated building of three halls with many donated

objects inside, brought in by the worshippers, many of them fishermen of Cheung Chau. But the finest object is a remarkable large, double-handed sword, which was 'fished out' by a fisherman in the bay and estimated to belong to the Song dynasty (AD 960–1279).

Unlike other temples, in which the name of the deity is engraved on the stone lintel above the entrance, Pak Tai's name is not engraved at this temple, but the three-characters which appear on the lintel may be translated as the 'Temple of the Jade Emptiness',

presumably the abode of the Emperor of the North.

Today, visitors will find that the temple is approached by splendid and wide granite steps, obviously not yet in existence when the above photograph was taken. The steps were probably added after 1928 in one of the temple's several extensive renovations.

The popular Cheung Chau Bun Festival, which features colourful processions and towers made of buns, is not actually the festival of Pak Tai, but the deity features prominently in the event.

Hongkong Telegraph 31 December 1914

BUSY HONGKONG: It is interesting to note, remarks the London and China Express, that almost one-third of China's foreign commerce in 1913 was transacted through Hongkong.

❖   *A nice note on which to finish the year.*

Interior of a Private Residence, Hong Kong, c.1900
A young European couple is enjoying a restful moment inside their house. The lady is sitting by the opened piano. The house may possibly be located in the Mid-Levels or in the Peak area. The interior is typical of a reasonably well-off expatriate family. It is comfortable without being pretentious; note that some of the furniture is made of rattan which in the hot summer months is cooler than the upholstered kind. The many family photographs add to the warm cosy atmosphere of the house. Neither the house not its occupants have been identified.

1915

In imposing a fine of $10 on each of eight men for riding bicycles to the common danger in Kowloon, Mr. Hazeland this morning observed 'the roads in Kowloon are not safe since this bicycle mania started'.

Hongkong Telegraph
2 January 1915

❖ *How the times have changed. Some would have wished the bicycle mania had returned to replace the motor car mania.*

Hongkong Telegraph
12 January 1915

A Government official was handing out some farm permits in the New Territories. He mentioned a name. 'That's your name, isn't it?' he asked one woman. 'How should I know? I am only a woman' was the perfectly serious reply.

❖   *One tends to doubt the story. However, a good deal of misunderstanding occurred because of the officials' poor knowledge of the language. Also, the village folk had their own brand of humour: an absurd question deserved an absurd reply.*

Hongkong Daily Press
14 January 1915

The footpaths under the verandahs in Nathan Road, Kowloon, are now lighted by night by powerful lamps, and the improvement is one that will be appreciated by the people residing this side of the water.

❖   *For many years, Hong Kong Island and Kowloon were like two separate cities. Even as late 1930s, it was common to meet people on either side of the harbour who had never visited the opposite side.*

Hongkong Daily Press
19 January 1915

Among the many peculiarities found prevailing in the currency and exchange of Hongkong there is none more striking than the fact that the Hongkong silver dollar [the legal currency of the Colony] is at a large discount when compared with the notes of the Hongkong and Shanghai Banking Corporation.

❖   *Currency was a confusing subject in the early days of Hong Kong. The Mexican silver dollar continued as legal tender well into the 1880s. A serious fall in the price of silver may have been the reason for the preference of the Hongkong Bank notes.*

China Mail
20 January 1915

London Dec. 11th: The news of the British naval victory off the Falkland Islands is big news indeed.

❖   *In this battle, British fleet under Admiral Sturdee won a victory over Admiral von Spee of Germany.*

Chinese Soldiers (Qing Dynasty) on Parade, c.1890
An impressive review of Qing Imperial troops is taking place on a large parade ground, probably at the south-western corner of the Old City of Canton. Many banners are displayed. The men in the middle column appear to be carrying heavy, probably swivel, guns. The soldiers lined up in the foreground are armed mainly with bows and arrows, the latter carried in a quiver.

Modern science is largely responsible for modern warfare. ... Every advance of engineering, while being directed primarily toward the ends of civilization and prosperity, has facilitated and intensified warfare by extending the means of transport and communication ... and by placing enormous physical forces at the disposal of man.

China Mail
25 January 1915

❖ *This is becoming more relevant with every decade. Without being cynical, one may wonder if the above should read '... towards the end of civilization'.*

The stranger who visits Hongkong will find very little external evidence that Britain is at war. The business of the Colony is carried on as though the Empire were on terms of the most complete amity with the rest of the world instead of passing through, perhaps, the most critical period of its history. Equally sport goes on ... as far as possible.

South China Morning Post
27 January 1915

❖ *Sport always goes on. An American visitor in London during World War II was shocked to see newspaper headlines 'England Collapses'; this, of course, referred to the test match.*

China Mail
28 January 1915

The month that saw the occupation of the Island, some seventeen years later saw a most atrocious attempt at poisoning the whole of the European population of Hongkong. After eating their breakfast on January 15th, people were taken mysteriously and seriously unwell. No-one appears to have died … it was discovered that the bread which came from the bakery of one of the principal compradores of the city was heavily dosed with arsenic.

❖ *This refers to the notorious 'bread poisoning' case in January 1857. It was widely believed at the time to have been instigated by the Chinese officials at Canton. Baker Cheong Ah Lum and many of his workers were implicated, but no convictions resulted from lack of evidence. Ah Lum, however, lost his business. There were no fatalities, ironically not because there was too little arsenic, but because too much was put in, resulting in vomiting thus getting rid of the poison.*

Hongkong Telegraph
2 February 1915

As most of us are now acquainted with the fact that war has broken out between Britain and Germany, how would it be to clean down the outside walls of the Post Office?

Hongkong Telegraph
3 February 1915

It was in 1861 … that Kowloon was handed over to the British with due form and ceremony, Saturday afternoon, January 19, being the time and date. The British representative journeyed to Kowloon — without the use of a ferry — landed on the mud bank and beach that existed, and met four Chinese mandarins. They handed the British a handful of earth wrapped up in paper, and Kowloon had been transferred. That handful of earth represented about four square miles of land.

❖ *A fascinating bit of history, probably unknown or forgotten by most. A pity, a similar transfer in the opposite direction was not suggested for the return of all the territories in 1997, though a wheel-barrow of earth, with a couple of toy skyscrapers thrown in, might have been more appropriate.*

Hongkong Telegraph
9 February 1915

A change came when the Sikh Police Force was introduced into Hongkong for the first time. … The men that they started with were of a good stamp, for most of them wore the medals of the Mutiny and the China War. The experiment was so successful that the Deputy Superintendent of Police again went back to India, bringing further reinforcements, and the new institution gained a hold upon the affection of the authorities which it holds to the present day.

Sikh Policemen, Police Headquarters, Hollywood Road, Hong Kong Island, c.1905–10

The photograph shows Sikh policemen lined up on parade in front of the police headquarters. The police force in Hong Kong had a slow and unhappy start, around 1844, relying at the time mostly on discharged British and Indian soldiers untrained in police duties. It was not until 1855, under Governor Bowring, that progress was made, much of which was due to the recruitment and growing efficiency of Chinese constables. Sikhs were first recruited in 1867, by Governor Macdonnell, and were initially used as jail guards. Enrolled later into the police force, they proved efficient and reliable.

The authorities in China who, a year or so ago, talked of abolishing their big national festival and following the Western Calendar where the observance of New Year is concerned, must have realised by this time that such radical changes are more easily planned than accomplished.

Hongkong Telegraph
13 February 1915

The Chinese like plenty of noise to be sure; but the commotion created by the letting-off of fire works is less offensive than the catcalling and drunken minstrelsy of Britishers when they celebrate their own New Year.

Hongkong Daily Press
16 February 1915

Hongkong Daily Press
18 February 1915

According to Manila papers ... Dr. Sun Yat-sen has been pardoned by the Chinese Government. ... [He] has been living in Japan since the failure of the revolt, of which he was a leader, to overthrow the present government.

❖ *Although the father of the Chinese Revolution of 1911, this extraordinary man and his revolution had suffered almost immediate reverses at the hands of Yuan Shih-kai and his military allies; Yuan even managed to proclaim himself emperor for a short time. It had taken fully 17 years to wipe out these abuses and establish an undisputed political authority over the whole of China.*

Hongkong Daily Press
22 February 1915

The request for mouth-organs for the troops at the Front seems to imply that Tommy* is bent on punishing Germany with her own instrument of torture.

❖ *This presumably refers to the virtual monopoly which Germany had for many years on the manufacture of mouth-organs. Its invention, however, is attributed to Sir Charles Wheatstone, in the early 19ᵗʰ century.*

Of course it is an understood thing that the P.W.D. [Public Works Department] lays a new road down solely for the pleasure of being able to look forward to tearing it up again at an inconvenient season.

❖ *How very true to this day.*

Hongkong Daily Press
23 February 1915

Some choice examples of schoolboy 'howlers' are quoted ... among them are the following:
'The Philistines are Islands in the Pacific'
'Australia sends to England wine made from a bird named the emu'
'Cologne is famous for the odour made there'
'To germinate is to become a naturalised German', and
'A refugee keeps control at a football match'.

Hongkong Telegraph
3 March 1915

KOWLOON CANTON RAILWAY (BRITISH SECTION): The public is hereby notified that ... tiffin will be served on the train leaving Kowloon at 1.35 p.m. to first-class passengers only. The charge for tiffin will be $1.25.

---

* 'Tommy' — popular and somewhat affectionate nickname for a British soldier.

In … Sheung Shui, this morning, the villagers having complained to the police of the presence of a tiger in the locality, P.C. Croucher and a constable … went to investigate the complaint. … A coolie standing close by carelessly threw a stone into the bush … a monster tiger, likened to the size of a pony, sprang from the bush, caught P.C. Croucher in his claws and — though the Constable is some 6 feet in height and turns the scale at 15 stone — tossed him about like a shuttlecock. His friend went to his assistance and … fired two shots. … One of the shots is supposed to have struck the tiger, and he dashed back into the bush, but not before he had torn four holes in the back and one in the shoulder of the Constable, severely lacerating his body all down one side.

Hongkong Telegraph
8 March 1915

❖ *No longer a rumour but a most unpleasant encounter. Croucher and a Chinese villager, badly wounded, later died of their injuries. An armed party took up the chase the following morning and killed the tiger, but not before it had succeeded in killing an Indian Constable. Three victims! The killed tiger was exhibited at the City Hall to thousands of people. It was later skinned by the Dairy Farm butcher!*

Tigers are long gone from the New Territories. Today, one cannot help feeling sad for the poor animal, which at the time was probably nearing extinction in the region, but for the villagers living in there the danger was very real.

Successful Tiger Hunt, New Territories, 8 March 1915
Although uncommon, tigers have been reported occasionally in the New Territories. The slain tiger in the photograph had attacked and badly wounded a villager and a European constable (Croucher) in the vicinity of Sheung Shui; both later died of their injuries. An armed party led by the District Superintendent, D. Burlingham, hunted down the animal and killed it, but not before it succeeded in killing an Indian constable.

The photograph depicts the successful hunters with their trophy. It was reported that the animal measured 8 ft. 6in. from nose to tail tip and weighed 289 lbs.

Hongkong Telegraph
10 March 1915

The village of Thai-long, in the New Territories, near the entry of Mirs Bay, has just celebrated the golden jubilee of its conversion to Christianity, says the Bulletin of the Catholic Women's League. Being the first village to come over to the Faith as a whole, since the Italian priests of the Catholic Mission from Hongkong penetrated into the interior, the matter assumes a peculiar interest. The honour of having received the village into the Church, and of having erected the first Chapel ... belongs to the then Father Volunteri ... the first to go, unsupported and alone, over the entire district of the present Mission.

❖ *The Catholic Church was very successful in the 19th century, especially in Sai Kung district, where Thai-long (Tai Long) is located, but its influence had gradually waned mainly due to the depleted population. Today, a number of empty churches in the villages of Sai Kung testify to this.*

Hongkong Daily Press
22 March 1915

A district Post Office known as the 'Wantsai Branch Post Office' has been established in Queen's Road East, adjoining the premises of the Sanitary Department.

❖ *This quaint but attractive little building was recently preserved and protected as a historic building.*

Hongkong Daily Press
12 April 1915

HONGKONG TRADE: EXPORTS: The prices of Feathers are unchanged during the last two months. ... The condition of Ginger is unchanged and there is nothing doing in Galangal or Cassia Oil. Star Aniseed Oil is easier, but the demand is slow. No business has been done in Wood Oil or Soy. Human Hair is quoted at prices per picul f.o.b. Hongkong. There is nothing doing in Quicksilver, Saigon Cassia or Gall Nuts. As for Bristles, there are no stocks on hand and no forward business is possible for the present.

❖ *This is a fascinating insight on the articles of trade of the time. In case someone is wondering what is galangal (or galingale), it is an aromatic root stem of various East Indian plants of the ginger family.*

Wan Chai Post Office, 1983

Hong Kong's first post office was established in 1842 and located with the government offices, on top of Battery Path. However, it was under the control of the postal authorities in England, issued no stamps, and derived no income.

In 1860 Hong Kong assumed control over its postal service, and in 1862 issued its first stamps with the picture of Queen Victoria, and with the strange denominations of 2, 8, 12, 18, 24, and 96 cents.

Of the early post offices in Hong Kong, the Wan Chai Post Office is the only survivor. It was opened on 1 March 1915 in Queen's Road East on Hong Kong Island. Small, architecturally undistinguished, and of minor historical importance, it evinced little interest initially among the Hong Kong conservationists of the 1970s, and even less enthusiasm with the Antiquities Advisory Board. But as the number of historical buildings dwindled under the hammer of redevelopment, the little post office came into its own, and in 1990 it was officially gazetted as a historical building, protected under the Antiquities & Monuments Ordinance.

It is an L-shaped building with a pitched roof and a mixture of Chinese and Western styles. Small and undistinguished it may be, but it is well constructed and possesses undeniable charm.

Hongkong Daily Press
15 April 1915

Herr Ludwig Ganghofer the German publicist with the German Army, has an article … in praise of the enemy's organised methods of pillage in France and Belgium. 'The great principle' he says, 'is to bring as little from Germany to supply the needs of the Army, to take as much as possible from the conquered territory, and to send anything useful to Germany.'

❖ *The World War was in full swing and both sides used a great deal of propaganda. Here are a few verses from the* London Scottish Regimental Gazette:

> Hans Dudelheim voss braver more
> Dan any mans dot voss;
> All by himsebst he burn a church
> Undt gets der Iron Cross.

> Some vomen undt some children too,
> Another day he shot,
> Undt so, for making frightfulness,
> Vonce more der Cross he got.

> ………………………………

> So vinning Crosses all der time
> He vent his kultured vay
> His chest vos covered op mit dem
> He von dem twice a day.

Hongkong Daily Press
16 April 1915

It is reported that the Allies have landed at three points in the Gallipoli Peninsula … April 24th.

❖ *The Gallipoli landing, the brainchild of Winston Churchill, designed to strike at Turkey and eliminate her from the War, went disastrously wrong. After suffering heavy casualties, the campaign had to be abandoned.*

RANDOM REFLECTIONS: Cannot something be done to dispose of the many physical wrecks who act as chair and ricksha coolies? The verb is not intended to mean anything brutal or final ... but cannot they be diplomatically informed — that their day's work ... in such strenuous employment ... is over, and that they should seek work ... compatible with their physical capabilities? ... The subject is really not one of levity; the sight is often sickening and saddening.

Hongkong Daily Press
26 April 1915

❖   *Without doubt, the condition of these men was one of the saddest and most reprehensible aspects of the old Hong Kong. The correspondent here displays pity but little understanding of the problem. Happily, it no longer exists today; the few rickshaws, at the Star Ferry Pier, who carry only tourists a short distance to be photographed, are well paid and look well nourished.*

British Soldiers in Hong Kong, c.1908
In this photograph, units of the Royal Garrison Artillery (R.G.A.) with their band are mustering for a parade on Chater Road near the Queen Victoria Monument, with the Prince's Building in the background. Just visible, on the left, is the Supreme Court still under construction. In 1898, the Royal Artillery Regiment was split into Horse, Field, and Garrison branches, and the units in Hong Kong were titled Royal Garrison Artillery. This division came to an end in 1924, when the three units were reunited again as the Royal Regiment of Artillery.

Hongkong Daily Press
10 May 1915

From the Editorial:

COLOSSAL MURDER: All the other incidents of the great war are for the moment eclipsed by the amazing and atrocious act of piracy committed in the Irish Sea by a German submarine in sinking, without warning, the giant liner 'Lusitania', and causing thereby the loss of nearly 1,500 lives — non-combatants, a large number of them women and children.

❖ *The sinking of the passenger liner* Lusitania, *on May 7, by a German submarine had a far-reaching effect on the war. Among some 1,200 people lost were 128 US citizens. Anger over the attack helped to generate support for the USA's entry into the war on the side of the Allies two years later, thus sealing Germany's fate.*

Hongkong Daily Press
24 May 1915

Few British Colonies can scarcely show more substantial proofs of loyalty than Hongkong. We are comparatively an atom of the Empire, yet we have sent many men to the front, plenty of money to England, and heaps of clothing and tobacco to the very trenches themselves. Now we are to follow all this up by supplying ... aeroplanes! Already one can see ... Hun soldiers looking at a couple of aeroplanes through their glasses, glancing at one another with scared faces and exclaiming 'Ach Himmel, vun more country against us; vere is der Hongkong?'

❖ *Two aeroplanes were in fact bought and presented to the British Government. One was paid entirely by the subscriptions of the partners of the Tai Yau Bank, among them — Messrs Lau Chu-pak, Ho Tung, Ho Fook and Ho Kam-tong.*

Hongkong Daily Press
4 June 1915

KNIGHTHOOD FOR MR. HO TUNG: A telegram from the Secretary of State for the Colonies ... 'It gives me much pleasure to inform you that His Majesty has been graciously pleased to approve of a Knight Bachelorship for Mr. Ho Tung.' Mr. Ho Tung will take the name of Sir Robert Ho Tung.

❖ *A fitting reward for this remarkable man. Against the background of the period when the gulf between locals and expatriates was enormous, this achievement of a local man was exceptional.*

The Daily Press *continued with the new knight's career:*
Sir Robert Ho Tung who is 52 years of age — born in Hongkong — lived here practically all his life — educated in private Chinese schools and Queen's College ...

❖   *The account of his career continued for another two pages, all the way from a humble junior compradore to a powerful merchant and philanthropist. One curious fact though emerges — he never sat on the Legislative Council.*

Robert Ho Tung (1862–1956), Hong Kong, c.1910–20
Benefactor and philanthropist, step-brother of Ho Kam-tong and Ho Fook, his business interests were very extensive. He was the chief compradore for Jardine, Matheson & Co. and subsequently had built a business empire for himself. Made numerous donations and endowments, among them the chair of clinical surgery at the University of Hong Kong. Life member of the University Court, he was knighted in 1915.

DRAGON BOAT FESTIVAL: Aberdeen, in ordinary times ... quiet, picturesque little harbour ... yesterday, it was the most animated portion of the island ... those aquatic centipedes rush along: for when dragon boats are ... propelled at top speed one can just discern a long dark body with multitudes of small legs which churn up the water ... in a gigantic effort to out-leg the other centipedes ... Yet really, those centipedes were dragons ... with awesome looking heads, and green tails which wagged viciously, and the long bodies were full of brown and brawny men — 50 odd in each body who strained and sang to the beat of their drum ...

❖   *A very good description of a dragon boat race (see p.177).*

Hongkong Daily Press
18 June 1915

Questions in class: 'What do you call the system under which a man is not allowed to have more than one wife?' Answer: 'Monotony'. Question: 'What do you call the system under which a man may have 100 wives?' Answer: 'Monopoly'.

Hongkong Daily Press
22 June 1915

**Hongkong Daily Press
25 June 1915**

Anti-malarial measures first inaugurated in the Colony in 1899. Sanitary inspectors search breeding places … dense tangles of brushwood in the neighbourhood of houses is cut down, quinine is administered to children in certain districts, and nullahs are regularly swept … The money spent on anti-malarial measures is well spent … and a steady continuance of warfare against the mosquito in residential districts, will be rewarded by a continuous decline in the number of deaths from malaria.

❖   *One is inclined to doubt the efficacy of these measures, since the real reservoir of disease was in the rural areas where cattle was raised and mosquitoes flourished. In the 1930s and 40s, it was still virtually impossible to escape from at least a few bouts of malaria.*

**Hongkong Daily Press
13 July 1915**

HONGKONG MAN AT GALLIPOLI: A letter from Sergeant-Major Brayfield: 'Having a few minutes in hand during a lull in the almost everlasting rain of shrapnel, I am taking the opportunity of dropping you a line. I had a pretty close call two weeks ago. I was out in the firing line … about 300 yards from the Turkish lines, when a bullet got me. … The bullet went through the top of my right ear, grazed my right temple … Luckily there is no harm done and I shall have only a small scar. On the night of 27th May poor Robinson was killed. He was with others of his section in a night advance, when a bullet caught him. … I shall miss him … often used to go to his dugout and chat about Hongkong.'

❖   *One simple letter straight from the trenches speaks more eloquently of the horrors of war than ten official communiques. By the way, Robinson worked at Taikoo Dockyard; he was an excellent rugby player.*

**Hongkong Daily Press
16 July 1915**

It would be difficult to exaggerate the gravity of the position created by the floods which besides devastating the entire valley of the West River, have wrought unparalleled disaster to the city of Canton. Three fourths of that large and densely populated city are flooded to a depth of seven to ten feet, and on top of this calamity has followed a fire which has destroyed upwards of two thousand houses.

❖   *It was one of the worst disasters in Canton's history. The fire was believed to have been started by the looters. Nearly ten thousand people perished. The Hong Kong Government contributed $50,000 towards the relief.*

Another of those well-meaning but impossible situations towards peace has been made as an American contribution. ... Mr. John Wanamaker, head of the largest department stores in New York and Philadelphia proposed that the US should purchase Belgium from Germany for twenty thousand million sterling and then return Belgium to its own people.

❖ *There used to be a general impression the Americans regarded everything as purchasable. There was a story, no doubt apocryphal, of an American millionaire, who on seeing Victoria Falls, cabled home: 'Sell Niagara'.*

Hongkong Daily Press
16 August 1915

Hawkers' Stalls, Wan Chai, Hong Kong Island, c.1920
This photograph shows a market lane with numerous hawkers' stalls selling a great variety of merchandise. At the time, the lane led from Wan Chai Road (in the foreground) to Queen's Road East. At the far end, the English Methodist Church is seen, on the corner of Kennedy Road and Queen's Road East. Street trade run by licensed (and unlicensed) hawkers is very typical of Hong Kong street scenes.

Hongkong Daily Press
30 August 1915

The cries of Kowloon's hawkers have become more frequent and lusty, and an entirely new brand of cries, much more nerve-wracking than any which have been rendered before, have been introduced. ... They consider themselves to be at liberty to carol and cry and weep and wail just as much as they like. They really make the early morning hideous.

❖ *Another dismal failure of expatriates in the past to appreciate the uniquely interesting feature of the local customs. One had wished that a recording was made of these sounds, now no longer heard, a subject fit for anthropological study. See Hawkers' Stalls, p.333.*

Hongkong Daily Press
27 September 1915

According to a Gazette notice, Robinson Road and Seymour Road have been added to the list of roads which may be used by motor traffic.

Hongkong Telegraph
11 October 1915

OUR PRAYA: Can nothing be done to make the stretch of Praya between Connaught Statue and the Harbour Office a little more endurable? It is true that we have to thank the Government for improving the roadway itself in that neighbourhood; owing to the energies of the PWD it is now possible to ride there in a ricksha without being jolted to death by the holes in the road. But in an important place like Hongkong the residents have surely a right to demand something more than tolerably well-made thoroughfares. The junkmen and sampan people litter the roadway just as they choose. ... And always, above and beyond everything, we have the Sanitary Board's sulubrious quarters near the Yaumatei Ferry, proclaiming their presence ... by the foulest stink in the Far East. And yet that stretch of Praya might be one of the Colony's beauty spots ... and what is now more like a dungheap could, with the next to no expense, be converted into a fine esplanade. But, after all, does Hongkong really care?

Old Marine Department Building, c.1920

As a port, with rapidly increasing shipping movement and harbour facilities, Hong Kong has had to develop a strong and efficient Marine Department. It is likely that initially, in early 1841, ships' movements were controlled by the office stationed on board a ship in harbour. By 1843, the Harbour Office was located on shore, on a hill by the side of the present Wyndham Street, with Lieutenant Pedder of the Royal Navy as the first harbour master.

After several moves, between 1845 and 1880, in which the Harbour Office had been in search of wider and clearer view of the harbour, construction began, in 1901, of a building on the praya, the present Connaught Road Central.

It was completed in 1906; this is the building in the photograph. High and commodious, and conveniently placed, it was an entirely satisfactory building for fulfilling its functions. It was situated at the junction of Rumsey Street and Connaught Road Central, the latter being at the time the waterfront.

There was nothing in front of the building to obstruct its view of the harbour and its signal tower, in the form of a corner turret, had a full view of the entire harbour.

A fine building of a 'modified' Renaissance style, with arched openings for windows and verandahs, with its dominating and interesting signal tower, it was a splendid landmark of the waterfront. Inside, there were many fine features, including a grand staircase with wrought iron railings in the main entrance hall.

Like many of the great buildings of that period, it was demolished in 1979 — another victim of the massive development and redevelopment fever which has consumed Hong Kong in the last three decades.

Shameen, Canton, c.1930

Prior to the cession of Hong Kong to Britain, and for some years after, foreign traders were accommodated on the waterfront of Canton City in the so-called 'factories' — a misleading term, derived from the word 'factor' or agent. In 1856, at the beginning of the Second Opium War, between China and Britain, the factories were burned down.

Although by the end of the war, in 1860, most of the foreign merchants were firmly settled in Hong Kong, some wished to open branch offices in Canton. To replace the factories, as a place where foreigners might reside and work, Shameen was chosen.

Meaning 'sandy face', it was at the time a sand spit of irregular shape, close to the site of the former factories. The sand spit was enlarged, bunded, and by 1861 was an oval-shaped island ready for building.

Shameen developed as a foreign enclave with its own commercial, social, and cultural life, most of its building constructed in Western style. Two churches, Anglican and Catholic, were built to serve the religious needs of Shameen's foreign community, the former is seen on the left in this photograph. Shameen remained a foreign settlement until World War II.

Today Shameen is still a pleasant spot to visit, with many trees and not a few old buildings still preserved. For those requiring comfortable accommodation, the recently built White Swan Hotel provides luxury accommodation and excellent food.

Hongkong Telegraph
16 October 1915

GERMANS IN SHAMEEN: In the House of Commons, Colonel Yate ... asked if Germans were still permitted to reside in the Shameen Territory of Canton, which was leased to Great Britain, and if the German Consulate, Bank, and Post Office there were still allowed to do business. Lord Cecil, replying, said that China retains the sovereignty of Shameen; therefore the forcible ejection of German tenants, unless they break the conditions of their leases, would be a breach of the neutrality of China.

Permission having been received for another twenty members of the regular Police Force of Hongkong to proceed Home to join the Army, we learn that practically every member of the European force volunteered. ... In the first instance twelve men were selected who had seen previous war service.

Hongkong Telegraph
27 October 1915

HONGKONG UNIVERSITY ATHLETIC GROUND: At the last annual general meeting of the Hongkong University Union, the Hon. Treasurer (Professor Middleton Smith) made an appeal for $10,000 in order to build a Pavilion for the New Athletic Ground near Pokfulam Road ... In four days a sum of $5,000 was raised, and in less than a fortnight over $10,000 was promised.

Hongkong Telegraph
17 November 1915

❖ *A handsome pavilion was built in due course and was formally opened by the Governor Sir Henry May on the 3rd of May 1916. Sadly, it was demolished in 1993 or 94 reputedly to make room for an extra tennis court! See also p.338.*

From Peking Correspondent:
The monarchial issue has been decided. China is committed to a future as an Empire and not as a Republic. The momentous decision was reached on Saturday. The previous day witnessed the impressive assembly of the electors of Peking with the Manchus, Mongolians and others, on which occasion Prince Pu Lun proposed that the form of government be changed and that the Great President [Yuan Shih-kai] be invited to ascend the Dragon Throne.

Hongkong Telegraph
25 December 1915

❖ *Yuan Shih-kai had manipulated powers to undo the benefits of the revolution. The monarchy was not inaugurated immediately and, in the event, had lasted a mere nine months.*

Hong Kong University Pavilion, c.1920

No true British university can exist without a cricket pavilion, which is a traditional structure where cricketers change and from which they leisurely emerge (not so leisurely any more) to take their places in the field.

The University of Hong Kong, steeped as it was in the British sporting tradition, was no exception. Built during the governorship of Sir Francis May (1912–19), himself a keen sportsman, the University Pavilion was a handsome circular structure standing at the corner of the University Sports Ground on Pokfulam Road. There was no lack of keen players in those days, and a game of cricket could be observed in progress every Saturday afternoon in front of the pavilion.

In this photograph can be seen Claude Severn, the Colonial Secretary, and Richard Ponsonby-Fane, another civil servant, both devout cricketers, seated fifth and seventh from left respectively.

Two university professors from the engineering faculty, Middleton-Smith and Redmond, are standing in the next row third from left and second from right. D. K. Samy, later a prominent physician in Hong Kong, is standing on the extreme left in the same row.

1916

ATTEMPTED ESCAPE OF GERMAN PRISONERS OF WAR: Another attempt to escape from the internment camp at Hunghom was revealed yesterday ... by the discovery of a tunnel leading from the latrine to the far side of the railway track which runs alongside.

❖   *They were not true prisoners-of-war but internees, German civilians or seamen whose ships happened to be in Hong Kong when the war broke out. Unable to maintain these internees in Hong Kong, arrangements were made subsequently to transfer them to Australia; the cost of maintaining them there, however, was borne by Hong Kong.*

Hongkong Daily Press
5 January 1916

Many Peak residents must have had their tempers ruffled when passing the building at the top of Battery Path which is being demolished. With sublime disregard for passers-by, only ramshackle guards have been placed around the building, so that brick dust fills one's eyes and the bricks which ever and anon come hurtling through the air, have a better chance of finding a human target.

❖   *The correspondent was in error. The building was not being demolished but extensively rebuilt by the French Mission which had recently acquired it; a chapel was added in its north-west corner. This fine building is still standing, protected as a historic structure. See French Mission Building, p.340.*

Hongkong Daily Press
11 January 1916

His Excellency the Governor opened the handsome little Harbour and Yaumatei Dispensary at Yaumatei yesterday. It is the eighth of its kind ... erected as a result of voluntary subscriptions on the part of the Chinese community. ... The number of people both ashore and afloat to whom the dispensary has given a helping hand ... is by no means small.

❖   *Chinese dispensaries, with a Chinese doctor (trained in Western medicine) in charge were first opened after the great plague epidemic of 1894. At first started on Hong Kong Island, they spread outwards, and by 1914 had treated thousands of cases, all funded by voluntary contributions by the Chinese community.*

Hongkong Daily Press
26 January 1916

French Mission Building, Central District, Hong Kong Island, c.1930
The red-brick, architecturally attractive building stands at the top of Battery Path; it has been gazetted and protected as a historic building. And so it is, its history being as long as it is varied. It began around 1850 when it was built by the Hong Kong Government and used for a while as the residence of the governors. It was then acquired by a rich businessman, E. R. Belilios, and in 1915 sold to the French Mission (*Mission Étrangères*), by whom it was extensively rebuilt and a chapel added; the photograph belongs to this period. After the Second World War, the Mission sold it back to the Government which had used it in a variety of ways, including the Education Department, Victoria District Court, Information Services, and even, for a short time, as the Supreme Court. Now, it houses the Court of Final Appeal.

Hongkong Daily Press
31 January 1916

As a result of a collision between the Yaumatei ferry boats *Wui On* and *Lee Sang* … the former was sunk in the Harbour, and carried with it twelve bags containing cricketing outfits, bats, etc. belonging to the Hongkong C.C. [Cricket Club]. … fortunately other launches were able to rescue all the passengers. … Twelve bags went down … along with the score book.

The street adjoining the North Boundary of Inland Lot. No. 2093 and extending from Ship Street in a Westerly direction towards Inland Lot No. 199 will be known as Schooner Street.

Hongkong Daily Press
6 February 1916

❖ *I must admit I was puzzled by the names — why the nautical references in Wan Chai, far from the seashore? But both Schooner Street and Ship Street can be found in the* Hong Kong Guide to Streets and Places, *branching off Queen's Road East.*

ORIGIN OF BARBED WIRE: ... is traceable to an American, a certain Mr. Hunt, who could never succeed in keeping animals within the bounds of a plain wire fence. [He] garnished the wire with small eight-pointed stars of sheet iron and fixed them at equal distances. As the device was a success he patented it in 1873.

Hongkong Daily Press
8 February 1916

❖ *The interest in barbed wire was prompted by its extensive use in the trenches in the war raging at the time. My source, however, ascribes its invention to an American farmer, Joseph Glidden, who patented it in 1873.*

Some 'howlers' from a university:
A blizzard is the inside of a hen.
A vacuum is a large empty space where the Pope lives.
George Washington married Martha Curtis and in due course became the father of his country.
The government of England is a limited mockery.
Typhoid fever is prevented by fascination.

Hongkong Daily Press
10 February 1916

At the Magistracy ... a ricksha coolie [was charged] with rushing at pedestrians near Blake Pier ... And with assaulting the police in the execution of their duty. ... The constable deposed that the coolie knocked down a woman and child with his ricksha. ... The coolie then assaulted the policeman, biting his arm in several places. ... The first charge was dismissed, but for assaulting the police the coolie was fined $15 or 14 days' imprisonment.

Hongkong Daily Press
22 February 1916

❖ *Clearly, knocking down a woman and a child was not considered serious compared to biting a policeman!*

Hongkong Daily Press
23 March 1916

The Hongkong Fire Brigade has received a very valuable addition to its equipment ... a new and most up-to-date motor fire-engine ... The engine is of 60-horse-power, and is capable of a speed of 30 miles per hour. It is fitted with a Hatfield pump, which has a capacity of 400 gallons.

Hong Kong Fire Brigade, Hong Kong, 1926
The photograph shows the Fire Brigade in action during the fire which broke out at the Hongkong Hotel in the early hours of 1 January 1926. Two fire engines can be seen at the scene of the fire. The fire was extensive and a large portion of the hotel was damaged. The only fatality was a seaman named Edward Batchelor who volunteered to assist the fire-fighters.

Hongkong Daily Press
28 March 1916

THE ARCTIC EXPEDITION: For the past eighteen months attention has been concentrated on the war ... [and the] public [have] almost forgotten about Sir Ernest Shackleton and his brave companions ... [who] set out from London September 18th 1914 with the object of crossing the South Pole Continent. ... no word has been received since February 8th last year, when he announced he did not see any prospect of getting through the ice that season.

❖ *Shackleton failed in his effort. His ship* Endeavour *was crushed in the ice, but he and his men managed to escape using sledges and boats.*

Hongkong Telegraph
17 April 1916

In order to set example of domestic economy, His Excellency the Governor has decided that from now until the end of the war, alcoholic beverages consumed at the Government House will be limited to — Light White Wine, Light Claret, Whiskey, Beer — and that none of these beverages will be consumed between meals.

A magnificent new building which adorns the terminus of the Kowloon-Canton Railway, and which has only just been completed, has unfortunately not been accorded a ceremonial opening. We have now what is the finest railway station in South China, if not in all the country. ... when one realises that the linking up of Canton and Hankow has long been begun ... that there will be direct communication between Hongkong and North China, and, consequently, with Europe via Siberia, it will be readily grasped that Kowloon terminus will be the terminus of one of the most important railway lines in the world.

Hongkong Telegraph
29 April 1916

❖ *Alas, 60 years later this was still not grasped by the pundits of the Hong Kong Government. This magnificent building was torn down in 1978 against loud but futile protests of the conservationists. The clock tower remains to remind us of this folly.*

Kowloon-Canton Railway Terminus Building, Tsim Sha Tsui, c.1914
Photograph of the Terminus Building in the final stages of construction. This superb building in classical style, with colonnades and clock tower, was completed in 1916, though the clock was not installed until 1920/21. The Kowloon-Canton Railway (the KCR) was one of the most important joint Anglo-Chinese projects. After years of protracted and difficult negotiations, and even more difficult financing problems, the work on the railway finally began in 1906. The British section of the railway was completed in 1910 and the Chinese the following year. The line was fully operational in 1913, linking two major cities in South China. The railway's terminal building and its clock tower came to be regarded by many as structures of great public interest and historical importance. It was in effect the eastern terminus of a railway link all the way to Europe. In 1978, the terminus building was demolished to make way for the construction of the new Cultural Centre and the terminus moved to Hung Hom. The decision to demolish the building was taken after a long and bitter dispute between the Government and the local conservationists. The clock tower, however, was spared as a compromise, and is still standing dominating the Kowloon waterfront — a proud landmark familiar to travellers world-wide.

Hongkong Telegraph
5 May 1916

THE LENGTH OF A KISS: Some comment has been aroused by the regulation of the Ohio 'cinema' censorship that a kiss must not be more than ten feet long, each foot representing a second by the clock. 'It makes no difference whether it is a mother kissing her son, a brother kissing his sister, or a wife a husband. If the kiss exceeds 10ft. in length it has to be cut down'. Just about the point where it ceases to be a kiss and becomes an asphyxiation.

Hongkong Telegraph
7 June 1916

SPECIAL CABLE: President Yuan Shi-k'ai died yesterday morning from kidney trouble. … The Foreign Ministers met the Premier, who gave satisfactory assurances for the maintenance of peace in Peking. It is presumed that Li Yuan-hung [Vice-President] will succeed to the Presidency.

Hongkong Telegraph
16 June 1916

The Canton-Kowloon express [train], which left Canton yesterday morning … was wrecked by robbers at Sum Long … at one of the most desolate portions of the line. … there were some 180 passengers aboard the train when it left Canton. … the engine driver and stoker apparently not having observed that the metals came to an abrupt end, for the robbers had completely taken up the whole length of the … rails … the two front coaches rocked … and ultimately turned over. … in addition to three people killed, about thirty others were injured; some seriously. Immediately the train left the rails, the robbers … came out of their ambush and proceeded to systematically rob all the passengers … even the injured had all their belongings taken away.

Hongkong Telegraph
31 July 1916

The river boats continue to bring down to Hongkong large numbers of refugees [from Canton] and it is stated … that further trouble is looked for round about Canton at an early date … disconnected and contradictory stories as to fighting in and around Canton are being passed round … among the Chinese.

❖ *Nearly 1,500 persons were arriving in Hong Kong every day. Sporadic fighting in Canton had been frequent during the transition period from empire to republic.*

The 'Amah Rock', Sha Tin, New Territories, c.1930s

The curious granite outcrop on top of a hill in Sha Tin, near the Lion Rock Tunnel, when viewed from a certain angle resembles a woman with a child on her back; hence the popular name the 'Amah Rock'. The legend relating to the rock is old and of some significance to the local inhabitants, as it is mentioned in the Chinese Gazetteer of the local district, New Peace County, last published in 1819. The Gazetteer's name for the rock, translated into English, is 'Waiting Wife Rock', and the legend relates how this faithful woman and her child waited in vain for her husband who had gone off to war, and when he failed to return after a long time, they turned into stone.

The 'Amah Rock' is sometimes confused with the 'Lovers Rock' shown below.

The 'Lovers Rock', Bowen Road, Hong Kong Island, photo 1987

Located on the hillside above Bowen Road, this strange outcrop of rocks has long been known as 'Lovers Rock', or 'Marriage Rock'. It is a popular place of worship especially with unmarried women who pray for happiness in marriage. Others come to pray at this rock for other blessings.

**Hongkong Telegraph
30 August 1916**

The Chinese Mid-Autumn Festival having begun, the shops ... are displaying their accustomed stock of 'mooncakes'. Outside such shops, as usual, elaborate pictures are hung, sign-board fashion, and, as many of these have more or less a topical or political significance, interested crowds are to be seen inspecting them — and, incidentally, blocking up the path-way.

**Hongkong Telegraph
6 September 1916**

MONKEY IN COURT: Some excitement was caused in Mr. Wood's court at the Magistracy this morning, when a large black monkey, belonging to Chief Detective Inspector Murison ... entered the court by the open window. ... After making acquaintance with Usher of the Court, the monkey was taken in hand by Sergeant Cockle, and quietly allowed itself to be led away.

**Hongkong Telegraph
12 September 1916**

HELENA MAY INSTITUTE, OPENING CEREMONY: The opening of the Helena May Institute, which is taking place this afternoon, marks an important event in the social life of the Colony. ... To those who are not intimately acquainted with the many spheres of philanthropic ... work of the ladies of Hongkong, the purpose of such an institute ... seems a little obscure, and, to some, even trivial. ... but to those who know otherwise this building represents the centralization and consolidation of a mass of energy, the absence of which would make the Colony infinitely poorer. ... For many years past the want had been acutely felt by many ladies of a suitable building wherein meetings could be held and social activities enjoyed.

❖   *There was a large gathering at the opening. The ceremony was, appropriately, performed by Lady May, and subsequently those present made a tour of the fine premises. Speeches were made by the Governor, and by Mr Ellis Kadoorie and Mr Ho Kam-tong, the two main contributors of the funds. The newspaper, however, by emphasizing the social element of the institute, misses the main object of the institute, which was clearly stated as 'to provide accommodation for single working women either resident or passing through'.*

Opening of the Helena May Institute, Garden Road, Hong Kong Island, 1916
The photograph depicts guests gathering near the main entrance of Helena May Institute at its opening. The Helena May (as it is now called) was completed in 1916 as a hostel for 'working women of moderate means'. The idea (and the quotation) was originated with Lady Helena May, the wife of Sir Henry May, then Governor of Hong Kong. Mr (later Sir) Ellis Kadoorie and Mr Ho Kam-tong, both noted philanthropists, provided the funds. It is a handsome three-storey building and its white main facade faces Garden Road on Hong Kong Island. Its architectural style may be described either as Late Victorian or Edwardian Classical Revival.

In addition to housing single working women, the Helena May has contributed much to the cultural life of Hong Kong as a venue for concerts, lectures and a variety of classes, and through its library.

One pair of binoculars, contributed by H.E. Sir Henry May, KCMG, is now to be added to the list of glasses received and forwarded to the Lady Roberts Field Glass Fund. The total now stands: One stand telescope, eleven hand telescopes, thirty-eight binoculars and a donation of $75.

❖   *Not a patriotic effort Hong Kong could be proud of?!*

**Hongkong Telegraph
22 September 1916**

Sir Aurel Stein, who has just returned to England on the conclusion of a two and a half years' journey through Central Asia … made some fascinating discoveries in Eastern Turkestan and along the Perso-Afghan border. After crossing into Chinese Turkestan, Sir Aurel Stein made his way … towards the desert round the dried up Lop Nor.

❖   *His main objective was to trace ancient caravan routes between China and the West. He is credited with the discovery of the famous Cave of a Thousand Buddhas, near Tan Huang.*

**Hongkong Telegraph
28 September 1916**

Hongkong Telegraph
17 October 1916

ANGLO-INDIAN SCHOOL: The handsome new school ... in the Soo Kan Poo Valley is the generous gift of Mr. Ellis Kadoorie to the Hongkong Government ... opened last evening by His Excellency the Governor. ... the building will accommodate about 240 boys and has been built at a cost of $35,000.

❖   *This prompted and editorial which said, in effect, that while there was a strong need for an Indian school and Mr Ellis Kadoorie's generosity was to be applauded, 'but what about the poor British boys? When is their turn coming?'*

Hongkong Daily Press
13 November 1916

Telegrams have been pouring in from the provinces, says the Peking Gazette, promising to take the most stringent measures for the suppression of poppy planting and opium smoking. It is expected that the whole country will be completely free of opium when the special British opium inspector arrives in China.

❖   *The ultimate irony! After introducing opium into China, Britain was now responsible for eliminating it. By 1890, most of the well-established merchant firms in Hong Kong had stopped trading in opium. In 1911 an agreement was reached with China to eliminate Indian opium completely by 1917.*

Hongkong Daily Press
24 November 1916

From the Editorial:
The enormous volume of traffic between England and France ... has given advocates of the Channel Tunnel a new and powerful argument in favour of the scheme. The example of the Channel Tunnel would not be lost on other communities ... we speculate whether Hongkong and Kowloon will ever be joined together in a similar manner. Similarly, the proposal to cut a tunnel through the island from the city of Victoria to Deep Water Bay, seems very chimerical.

❖   *All three are now realities. There is, however, nothing prophetic about this: the ideas are obvious enough, with only the technological limitations standing in the way of their achievement.*

Tung Chung Fort, c.1920

Little is known about coastal defences of South China prior to the Ming dynasty (AD 1368–1644). Chinese archives record that during the Ming dynasty coastal defences of South China were strengthened to protect areas from the increasing menace of local pirates. It is likely that the concern also extended to the appearance of foreign trading ships in local waters.

There are several old Chinese forts in Hong Kong, but none can be dated earlier than the Qing dynasty, around the middle of the 17th century. The Tung Chung Fort is a large walled enclosure, about 1km south of Tung Chung village, on the northern shore of Lantao Island.

A carved granite slab above the entrance bears the date 1832 — probably the date of the construction or the renovation, but it is possible that an earlier fortified structure existed on the site.

The size, location and the layout of the fort point to its role as a military administrative centre rather than a fort, similar to the Kowloon Walled City, exercising control over a number of coastline forts.

This was dramatically confirmed by the discovery, in 1980, of a smaller fortification, on the coast near the village, previously completely hidden by the dense vegetation. Other similar fortifications along the coast are perhaps still to be found.

On top of the north wall of Tung Chung Fort (the name 'fort,' by which it has long been known, has been retained), are six cannons (three are seen in the photograph) with Chinese inscriptions, but there is, however, some doubt if they belonged originally to the fort.

After the lease of the New Territories, in 1898, the fort was occupied, first as a police station and later used to house a school. Today the Public Primary School of Tung Chung is still located inside the fort.

In the last 10 years, the fort has been renovated and restored, and is definitely a feature not to be missed during a visit to the island.

Hongkong Daily Press
1 December 1916

From the Editorial:

The common conception in Europe of the Chinese people used to consist essentially of pigtailed men and small-footed women. The first of these characteristics has now practically vanished. ... The campaign against foot-binding is far older than that against the queue ... Foot-binding far ante-dates the Ch'ing dynasty — its origin is usually placed in the tenth century A.D. The Manchus were never in favour of the practice, but had to accept it. ... The new Republic Provisional President — Yuan Shi-Kai in one of the first official acts, produced a mandate describing foot-binding as a 'truly revolting practice', and dwelt on the necessity of abolishing it. ... The practice will, we are sure, die a natural death as female education advances in China.

❖ *Foot-binding is now a thing of the past; it would be hard to find today anyone old enough to have seen the so-called 'lily-feet'. Not everyone in old China admired the crippled, misshapen feet; the famous poet of the Tang Dynasty, Li Po, wrote poems extolling the beauty of the unspoilt, unbound feet of native girls of the southern tribes, which, incidentally, places the custom earlier than the 10th century AD.*

Bound Feet of a Chinese Woman, Place and Date Unknown

The picture's purpose is to show bound feet and the extent of mutilation produced by the binding. The custom which prevailed in the old China had certain social distinction since the poorer families, and especially farmers, could not afford to have their daughters handicapped when their help was needed in the house or in the field. The painful binding process would begin at the age of four or five when the feet were tightly bound and compressed. The bound feet had the effect of producing a swaying gait which, it was said, men found attractive.

There was a large gathering at Hongkong University last evening when the first Congregation was held for the conferring of degrees. ... His Excellency the Chancellor declared the Congregation open, after which the Vice-Chancellor read a remarkable message in the form of a poem from the President of China.

Hongkong Daily Press
15 December 1916

A nice little pavilion ... on the jetty of the British Concession, Shameen, has been presented to the British Municipal Council to perpetuate the memory of Wassiamull Assomull by his brothers, at a cost of $2,000. A welcome addition ... will serve to remind the community of the long connection of this pioneer of British India trade in the Far East.

Hongkong Daily Press
18 December 1916

❖ *The firm of Wassiamull Assomull, of Sindhi origin, started trading modestly in Hong Kong in 1890s, and grew to become a large and important trading firm in the 20th century, with 64 branches in different parts of the world, 20 of them in China alone.*

Discovery of Han Dynasty Tomb at Lei Cheng Uk, Kowloon, August 1955
The photograph depicts an historic event — the discovery of a Han Dynasty tomb in Kowloon. A crowd has gathered to look at the tomb, revealed as a gaping tunnel when workmen were levelling a hill to make a site for the Lei Cheng Uk housing estate. Subsequent examination and excavation of the design and the nature of its contents, established the date of the tomb as the Eastern Han (AD 25–220). While many similar tombs of the period have been unearthed in Guangdong province, this was the first, and so far the only one, to be discovered in Hong Kong territory. It is one of the most important ancient monuments in Hong Kong and the clear indication of the presence of the Han Chinese in this area. The tomb has been restored and preserved as the branch of the Hong Kong Museum of History and is open to the public.

Hongkong Daily Press
21 December 1916

[The] small-pox epidemic shows no signs of abating. Within the last seven days 76 cases [were] reported or discovered. … Dr. Woodman … and six assistants are busy vaccinating people at a rate of 1,000 per day … The chief cause of the spread of the disease is the dumping of bodies of small-pox victims in lanes and in the streets.

❖   *A not-so-happy look at Hong Kong of yonder days.*

1917

Hongkong Daily Press
3 January 1917

The pitfalls that beset the path of those who aspire to a knowledge of Chinese were amusingly illustrated the other day, when one of the students at the Language School recently opened by the Hongkong Chamber of Commerce asked his 'boy' if he had been vaccinated and by way of reply, was presented with an onion. It seems that he had omitted to sound his aspirates.

Hongkong Daily Press
10 January 1917

At the Degree Examinations held last June in the University of Hongkong, the Board of Examiners of the Faculty of Engineering, awarded degrees to twelve engineering undergraduates.

❖   *By way of comparison, at the 150th Congregation held in November 1995, there were 446 first degrees awarded to undergraduates of the Faculty of Engineering!*

Hongkong Daily Press
23 January 1917

Much has been written and said of late concerning education in Hongkong, but nobody has explained how it is, that the principal prizes are always carried off by Chinese students, while English boys come in at finish for good conduct, scripture, cricket, tennis and football.

❖   *Traditionally, Chinese have valued scholarship very highly, while sports, martial arts and similar pursuits came low on the scale of achievement.*

St. Paul's Girls' College, Hong Kong, c.1920
Graduates of the college photographed on the steps of the college premises.
The college was founded in 1915 and moved to Macdonnell Street in 1927. It
became St. Paul's Co-educational College after the Second World War.

Hongkong Daily Press
10 February 1917

From the Editorial:

We publish a very important proclamation by H.E. the Governor appointing a commission to enquire 'Whether and to what extent, having regard to both Imperial needs and local conditions, it is practicable and expedient that male British subjects of military age, resident in the Colony, who wish to volunteer for active service with His Majesty's Forces outside the Colony, should be allowed to leave the Colony for that purpose.'

❖ *The result was the enactment of the Military Service Ordinance, which made every British male between 18 and 55 liable to military service unless exempted on legitimate grounds.*

Hongkong Daily Press
22 February 1917

On Sunday, Mr. Owen-Hughes and Mr. Forbes circled the island in a small motor-car. Though this is not the first occasion upon which this feat has been achieved, the gentlemen may claim to be the first amateur motorists to complete the round trip. Some years ago an attempt was made with a large car, but gangs of coolies had to be requisitioned to lift it round sharp and narrow bends.

❖ *The time taken for the round trip was two and three quarter hours. Harry Owen-Hughes, of H. Wicking & Co., was a prominent Hong Kong businessman, sportsman and a keen member of the Hong Kong Volunteers.*

Hongkong Daily Press
28 February 1917

A man who is on trial … in connection with a charge of defrauding an insurance company endeavoured to commit suicide by swallowing coins. … He swallowed nine copper cents, six cash and three ten pieces. He was taken to hospital and it is alleged that patients in adjacent beds are complaining of having their rest disturbed by the noise he makes as he turns in his sleep!

Hongkong Daily Press
17 March 1917

Pirates are still at large along the West River. Captain Jones — Master of river steamer *Kochow* — reported while on a voyage from Waichow to Hongkong. … five passengers suddenly produced revolvers, took possession of the vessel, overpowered the master — who was wounded by revolver shots. They stole $8,000 from a Chinese official and $1,200 from the Compradore. They then left the ship by [the] ship's boats.

From the Editorial:
… on the remarkable career of the late Towkay Loke Yew in Malaya. From humble origins this remarkable Chinese rose to a position of great affluence. … he was a most practical friend of Hongkong University … he heads the original list of donors to the original endowment fund, and not long ago, handed over a sum of half-a-million dollars without interest for twenty one years. … He desires to offer learning to others which had been denied to him.

❖ *Loke Yew prospered from tin mines. In 1956, the University Great Hall was renamed Loke Yew Hall.*

**Hongkong Daily Press
21 March 1917**

In the early hours of yesterday morning while a ballast train was on its way to Kowloon from Shatin, when nearing Shatin tunnel, a wheel from one of the trucks came off. … several trucks derailed … a number of railway coolies or gangers were travelling on the train, and one of their number was killed as a result of the impact. … ten are in the Government Civil Hospital suffering from more or less serious injuries.

❖ *This was the first serious accident of the Kowloon-Canton Railway. One of the injured had subsequently died making the total fatality of two. It may be assumed that the word 'coolie' comes from the Hindustani 'quli', meaning 'hired servant', but in Hong Kong and other places in the Far East, it seems to refer to an unskilled labourer usually working for little pay.*

**Hongkong Daily Press
29 March 1917**

Hongkong Telegraph
8 May 1917

VOTES FOR WOMEN: Mr. Lloyd George made a declaration in the House of Commons today in favour of women suffrage. … Ex-Premier Asquith said his opposition to women suffrage always had been based solely on consideration of public expediency. The women had now worked out their own salvation. The war could not be carried on without them.

❖ *Women received their voting rights in 1918, but only those over 30 years of age. In the USA women's voting rights were accepted in 1920, and in Switzerland not until 1971!*

Union Church, Kennedy Road, Mid-Levels, Hong Kong Island, c.1910
The church is located close to the Peak Tram Kennedy Road Station, opposite the Botanical Gardens. The photograph shows the western face of its tower. Of Protestant denomination, the church was originally located on Elgin Street, Mid-Levels, and moved into the new building on Kennedy Road in 1891. It is a fine building, in the Italian style, capable of accommodating over 500 worshippers.

UNION CHURCH: The new organ erected at the Union Church was dedicated yesterday morning, when a special service drew a large congregation which included His Excellency the Governor and Lady May. Mr. E.J. Chapman, the Church organist, was at the instrument, which was shown to be of very fine tone and capacity.

Hongkong Telegraph
21 May 1917

To-day is Empire Day … the day has been marked by several events calculated to remind residents of the glories of the Empire, of which the Colony forms so important an outpost. At nine o'clock this morning special services were held at the Anglican and Roman Catholic Cathedrals for school children … and later … the members of the Hongkong Club gathered together to toast the future prosperity and welfare of the Empire.

Hongkong Telegraph
24 May 1917

❖   *The 'Empire' is, of course, the thing of the past. But the world has still one emperor — the emperor of Japan — though he can hardly be said to rule an empire.*

Advertisement:
CHEUNG CHAU: Seaside Health Resort. Within Easy Reach of Hongkong. Bathing, Boating, Fishing, Walking, Invigorating Breezes. For Houses or Accommodation, with all particulars address S.D. Hickle, Act. Hon. Secretary.

Hongkong Telegraph
28 May 1917

Vicar's Point, Cheung Chau, Hong Kong Waters, c.1910
Mentioned earlier on p.269, Cheung Chau has a rich historical past and folklore, and abounds in interesting places and names. The rocky point of a small headland, depicted on the photograph, has been known in the past as 'Vicar's Point', probably the result of the island's undue popularity with missionary bodies whose members have long favoured it for rest and retreat.

Hongkong Telegraph
4 June 1917

KNIGHTHOOD FOR MR ELLIS KADOORIE: … this news will, we are sure, be received with feelings of general pleasure, for no resident of Hongkong has better deserved the honour which has been bestowed on one of the Colony's biggest benefactors. Sir Ellis Kadoorie's benefactions have been numerous and most liberal. They have been chiefly associated with education … Schools bearing his names were erected in Hongkong, Shanghai and at Honan. … Quite recently, too, he presented to the Colony the building at Soo Kun Poo Valley in which the School for Indians is housed. He was also a large benefactor to the Hongkong University. … Another project in which Sir Ellis is deeply interested is the Helena May Institute, for the erection of which he was primarily responsible.

❖ *Benefactions have continued by Sir Ellis's sons. Horace had promoted and assisted farmers of the New Territories for which he was knighted, while Lawrence became Hong Kong's first peer.*

Hongkong Telegraph
11 June 1917

AMERICA ENTERS THE WAR: 'We are' General Pershing is reported to have said … 'glad to be the standard bearers of America in the Great War of Civilization'. The American Government and the American people knew well the serious step they undertook in combining their forces with those of the Allies.

❖ *There is little doubt that the American entry into the war on the side of the Allies had swung the balance into their favour very significantly at the time when the war was practically at a stalemate.*

Hongkong Telegraph
21 June 1917

Before Mr. Dyer Ball, at the Police Court this morning, Mr. Ho Sai Wing, compradore of the Hongkong and Shanghai Bank, was summoned for keeping a dog accustomed to annoy passers-by.

❖ *The interest of this snippet lies not in the charge brought against the compradore, but in the person of Mr Dyer Ball. All who are interested in Chinese culture and customs will no doubt be familiar with his invaluable volume 'Things Chinese'. A remarkable man by any standard, he entered the Hong Kong Civil Service, in 1866, not through the usual cadet system. A master of Cantonese and other local dialects, his book, first published in 1892, became a standard reference book on the subject. Among those who devoted their lives to the understanding and promoting the study of Chinese culture, he stands out as a man of great achievement.*

Staff of Victoria Gaol, Hollywood Road, Mid-Levels, Hong Kong Island, c.1905
An impressive photograph of the prison staff, which includes Chinese, Indian and European warders, taken probably in the courtyard of the gaol. The initial prison, built on Hollywood Road in 1841, was very small. It was reconstructed and enlarged in 1865, and again later until, at the time of this photograph, it was big enough to accommodate over 200 prisoners.

THE LATE GENERAL BROADWOOD: There will be many in Hongkong who will have read with the greatest regret of the death from wounds received in action, of Lieutenant General R.G. Broadwood, C.B.,* who commanded the troops in South China from 1906 to 1910. ... Though General Broadwood's stay in Hongkong was not marked by any unusual military changes, it can be said that he was one of the most popular G.O.C's** the Colony ever had. ... His name is perpetuated in the Colony by Broadwood Road.

Hongkong Telegraph
25 June 1917

❖   *As far as can be gathered, his popularity in Hong Kong rested upon him being interested in racing, and his stewardship of the Jockey Club.*

---

* C.B.: Companion of the Bath
** G.O.C.: General Officer Commanding

Hongkong Telegraph
30 June 1917

AN IMPENDING CALAMITY: The blow fell … Telegraphic advice received from Home yesterday stated that no more cargoes of gin can be shipped for the Far East. There is a ray of hope in the statement made by a prominent wine and spirit firm, that the stocks in Shanghai are sufficient to last several weeks.

❖　*In the times when the Hong Kong expatriate community was practically sustained by 'pink gins', it was a calamity indeed! But surely, the* Telegraph *wrote this tongue-in-cheek?*

Hongkong Daily Press
5 July 1917

THE RESTORATION IN CHINA: The Foreign Legations are taking precautions as a military clash is believed to be imminent. The Empress Dowager and Shih Hsu are opposing the restoration but Chang Hsun will not listen to them. … The President escaped last night. … sought refuge in the Japanese Legation … he issued mandates requiring the Vice-President establish Provisional Government at Nanking.

❖　*The attempted* coup d'état *by the unscrupulous general Chang Hsun did not succeed. The Republican troops encircled Peking and Chang Hsun had resigned. An edict cancelling the monarchy was issued. The restoration of the Manchu Dynasty had only lasted one week.*

Hongkong Daily Press
25 July 1917

A dancer named Marguerite Dell, and known as 'Matahari', who was born in the Dutch East Indies, has been sentenced to death for espionage.

❖　*She was executed by the French firing squad. Matahari was, if not the most famous, certainly the most glamorous spy of all times. It is now generally accepted that she was innocent, but was simply a scapegoat of French military ineptitude.*

Hongkong Daily Press
15 August 1917

China has declared a state of war against Germany and Austria-Hungary, beginning at ten o'clock today.

Hongkong Daily Press
27 August 1917

DECIMAL MONEY: The Institute of Bankers [in England] recently published the report of a Committee appointed to enquire into the adoption of decimal coinage and the metric system of weights and measures. The report states that the present system of weights and measures is an obstacle to the extension of foreign trade. … The Committee recommends the adoption of decimal coinage, chiefly with a view to the introduction of the metric system of weights and measures. The Committee recommends that the change shall not become effective until some time after peace is declared.

❖ *An interesting observation especially as England stuck to its archaic system of coinage, weights and measures until well after the Second World War.*

A duck made its appearance in Mr. Wood's Court. ... a man and a woman were charged with the theft of the duck from Kowloon City. The complainant said ... he knew that the one was stolen ... because he had made marks on its feet. The defendants said that they had bought the duck two months before and put marks on its feet. To prove his story the complainant took the duck into the witness box, but while here the bird quacked so loudly and persistently, that the evidence was very broken, and in the end, Mr. Wood decided to discharge the defendants.

Hongkong Daily Press
1 September 1917

❖ *How the times have changed! It seems inconceivable that a leading newspaper in Hong Kong today would have reported such a case.*

Duck Farming, New Territories, c.1910
A farmer is leading a flock of ducks. Duck-breeding is a common industry especially in the New Territories, often associated with fish farming. Duck feathers are also a useful by-product of the industry. Since the Chinese are very fond of duck dishes, duck breeding has been found to be very lucrative.

Hongkong Daily Press
6 September 1917

THE KING'S FAMILY NAME: At a special meeting of the Privy Council held at Buckingham Palace ... the King signed ... a proclamation declaring that the name Windsor is to be borne by his Royal House and Family and relinquishing the use of all German titles and dignities.

❖ *As the Royal Family seldom used family names, it is difficult to be sure what was their name before; I think it was Saxe-Coburg, and before that, ending with William IV, it may have been Guelf.*

Hongkong Daily Press
22 September 1917

At the present time worms roused from their earthly reveries in the fields are looked upon as a distinct luxury on the tables of certain Chinese houses, and worm gatherers and hawkers are making a plentiful harvest of money. ... They were sold at fish stalls not vegetable stalls. ... They were only collected at the time the paddy was cut.

❖ *While there are many erroneous notions about the food habits of the Chinese, worms, fresh from the fields, used to be enjoyed in the past. All nations have their peculiarities in the choice of food; European fondness for cheese may seem strange to the Chinese.*

Hongkong Telegraph
1 October 1917

We desire to-day to join most heartily with many others in offering our congratulations to the *Daily Press* on the celebration of its diamond jubilee. ... Sixty years is a long span in the life of any newspaper, and in the case of our contemporary it extends over practically the whole of the history of Hongkong as a British possession.

❖ *The* Hongkong Daily Press *continued right up to the outbreak of the war with Japan in December 1941, but did not resume after the war.*

Hongkong Telegraph
30 October 1917

Visitors to Old Kowloon City must have often noticed the ... old Chinese cannon lying about inside the walls ... more than half buried in filth. ... the thought must suggest itself as to why no steps were taken to preserve these interesting old relics ... [they] form an interesting link with the past and ought, to our way of thinking, to have been saved as a memento to future generations.

❖ *Two fine cannon, dating from the early 19th century, remained neglected like the rest of the old Kowloon City due to its ambiguous political status (see p.185–186). In the period 1992–1995, the old City, by now reduced to a slum area, was cleared, restored and opened to the public, and the old cannon proudly displayed.*

Cannon of the Kowloon Walled City, Kowloon, c.1939
The two cannon, mentioned in the text, are lying neglected on the ground in this photograph. They would eventually be properly displayed as items of historical interest when the Kowloon Walled City was converted into a public park, in 1990s.

THE LIZARD SELLER: A grey-bearded old man appeared … at the Police Court this morning in answer to a charge of hawking lizards without a licence. … He said he sold the lizards at the rate of two cents each, to people who had a sick cough. His Worship discharged him but said if he was brought up again he would be fined.

Hongkong Telegraph
1 November 1917

Hongkong Telegraph
15 November 1917

TYTAM TUK RESERVOIR: We are officially notified that a memorial stone to mark the completion of the large new dam and contingent works will be laid by His Excellency the Governor at Tytam Tuk on Sunday December 22nd. ... The public will be notified later ... .

❖   *An important reservoir, the construction commenced in 1912. Its storage capacity was 1,419 million gallons, and its dam was 1,255 feet in length. The memorial stone is still there and the reservoir is still performing a useful function for the Hong Kong Island.*

Tai Tam Tuk Reservoir and Dam, Hong Kong Island, c.1920s
The reservoir, located south of Mount Butler and north of Stanley, appears full in this photograph. It was built in two stages: the first section was completed and opened in 1907 by F. H. May (later Governor of Hong Kong), and the second section was built between 1912 and 1917. An earlier reservoir, known as the Tai Tam Reservoir, north of the Tai Tam Tuk, was built in 1883. Combined, the two reservoirs represented a very considerable storage capacity of water, much needed in the face of the rapidly increasing population.

Hongkong Telegraph
11 December 1917

DEATH OF INVENTOR OF FINGERPRINTS: The death occurred recently at Reading [England], at the age of 84, of Sir William Herschel, grandson of the distinguished astronomer. ... he was an eminent member of the Indian Civil Service and the discoverer of the finger-print system of identification. It was in 1859 that he hit on this idea, and, after proving the individuality of the prints and their persistence for fifteen years, he initiated the system for civil purposes in Bengal in 1878.

❖ *Herschel, however, did not adopt fingerprints for identification of criminals; this was first developed in 1890 by Edward Henry, the police inspector-general in Bengal.*

The Chinese junk, that picturesque craft which has figured so largely in the sea lives of the Chinese, is gradually disappearing from the ocean trade routes … The two reasons given for the decline in the junk trade are the invasion of steam craft and the losses incurred through the brigands. Statistics from practically every port in China furnish ample evidence that the day of the junk is passed.

❖ *One could still see the handsome junk with sails in coastal waters until the 1960s, when motor engines had replaced sails entirely.*

Hongkong Telegraph
15 December 1917

Chinese Fishing Boat, Hong Kong Waters, Date Uncertain
Photograph of a three-masted trawler, off a sheltered bay somewhere in Hong Kong waters. Fishing has always been a very important occupation (one might even call it an industry) in Hong Kong, much encouraged and helped by the government. Two local communities, the Tanka and the Hoklo, have been traditionally engaged in fishing since the early times.

1918

Hongkong Telegraph
2 January 1918

The Chinese Ministry of Education has issued an order ... stating that 'as most of the girl students ... have assumed diverse forms of dress ... and have behaved according to their own fancies ... we have fixed the following five regulations:

1. No girl shall be allowed to have her hair cut short in any Government school ...
2. No foot-binding shall be allowed.
3. No marriage without the parents' sanction shall be allowed ...
4. No leave shall be granted to girl students without sufficient reason nor shall they be allowed to promenade in the street in groups.
5. No girl over 13 years of age shall be allowed to attend a boys' school.'

Hongkong Telegraph
13 February 1918

EARTHQUAKE SHOCKS, EXCITEMENT IN HONGKONG: Considerable excitement was caused in the Colony ... this afternoon by a distinct earthquake shock, which threw the whole Central District into a state of panic. ... The just intimation of its presence was a fairly loud rumbling in the earth and then the buildings began to rock in an alarming fashion. Hundreds of people ... rushed out of buildings. ... The shock lasted about half a minute and was felt all over Hongkong and Kowloon. ... It is interesting to note that to-day is what is termed a 'bad day', or 'chak ho', among the Chinese. These days are set out on a calendar ... by certain so-called astrologers.

❖ *Mild tremors are frequent in Hong Kong and often passed unnoticed. The reported earthquake was much more serious in Swatow than in Hong Kong; in the former many buildings had collapsed and many lives were lost.*

Hongkong Telegraph
20 February 1918

CIRCUS AT CAUSEWAY BAY: On Monday next Harmston's circus, which is paying a visit to the Colony, will open its season at Causeway Bay, on the piece of ground behind the French Convent block of buildings. The attractions announced should be sufficient to draw large crowds, for an array of talent seldom seen in Hongkong is to perform. There is, in addition, a large menagerie.

From the Editorial:

Hongkong Telegraph
23 February 1918

THE SPRING OFFENSIVE: The news to hand as to the preparations that are proceeding with the forthcoming German offensive indicates that the Spring of 1918 is going to witness the decisive phase of the War. … We are told that after weeks of labourious training massed divisions are ready to make a last supreme effort.

❖ *The spring offensive did take place but was a failure sapping the last of the German resources and morale. The Allies counter-attacked, from July lasting until October, ensuring victory and the German surrender on 11 November 1918.*

The Race Course Fire, Happy Valley, Hong, Kong Island, February 1918
The photograph shows one of the biggest calamities in Hong Kong's history. In the afternoon of February 26, 1918, when thousands of people had gathered at the Race Course at Happy Valley, a huge fire suddenly broke out, engulfing the buildings — mostly rattan and bamboo matsheds. When the fire was finally brought under control and the dead were counted, 614 people were found to have perished. What caused the conflagration has been a matter of dispute for a long time afterwards, but overcrowding, fire-vulnerable structures, and the cooking fires of food stalls, were in part responsible. A public funeral was arranged and a special cemetery/memorial was built high up on a hill above the Government Stadium at So Kon Po for the victims of the fire. Two plaques, in English and Chinese, list the names of the dead. The memorial is looked after by the Tung Wah Group of Hospitals, but today it is largely forgotten and seldom visited. See also snippets to follow.

Hongkong Telegraph
26 February 1918

TERRIBLE CALAMITY AT RACECOURSE, MATSHEDS COLLAPSE, HUNDREDS OF PEOPLE BURNED ALIVE — FIRE RAGING NOW: As the ponies were going around to take their place in the China Stakes a terrible calamity occurred. The whole of the matsheds which were occupied by thousands of Chinese collapsed like a pack of cards and thousands of people were buried alive. ... Assistance arrived quickly, civilian, police and military rendering all the help they could. ... To make matters very much worse fire was seen to start ... stoves which were used to cook food overturned and the flames reaching the dried bamboo and leaves set fire to the whole, which burnt like tinder. ... It is feared that there will be many deaths. ... Fire is raging at the time we go to press.

Hongkong Telegraph
27 February 1918

THE RACECOURSE DISASTER, NEARLY SIX HUNDRED LIVES LOST: ... detachments of the various Garrison units ... kept guard all night and the Fire Brigade and the Police continuing their efforts to put the smouldering heap of refuse completely out. ... On enquiring after tiffin to-day a Telegraph representative was informed ... the latest accepted number of deaths is 576 definitely known ... With regard to the numbers in hospital there has not been a definite return given.

Hongkong Telegraph
11 March 1918

COLONY'S HEALTH: The return issued by the Medical Officer of Health shows that during last week there were 104 cases of spotted fever in the Colony, of which 55 ended fatally.

❖   *Spotted fever is the common name for typhus (not to be confused with typhoid fever).*

Hongkong Telegraph
4 April 1918

IMPORTANT HONGKONG WEDDING, MR. M.K. LO AND MISS VICTORIA HO TUNG: One of the largest and most socially interesting Chinese weddings that has ever taken place in Hongkong was celebrated to-day, when the contracting parties were Mr. M. K. Lo, the well known local solicitor. ... and Miss Victoria Ho Tung, the eldest daughter of Sir Robert and Lady Ho Tung. ...

❖   *Notes on this wedding, the guest list, and the list of presents took up three and half columns. Mr Lo's (later Sir Man Kam) firm of Lo and Lo is still a leading solicitors' firm in Hong Kong with their son, Mr T. S. Lo, at the head.*

REUTERS TELEGRAMS ... RICHTOFEN BROUGHT DOWN AT LAST, FAMOUS GERMAN AIRMAN KILLED: Reuter's Correspondent at British Headquarters ... says that the famous German airman Richtofen, was brought down yesterday. His body has been recovered and is being buried with military honours to-day. It is anticipated that the ceremony will be very impressive and worthy of the fallen airman's remarkable record.

Hongkong Telegraph
23 April 1918

❖ *Baron Manfred von Richtofen, nicknamed the 'Red Baron', was one of the most successful air aces of the First World War who was reputed to have shot down eighty Allied aircraft. Strangely enough, it remains uncertain who shot down Richtofen, though a Canadian Captain Brown was credited with the victory. It may be noted that he was shot down behind the British lines, and in a rare show of military gallantry, was buried with military honours by the British.*

From the Editorial:
It looks very much as if the notorious ... Dr. Sun Yat-sen has reached the end of the tether so far as his venture in the South is concerned. He has resigned the post of Generalissimo, to which he was appointed by a handful of his own supporters, and his intention is said to lie in the direction of going abroad. ... We have many times had occasion to say what we think of the doings of Dr. Sun, who is more highly thought of outside his own country than in it.

Hongkong Telegraph
11 May 1918

❖ *The interest of this snippet lies in the grossly insensitive and amazingly ignorant attitude of the* Telegraph. *In the history of Asia, if not the world, Sun Yat-sen stands out as shining example of a great political figure of unquestionable integrity. The facts were that he unselfishly stood aside to make way for Yuan Shih-kai as a president, only to find that the latter sought to make himself dictator. Dr Sun opposed him, was defeated and found himself again in exile. However, in 1923 he was back in Canton and elected president of the southern republic.*

Hongkong Telegraph
1 June 1918

'PEAK RESERVATION' It is notified that all persons now residing within the Peak District and all persons who may hereafter desire to reside within that District, must make an application in writing to the Governor in Council for permission to reside. Applications should be addressed to the Clerk of Councils.

❖ *Reference to this infamous rule, designed to keep the Chinese residents away from the Peak District, has been made earlier (p.76–77).*

The Peak, Hong Kong Island, c.1910–20
View south towards Lamma Island, seen above right. On the left, Aberdeen Bay can be seen. The private residences on the Peak were large and comfortable, occupied mainly by prosperous expatriate merchants or high-ranking civil servants.

Hongkong Telegraph
8 July 1918

Of all lethal weapons the machine gun is unquestionably the most efficient 'man-stopper'. … As a filler of graveyards and hospitals it holds a pre-eminent position on both sides of the line.

Hongkong Telegraph
19 July 1918

From the Editorial:
Some measure of constitutional reform would be useful, but self government here would be utterly impossible.

The news of the shooting of the ex-Tsar [of Russia] is now so authentic that there appears to be no doubt that the last of the Romanoffs has been murdered. ... Political exigencies no doubt, will be pleaded by the murderers ... to account for their crime, which, however, throughout the world will be resented as a dastardly and particularly cruel act.

❖ *In fact, the whole Royal Family was murdered. After Russia had discarded Communism, in the early 1990s, the remains of the Tsar and his family were found and reinterred, but there are no signs of Russia reverting to monarchy.*

Hongkong Telegraph
23 July 1918

The severe winter of 1340 gave us the blanket. ... Tradition has it that the inventor was Thomas Blanket, a Flemish weaver settled in Bristol and fallen on evil days.

Hongkong Telegraph
2 August 1918

From the Editorial:
The death rate in the Colony is high and is undoubtedly contributed to by over-crowding among Chinese, want of proper housing for Europeans, and by our antiquated conservancy and scavenging systems. The ordinarily accepted population of the Colony is just over half a million, but in the opinion of the present Medical Officer of Health, it is much nearer the million. ... The proper sewering of the Colony will have to come soon. ... The Colony is still in its infancy, and it needs a generous interpretation being given to the improvement schemes to keep reasonable pace with the automatic growth of its population.

Hongkong Telegraph
8 August 1918

Mr. Chiu Nam, of Hongkong, and his son, Mr. Kan Sat-hing, of Shanghai, both tobacco manufacturers, will donate three million cigarettes to the American troops in France.

❖ *A grand gesture by the standards of the time, but dubious by today's.*

Hongkong Telegraph
20 August 1918

Kobe [Japan] claims to have discovered a new postal record for the Far east. A post card mailed at Hongkong on November 28, 1913 was delivered at Kobe, as addressed, on July 1, 1918.

Hongkong Telegraph
24 August 1918

Hong Kong Island, c.1880–90
The photograph shows the densely built-up western portion of the Island. Overcrowding and poor sanitation in the early years resulted in high rate of disease and frequent fires.

Hongkong Telegraph
27 August 1918

A rental of $150 cannot be called exorbitant for a well-built house on the Peak, on account of the difficulty and expense of building there. But is there any reason why rents for roomy houses at Kowloon are very little below that figure?

Hongkong Telegraph
2 September 1918

Messrs. Lane Crawford and Co., are offering the whole of their present stock of smart dresses, blouses, shoes, skirts, coats, hats and hosiery at bargain prices in order to make room for new Autumn goods due to arrive shortly. ... A large and specially selected stock of the latest creations in lingerie, millinery and gowns will shortly arrive to take the place of the goods now being sacrificed.

❖ *One wonders if this is not one of the earliest attempts at what is at present widely and frequently advertised as 'Sale'?*

A message from Petrograd says Mr. Lenin has succumbed to his wounds.

Hongkong Telegraph
3 September 1918

❖ *The message is wrong. This was an assassination attempt but Lenin did not die. His health, however, declined progressively since the attempt, and he died in 1924.*

St. Joseph's College is to reopen on Monday, as well as Kowloon branch school. For the first time the College quarters will be at the old German Club which has been purchased, and is being adapted as an educational institution.

Hongkong Telegraph
7 September 1918

❖ *See Club Germania, p.194.*

There are many nuisances rampant in Hongkong, but among the worst is the disposing of rubbish by throwing it into the streets from verandahs. … There are other nuisances of a nature too disgusting to specify.

Hongkong Telegraph
12 September 1918

Since England made its momentous Declaration through Mr. Balfour in November last in favour of a National Home for the Jewish People being established in Palestine, Jewry throughout the world has been ablaze with enthusiasm at the prospect of the two thousand year dream being realised.

Hongkong Telegraph
16 September 1918

❖ *It has taken 30 years and another world war for the dream to be realized, and it is still beset with huge problems, as we know only too well from the almost daily newspaper reports from the 'Holy Land'.*

The war in Europe has been the chief factor in shaping the course of Hongkong's trade in 1917. On the whole the year was not a bad one for Hongkong's industries and commerce, ship building and sugar refining.

Hongkong Telegraph
18 September 1918

From the Editorial:
Despite the war, the financial condition of the Colony is decidedly solid.

Hongkong Telegraph
2 October 1918

❖ *Yes, there is profit to be made from the slaughter on the battlefields.*

**Hongkong Telegraph
5 October 1918**

The extent to which the Police Force of the Colony has been reduced through the war may be gained from the observation ... that no fewer than sixty-nine members have joined His Majesty's forces, of whom nine have been killed.

**Hongkong Telegraph
10 October 1918**

Although it is true that the war has deprived the Colony of many of its best players [of cricket], the same may be said of football and tennis, yet in both these spheres of sport, the League competitions are not being abandoned. The Happy Valley presented quite a lively appearance yesterday, golf, football, cricket and lawn bowls being indulged in.

Lawn Tennis Party, Hong Kong, c.1879
The occasion is said to be Christmas of 1879. There are several women in the party, but only men appear to be armed with tennis racquets, nor are they dressed for a sporting occasion! A small group on a verandah above seem to consist of spectators only. The entire group appears to consist entirely of Europeans, a common feature of the old colonial Hong Kong.

According to a Scottish correspondent it is impossible to obtain a bottle of Scotch whisky in Edinburgh, Glasgow, Greenwich or Dundee. Inquiries show that all stocks have been cleared ... This state of affairs is unprecedented.

Hongkong Telegraph
14 October 1918

The hand grenade is quite an old weapon of war. The French used it as early as 1594, naming it after the pomegranate, because of its resemblance to the fruit.

Hongkong Telegraph
23 October 1918

Dr. Johnson's famous dictionary contained 50,000 words. Since the date of its publication [1755] the English language has grown considerably for in the most recent dictionary there are over 450,000 words. ... The first of all dictionaries was one of the Chinese language. The feat of compiling it is credited to Pah On She who lived about 2,000 years ago.

❖   *The Chinese are the first again! Pity we are not told how many characters this first Chinese dictionary contained.*

Hongkong Telegraph
5 November 1918

In Ice House Street ... some person keeps about twenty cats, four dogs, some birds and a very noisy cockatoo, whose screeches are heard day and night. ... Perhaps the authorities will ... consider the question of restricting the number of dogs or other noisy pets which any one person may own.

Hongkong Telegraph
6 November 1918

GERMANY ACCEPTS ARMISTICE: The news that Germany had accepted the Allied armistice conditions was received this morning in Hongkong with the utmost jubilation. ... Flags of the Allied nations were soon in evidence. ... Many of the business offices closed for the afternoon, and a general holiday air has prevailed.

❖   *Certainly a historic occasion. The huge slaughter, in which the large portion of the youth of the warring nations had perished, had come to an end. But the official celebrations of the Peace took place in 1919. The Armistice on 11 November is still celebrated annually by the participating nations as the 'Red Poppy Day', from the fields of red poppy in Flanders where the major battles of the war took place.*

Hongkong Telegraph
11 November 1918

Hongkong Telegraph
28 November 1918

No-one can view the present insanitary state of large areas of the Colony without knowing that public health is greatly jeopardised thereby. It is … a standing disgrace to Western civilisation that this Colony should be more overcrowded and less healthy than the Chinese city of Canton.

Repulse Bay Hotel, Repulse Bay, Hong Kong Island, c.1920s
Affectionately known as the 'Grand Old Lady' of Hong Kong, the old Repulse Bay Hotel was officially opened on 1 January, 1920. Located away from the city's bustle and facing a calm, sheltered and popular beach, it seemed an ideal spot for rest and recreation. The enterprising Dragon Motor Car Co. undertook to start a bus service between Hong Kong and Repulse Bay at the charge of $1 for the return journey.

The opening of the hotel was marked by a distinguished gathering led by His Excellency the Governor, Sir Reginald Stubbs, while the evening dances featured the *Repulse Bay Waltz* specially composed for the occasion by Mrs Taggart, the wife of the manager. In the early 1980s, the Grand Old Lady went the way of many other fine old buildings of Hong Kong; it was pulled down and replaced by a new multi-storey hotel. Then, in a strange turnabout, perhaps bowing to popular demand, the owners recreated a replica of the facade of the old hotel.

The fact has long been known that the Hongkong Hotel Company intends erecting at Repulse Bay, one of the prettiest spots in the Colony, a modern hotel to be run on the most up-to-date lines. ... The main structure ... will be practically surrounded by large balconies. ... The Hotel will contain neither bars, billiard rooms, drawing rooms nor dining rooms, the idea being that, with a seaside Hotel of this description, the public much prefer a large space where they may see all the life and amusement, and where 'cabaret dinners', concerts and dances will be a feature.

Hongkong Telegraph
30 November 1918

❖ *The prediction was correct and the hotel did materialize, in 1920, as the previous photograph and caption describe.*

Airplanes, submarines, poison gas, and liquid fire are among the innovations which invested the Great War with peculiar interest.

Hongkong Telegraph
3 December 1918

❖ *They also seem to have invested the* Telegraph *with a peculiar cynical viewpoint.*

We are so accustomed to keeping watch dogs near the entrance of our rooms or houses that it will be a shock to many to be told that it is not the best way to guard your home. Keep one on the roof.

Hongkong Telegraph
5 December 1918

Hawker's licenses, we are told, cost $4 per annum. Unfortunately there is no hire purchase system prevailing in the issue of these passports. ... For a petty hawker to pay $4 in a lump sum to the Police for the privilege of crying his wares in the streets of the Colony is a piece of injustice which we trust the authorities will see their way to remedying.

Hongkong Telegraph
6 December 1918

A careful examination of the question of smoking ... has been made at the John Hopkins hospital, New York, and the general consensus of professional opinion now is that smoking in moderation is a clear protection against tuberculosis, colds, etc.

❖ *The tobacco companies would love this! Or is it a case of cure tuberculosis with cancer?*

Peace has been concluded between China and Thibet.

Street Cobbler Smoking a Pipe, Hong Kong, c.1910
Like most street trades, shoe repairing flourished in many Chinese towns and villages as well as in the early Hong Kong. The interest of this photograph, however, lies in the pipe smoking, which the man is clearly enjoying. Indeed, tobacco smoking is popular in China; it is said to have been introduced into China from the Philippines around AD 1500. The Chinese like to use long pipes, some made of metal, others — most popular — are made of bamboo, like the one depicted in the photograph, which may vary in length from a few inches to a few feet.

One of the prettiest sights in the Colony … is to be seen at the present time on the hillside adjoining the Helena May Institute. Here there are now in full bloom hundreds of poinsettias covering a considerable area, and a perfect blaze of colour meets one's eye when walking up Tramway Path.

Hongkong Telegraph **7 December 1918**

We hear that a deer stalking party went out in the New Territories yesterday, and that several deer were seen. One very fine specimen — a full-grown buck — was shot near Taipo.

Hongkong Telegraph **9 December 1918**

❖   *The Territory's barking deer. This lovely animal has all but disappeared from the New Territories, helped no doubt by this senseless killing for sport.*

A Picnic and Hunting Party, c.1880–90.
The group is having a picnic probably in Kowloon hills. The purpose may also be to combine the picnic with some hunting since several men are holding shotguns. This, of course, was long before the present-day concern for wildlife, when hunting was a popular pastime in Hong Kong. Such picnic/hunting parties were often organized by the local mercantile firms for their staff to relieve the boredom of colonial life in Hong Kong.

Hongkong Telegraph
16 December 1918

Cheap and rapid flights to England will probably be the experience of the next generation in Hongkong.

❖   *Rapid — yes, but cheap? No.*

Hongkong Telegraph
23 December 1918

From the Editorial:

In the matter of shipping facilities, as in all other spheres, we have to keep pace with the times. Bigger and bigger ships are coming to the Orient. We have to see that the Colony has adequate mooring and wharving facilities and the means for rapidly handling cargo. ... The Colony's share of plums will depend entirely on the measure of enterprise shown in improving the port's facilities and thus attracting trade to this great distribution centre.

Hongkong Telegraph
31 December 1918

From the Editorial:

The year 1918 will always remain in the annals of history as the year in which was decided once and for all whether the nations of the world were to be free or whether they were to be ground under the heel of Prussian autocracy. ... We in Hongkong have been more fortunate than many, and the new era finds us in a very happy and prosperous condition.

❖   *Alas, the hopes for a new bright era would come to naught. Twenty years later, these nations were plunged into another world war against the same enemy but in a much more evil guise than the Prussian militarists.*

Postscript

This, of course, is not a conclusion. *Voices From the Past* has only covered half of the British Hong Kong's history. By 1918 Hong Kong was still a staunch British colonial outpost, but subtle changes were taking place. The strict colonial veneer was softening, the community strata becoming blurred. The selected snippets reflect the amazing resilience of Hong Kong people in the face of many adversities. Starting with Hong Kong's inhospitable terrain, and continuing with periodic devastating typhoons, epidemics of plague, malaria, cholera and other crippling diseases, financial crises, Hong Kong seemed to weather them all and go on with ever increasing success. Hong Kong was born in war and conflict but had provided peace and stability for its people. *Voices From the Past* also reveals the gradual awakening of Hong Kong people's social, political and cultural aspirations which would not be stilled and would eventually, though not in this volume, bear fruit. There is also a lighter side of Hong Kong life with its day-to-day vicissitudes and its own peculiar brand of humour. It would become clear that Hong Kong was assuming a unique identity of its own which in time would create its own breed of undaunted people who would proudly refer to themselves as 'Hong Kong Belongers'.

It is hoped that the reader has enjoyed the *Voices From the Past* and perhaps discovered in it, as had the author in compiling it, new unsuspected and fascinating aspects of Hong Kong.

Sources

Newspapers and Periodicals

Friend of China & Hongkong Gazette
Hongkong Daily Press
Hongkong Telegraph
China Mail
South China Morning Post
Journals of the Hong Kong Branch of the Royal Asiatic Society

Others

Ball, J. Dyer.	*Things Chinese*. 1926. Reprint, Hong Kong: Oxford University Press, 1982.
Bard, Solomon.	*In Search of the Past: A Guide to the Antiquities of Hong Kong*. Hong Kong: Urban Council, 1988.
Bard, Solomon.	*Traders of Hong Kong: Some Foreign Merchant Houses, 1841–1899*. Hong Kong: Urban Council, 1993.
Eitel, E. J.	*Europe in China*. 1895. Reprint, Hong Kong: Oxford University Press, 1983.
Endacott, G. B.	*A History of Hong Kong*. London: Oxford University Press, 1958.
Fay, Peter W.	*The Opium War 1840–1842*. Chapel Hill, NC: University of North Carolina Press, 1975.
Hayes, J. W.	*The Rural Communities of Hong Kong*. Hong Kong: Oxford University Press, 1983.
Hutcheon, Robin.	*China-Yellow*. Hong Kong: The Chinese University Press, 1996.

Magnusson, M. (Ed.)   *Chambers Biographical Dictionary*. Edinburgh: Chambers, 1990.

Sayer, G. R.   *Hong Kong 1841–1861: Birth, Adolescence, and Coming of Age*. 1937. Reprint, Hong Kong: Hong Kong University Press, 1980.

Sayer, G. R.   *Hong Kong 1862–1919: Years of Discretion*. Hong Kong: Hong Kong University Press, 1975.